THE CAMBRIDGE COMPANION TO
GULLIVER'S TRAVELS

Jonathan Swift's satirical masterpiece, *Gulliver's Travels*, has shocked and delighted readers worldwide since its publication in 1726. At turns a humorous and harrowing indictment of human behaviour, it has been endlessly reinterpreted by critics and adapted across media by other artists. *The Cambridge Companion to Gulliver's Travels* comprises seventeen original chapters by leading scholars, written in a theoretically informed but accessible style. As well as providing detailed close readings of each part of the narrative, this *Companion* relates *Gulliver's Travels* to the political, religious, scientific, colonial, and intellectual debates in which Swift was engaged, and it assesses the form of the book as a novel, travel book, philosophical treatise, and satire. Finally, it explores the *Travels'* rich and varied afterlives: the controversies it has fuelled, the films and artworks it has inspired, and the enduring need authors have felt to 'write back' to Swift's original, disturbing, and challenging story.

DANIEL COOK is Associate Dean and Reader in English Literature at the University of Dundee. He is the author of *Thomas Chatterton and Neglected Genius, 1760–1830* (2013), *Reading Swift's Poetry* (2020), and *Walter Scott and Short Fiction* (2021), as well as co-editor of *Women's Life Writing, 1700–1850: Gender, Genre and Authorship* (2012), *The Afterlives of Eighteenth-Century Fiction* (2015), and *Austen After 200: New Reading Spaces* (2022).

NICHOLAS SEAGER is Professor of English Literature and Head of the School of Humanities at Keele University. He is author of *The Rise of the Novel: A Reader's Guide to Essential Criticism* (2012), co-editor of *The Afterlives of Eighteenth-Century Fiction* (2015) and Samuel Johnson's *The Life of Richard Savage* (2016), and editor of *The Cambridge Edition of the Correspondence of Daniel Defoe* (2022).

A complete list of books in the series is at the back of the book.

THE CAMBRIDGE
COMPANION TO
GULLIVER'S TRAVELS

EDITED BY

DANIEL COOK

University of Dundee

NICHOLAS SEAGER

Keele University

Shaftesbury Road, Cambridge CB2 8EA, United Kingdom

One Liberty Plaza, 20th Floor, New York, NY 10006, USA

477 Williamstown Road, Port Melbourne, VIC 3207, Australia

314–321, 3rd Floor, Plot 3, Splendor Forum, Jasola District Centre,
New Delhi – 110025, India

103 Penang Road, #05–06/07, Visioncrest Commercial, Singapore 238467

Cambridge University Press is part of Cambridge University Press & Assessment,
a department of the University of Cambridge.

We share the University's mission to contribute to society through the pursuit of
education, learning and research at the highest international levels of excellence.

www.cambridge.org
Information on this title: www.cambridge.org/9781108830195

DOI: 10.1017/9781108909488

First published 2024

A catalogue record for this publication is available from the British Library.

A Cataloging-in-Publication data record for this book is available from the Library of Congress.

ISBN 978-1-108-83019-5 Hardback
ISBN 978-1-108-82200-8 Paperback

Contents

Figures

Notes on Contributors

LIZ BELLAMY teaches English at City College Norwich and the Open University. She is the author of *Commerce, Morality and the Eighteenth-Century Novel* (1998), *Samuel Johnson* (2005), and *The Language of Fruit: Literature and Horticulture in the Long Eighteenth Century* (2019), as well as editor of Defoe's *Moll Flanders* (2008) and *British It-Narratives, 1750–1830: Money* (2012).

BARBARA M. BENEDICT is Charles A. Dana Professor of English at Trinity College. She is author of *Framing Feeling: Sentiment and Style in English Prose Fiction, 1745–1800* (1994), *Making the Modern Reader: Cultural Mediation in Restoration and Eighteenth-Century Literary Anthologies* (1996), and *Curiosity: A Cultural History of Early Modern Inquiry* (2001), as well as co-editor of Austen's *Northanger Abbey* (2006).

PADDY BULLARD is Associate Professor of English at the University of Reading. He is the author of *Edmund Burke and the Art of Rhetoric* (2011), co-editor of *Jonathan Swift and the Eighteenth-Century Book* (2013), and editor of *The Oxford Handbook of Eighteenth-Century Satire* (2019) and *A History of Georgic Writing* (2022).

DANIEL COOK is Associate Dean and Reader in English Literature at the University of Dundee. He is the author of *Thomas Chatterton and Neglected Genius, 1760–1830* (2013), *Reading Swift's Poetry* (2020), and *Walter Scott and Short Fiction* (2021), as well as co-editor of *Women's Life Writing, 1700–1850: Gender, Genre and Authorship* (2012), *The Afterlives of Eighteenth-Century Fiction* (2015), and *Austen After 200: New Reading Spaces* (2022).

J. A. DOWNIE is Emeritus Professor of English at Goldsmiths, University of London. He is the author of *Robert Harley and the Press* (1979), *Jonathan Swift: Political Writer* (1984), *To Settle the Succession of the State: Literature and Politics, 1678–1750* (1994), and *A Political Biography of Henry Fielding* (2009), as well as editor of *The Oxford Handbook of the Eighteenth-Century Novel* (2016).

BREAN HAMMOND is Emeritus Professor of English Literature at the University of Nottingham. He is the author of *Pope and Bolingbroke: A Study of Friendship and Influence* (1984), *Professional Imaginative Writing in England, 1670–1740* (1997), *Making the Novel: Fiction and Society in Britain, 1660–1789* (2006, with Shaun Regan), *Jonathan Swift* (2010), and *Tragicomedy* (2021), as well as editor of *The Double Falsehood* (2010).

JUDITH HAWLEY is Professor of English at Royal Holloway, University of London. She is the general editor of *Literature and Science, 1660–1834*, 4 vols. (2003), co-editor of *Sterne, Tristram, Yorick: Tercentenary Essays on Laurence Sterne* (2016), and editor of Elizabeth Carter's *Selected Works* (1999), Henry Fielding's *Joseph Andrews* and *Shamela* (1999), and Laurence Sterne's *Tristram Shandy* (2018).

IAN HIGGINS is Reader in English at the Australian National University. He is author of *Swift's Politics: A Study in Disaffection* (1994) and *Jonathan Swift* (2004), and co-editor of *Gulliver's Travels* (Oxford World's Classics, 2005) and *The Essential Writings of Jonathan Swift* (2010). He is a founding general editor of *The Cambridge Edition of the Works of Jonathan Swift* (2008–).

JOSEPH HONE is Lecturer in Literature and Book History at Newcastle University. He is the author of *Literature and Party Politics at the Accession of Queen Anne* (2017), *The Paper Chase: The Printer, the Spymaster, and the Hunt for the Rebel Pamphleteers* (2020), and *Alexander Pope in the Making* (2021), as well as the co-editor of the forthcoming *Jonathan Swift in Context*.

EMRYS JONES is Senior Lecturer in Eighteenth-Century Literature and Culture at King's College, London. He is author of *Friendship and Allegiance in Eighteenth-Century Literature: The Politics of Private Virtue in the Age of Walpole* (2013) and co-editor of *Intimacy and Celebrity in Eighteenth-Century Literary Culture: Public Interiors* (2018).

GREGORY LYNALL is King Alfred Chair in English Literature at the University of Liverpool. He is author of *Swift and Science* (2012) and *Imagining Solar Energy: The Power of the Sun in Literature, Science and Culture* (2019), as well as editor of a special issue of *La questione romantica* on 'Edward Rushton's Bicentenary' (2015).

JACK LYNCH is Professor of English at Rutgers University. He is the author of *The Age of Elizabeth in the Age of Johnson* (2002), *Deception and Detection in Eighteenth-Century Britain* (2008), *The Lexicographer's Dilemma: The Evolution of 'Proper' English, from Shakespeare to South Park* (2009), and *You Could Look It Up: The Reference Shelf From Ancient Babylon to Wikipedia* (2016), as well as the editor of *The Oxford Handbook of British Poetry, 1660–1800* (2016).

RUTH MENZIES is Senior Lecturer at Aix-Marseille Université, where she teaches literature and translation. She has published articles on Jonathan Swift and *Gulliver's Travels*, as well as on seventeenth- and eighteenth-century imaginary voyages in French and English and their rewritings and adaptations.

DIRK F. PASSMANN is author of *'Full of Improbable Lies': Gulliver's Travels und die Reiseliteratur vor. 1726* (1987), co-editor of *The Library and Reading of Jonathan Swift: A Bio-Bibliographical Handbook*, 4 vols. (2003), and co-compiler of the index to *The Correspondence of Jonathan Swift, D. D.* (2014).

MELINDA ALLIKER RABB is Professor of English at Brown University. She is author of *Satire and Secrecy in English Literature 1650–1750* (2007) and *Miniature and the English Imagination: Literature, Cognition, and Small-Scale Culture 1650–1765* (2019), as well as editor of Delarivier Manley's *Lucius: The First Christian King of Britain* (2000).

PAT ROGERS, Distinguished Professor Emeritus at the University of South Florida, has contributed to nine symposia on Swift since 1968, as well as articles in journals including *Eighteenth Century Ireland* and *Swift Studies*. He edited Swift's *Complete Poems* (1983). Aspects of Swift's work are discussed in his *Pope, Swift and Grub Street* (1980); *Literature and Popular Culture in Eighteenth-Century England (1985); and Documenting Eighteenth-Century Satire* (2012).

NICHOLAS SEAGER is Professor of English Literature at Keele University. He is author of *The Rise of the Novel: A Reader's Guide to Essential Criticism* (2012), co-editor of *The Afterlives of Eighteenth-Century Fiction* (2015) and Samuel Johnson's *The Life of Richard Savage* (2016), and editor of *The Cambridge Edition of the Correspondence of Daniel Defoe* (2022).

Abbreviations

BJECS	*British Journal for Eighteenth-Century Studies*
Correspondence	*The Correspondence of Jonathan Swift, D.D.*, 5 vols., ed. David Woolley (Frankfurt-am-Main: Peter Lang, 1994–2014)
ECS	*Eighteenth-Century Studies*
Ehrenpreis	Irvin Ehrenpreis, *Swift: The Man, His Works and the Age*, 3 vols. (London: Methuen, 1958–83)
ELH	*English Literary History*
GT	Jonathan Swift, *Gulliver's Travels*, ed. David Womersley, The Cambridge Edition of the Works of Jonathan Swift (Cambridge: Cambridge University Press, 2012)
Irish Political Writings after 1725	Jonathan Swift, *Irish Political Writings after 1725: A Modest Proposal and Other Works*, ed. D. W. Hayton and Adam Rounce, The Cambridge Edition of the Works of Jonathan Swift (Cambridge: Cambridge University Press, 2018)
JECS	*Journal for Eighteenth-Century Studies*
Journal to Stella	Jonathan Swift, *Journal to Stella*, ed. Abigail Williams, The Cambridge Edition of the Works

	of Jonathan Swift (Cambridge: Cambridge University Press, 2013)
MLQ	*Modern Language Quarterly*
MLR	*Modern Language Review*
MP	*Modern Philology*
Münster 1	*Proceedings of the First Münster Symposium on Jonathan Swift*, ed. Hermann Real and Heinz J. Vienken (Munich: Wilhelm Fink Verlag, 1985)
Münster 2	*Reading Swift: Papers from the Second Münster Symposium on Jonathan Swift*, ed. Richard H. Rodino and Hermann J. Real (Munich: Wilhelm Fink Verlag, 1993)
Münster 3	*Reading Swift: Papers from the Third Münster Symposium on Jonathan Swift*, ed. Hermann J. Real and Helgard Stöver-Leidig (Munich: Wilhelm Fink, 1998)
Münster 4	*Reading Swift: Papers from the Fourth Münster Symposium on Jonathan Swift*, ed. Hermann J. Real and Helgard Stöver-Leidig (Munich: Wilhelm Fink, 2003)
Münster 5	*Reading Swift: Papers from the Fifth Münster Symposium on Jonathan Swift*, ed. Hermann J. Real (Munich: Wilhelm Fink, 2008)
Münster 6	*Reading Swift: Papers from the Sixth Münster Symposium on Jonathan Swift*, ed. Kirsten Juhas, Hermann J. Real, and Sandra Simon (Munich: Wilhelm Fink, 2013)
Münster 7	*Reading Swift: Papers from the Seventh Münster Symposium on Jonathan Swift*, ed. Janika Bischof, Kirsten Juhas, and Hermann J. Real (Munich: Wilhelm Fink, 2019)

N&Q	*Notes and Queries*
OED	*Oxford English Dictionary*
PMLA	*Publications of the Modern Language Association of America*
Poems	*The Poems of Jonathan Swift*, 3 vols., 2nd ed., ed. Harold Williams (Oxford: Clarendon Press, 1958)
PQ	*Philological Quarterly*
Prose Writings	*The Prose Writings of Jonathan Swift*, 16 vols., eds. Herbert Davis et al. (Oxford: Basil Blackwell, 1939–68)
RES	*Review of English Studies*
SEL	*Studies in English Literature, 1500–1900*
SP	*Studies in Philology*
SStud	*Swift Studies*
Tale	Jonathan Swift, *A Tale of a Tub and Other Works*, ed. Marcus Walsh, The Cambridge Edition of the Works of Jonathan Swift (Cambridge: Cambridge University Press, 2010)
TSLL	*Texas Studies in Language and Literature*

Note on the Text

Parenthesised quotations from *Gulliver's Travels* refer to the Cambridge Edition of the Works of Jonathan Swift volume of *Gulliver's Travels*, edited by David Womersley (Cambridge University Press, 2012). They give part, chapter, and page number in the form II, ii, 150. Citations of prefatory sections or ancillary material in this edition are denoted by *GT*. The place of publication for pre-1800 works is London, unless otherwise stated. Publisher information for pre-1800 works is not provided.

Chronology

1696   Moving to Fetter Lane, Gulliver begins an unsuccessful medical practice
        War breaks out between Lilliput and Blefuscu
        Swift resides at Moor Park, in Surrey, as secretary to Sir William Temple

1699   Death of Temple (27 January)
        Gulliver sets sail on voyage to Lilliput (4 May)
        Swift returns to Ireland as chaplain to the Earl of Berkeley (August)
        Gulliver is shipwrecked on the coast of Lilliput (5 November), hauled to Mildendo (6 November), and meets the Emperor of Lilliput (7 November)

1700   Swift is appointed Vicar of Laracor in Co. Meath (February)
        Swift is appointed prebendary of St Patrick's Cathedral, Dublin

1701   The Act of Settlement (June)
        Swift is in England (April to September)
        Gulliver leaves Lilliput for Blefuscu (18 August)
        Death of James II (16 September)
        Gulliver leaves Blefuscu (24 September)
        Gulliver is rescued by Captain Biddel (26 September)

1702   Swift takes the degree of DD at Trinity College Dublin (February)
        Death of William III; accession of Queen Anne (March)
        Swift is in England (April to October)
        Gulliver arrives at the Downs, off the southern English coast (13 April)
        Gulliver sets sail on voyage to Brobdingnag (20 June)
        Gulliver winters at the Cape of Good Hope

1703   After encountering storms and monsoons, Gulliver lands in Brobdingnag (17 June)
        Gulliver sets out for Lorbrulgrud (17 August)
        Gulliver arrives at Lorbrulgrud (24 October)
        Swift is in England (November)
        The Great Storm (27 November)

1704   The Lindalino Rebellion against Laputa
        A Tale of a Tub is published (May)
        Swift returns to Ireland (June)
        The Battle of Blenheim (13 August)

1705   Gulliver is seized by an eagle; rescued by Captain Wilcocks

1706   Gulliver arrives at the Downs (3 June)
        Gulliver sets sail on voyage to Laputa (5 August)

1707   Gulliver arrives at Fort St George (11 April)
        Parliamentary union of England and Scotland (1 May)
        Swift spends the next two years in England
1708   Gulliver leaves the flying island (16 February)
        The Battle of Oudenarde (11 July)
1709   Gulliver arrives in Luggnagg (21 April)
        Gulliver leaves Luggnagg (6 May)
        Gulliver's interview with the Emperor of Japan (28 May)
        Gulliver arrives in Nangasac (9 June)
        Swift returns to Dublin (June)
1710   Gulliver lands in Amsterdam (6 April)
        Gulliver arrives at the Downs (10 April)
        Gulliver sets sail on voyage to the land of the Houyhnhnms (7
        September)
        Swift is a government propagandist in London for the next four
        years
1711   Gulliver is marooned in Houyhnhnm-land (9 May)
1712   The Bandbox Plot against the Lord Treasurer foiled by Swift (4
        November)
1713   Swift installed as Dean of St Patrick's Cathedral in Dublin
        The Treaty of Utrecht (11 April)
1714   Swift's *Public Spirit of the Whigs* declared libellous (February)
        Death of Queen Anne; accession of George I (August)
        An assembly of the Houyhnhnms discusses Gulliver's qualities (21
        September)
        The Houyhnhnms banish Gulliver (31 December)
1715   Gulliver leaves Houyhnhnm-land (15 February)
        Gulliver is picked up by Pedro de Mendez (20 February)
        Death of Louis XIV (1 September)
        Gulliver arrives at Lisbon (5 November)
        Gulliver arrives at the Downs, and returns home to Redriff (5
        December)
        Jacobite rising in support of James Edward Stuart
1720   Gulliver composes his narrative
        The South Sea Bubble crisis
1721   Robert Walpole becomes the first prime minister in effect
1722   Swift undertakes a six-month tour of the north of Ireland (April)
        Bishop Francis Atterbury is implicated in a Jacobite plot (August)
1723   Gulliver moves to Newark
        The trial and exile of Atterbury (May and June)

Swift undertakes a four-month tour of southern Ireland (June)

1724   Swift completes Part IV of *Gulliver's Travels* (January)

Drapier's Letters is published in separate pamphlets (March–December)

A bounty is offered for exposing the identity of the author of *Drapier's Letters*

1725   Swift is created freeman of the City of Dublin (April)

Swift completes *Gulliver's Travels*

1726   Swift is in London (March to August)

The first edition of *Gulliver's Travels* is published (28 October)

1727   Gulliver composes the prefatory letter to Richard Sympson, his print agent (2 April)

Death of George I; accession of George II (June)

Introduction

Daniel Cook and Nicholas Seager

The hero of *Travels into Several Remote Nations of the World. In Four Parts* (1726), Lemuel Gulliver, was barely five years old when the plague of 1665 terrorised London in real life; six, when the Great Fire tore through the capital city. As a young man he trained in medicine at Leyden, in the same period that his creator, Jonathan Swift (1667–1745), had entered Trinity College Dublin as an undergraduate. The Second and Third Anglo-Dutch Wars lumbered on during Gulliver's youth. And he was still a teenager when the Exclusion Crisis alarmed Britain – Swift was barely twelve. As a twentysomething Gulliver would have heard a succession of major news stories about the death of Charles II, the Monmouth Rebellion, James II's deposition and exile, the accession of William and Mary, and the Battle of the Boyne, which scarred the Irish landscape and imagination. Swift, during this period, also entered his twenties, and would later reflect on these and many other events in his political pamphlets and histories. While Gulliver spent the early 1690s voyaging to the East and West Indies, his creator had settled in England, and undertook postgraduate studies at Oxford. By 1694, the landlubber Swift had returned to Ireland in pursuit of an ecclesiastical career. A year later, as a newly ordained priest, he became a prebendary at Kilroot near Belfast.

Increasingly restless, like Gulliver, Swift soon returned to England, where he spent the rest of the decade working as personal secretary in the grand rural home of Sir William Temple. At this time, Gulliver opened his own medical practice just north of the Thames, though it soon proved unsuccessful. (In the yet-to-be-fabricated world of *Gulliver's Travels*, meanwhile, war breaks out between Lilliput and Blefuscu.) Shortly after this, Gulliver survives a shipwreck on the unchartered coast of Lilliput, on 5 November 1699, after six months at sea. In the first of the four voyages that comprise his *Travels*, Gulliver resides for nearly two years among people only six inches tall. Back in the real world, Swift had joined the staff of the Earl of Berkeley by this point, roughly six months after the

death of his employer and friend, Temple. Six months after that, he took
up a vicarship in County Meath, and then became a prebendary at St
Patrick's Cathedral in his hometown, Dublin. When, in 1701, Gulliver
summered in Blefuscu, Swift was back in England. Swift returned home in
September while Gulliver was lost at sea, and then finally rescued by
Captain Biddel. In February 1702, Swift gained the advanced degree of
D.D. – Doctor of Divinity – at Trinity College Dublin and seemed set for
advancement in the Church. Gulliver, meanwhile, could not slake a thirst
for further travel overseas.

   The author and his most famous character were both in England that
April, but Gulliver had begun his second major voyage by June. This
voyage proved particularly treacherous: after enduring storms and monsoons, the fantastical voyager finally landed in Brobdingnag almost exactly
one year later. Giving *Gulliver's Travels* an extra whiff of historical veracity,
the violence of the weather, which places Gulliver in a land of giants twelve
times his height, roughly coincided with the Great Storm which struck
Britain in November 1703. The fictional rebellion of Lindalino against
Laputa, the flying island inhabited by abstract philosophers that Gulliver
will encounter on his third voyage, coincided with the real Battle of
Blenheim (1704), Marlborough's greatest victory over the French in the
War of the Spanish Succession that had started in 1702. Gulliver would
embark on that third voyage on 5 August 1706, just months before the
ratification of the Anglo-Scottish parliamentary union. Although situated
in south-east Asia, Laputa might feasibly be construed as an imaginary
iteration of Ireland. Lindalino puns on the name Dublin (double-lin). On
Ireland's behalf, Swift was dismayed by the Union. As he argued in
a posthumously published religio-political fable, *The Story of the Injured
Lady*, Ireland might have been the more logical partner for England.
Written from the perspective of a woman (representing Ireland), the
story mocks the rival mistress (representing Scotland), who is 'of
a different Religion, being a Presbyterian of the most rank and virulent
Kind'. More egregiously, the rival enters into a union with the wealthy
Gentleman (representing England) though 'she still beareth him an invin-
cible Hatred; revileth him to his Face, and raileth at him in all Companies'.
Growing 'pale and thin with Grief and ill Usage' after being spurned, the
Injured Lady wastes away.[1] Channelling Swift's increased Hibernian pride,

[1] Jonathan Swift, *Irish Tracts 1720–1723 and Sermons*, ed. Louis Landa (Oxford: Basil Blackwell, 1948),
3–9 (4).

the residents of Lindalino take matters into their own hands by rebelling against Laputa.

On a more personal level, Gulliver, like Swift, seemed unsettled in the new century. During its first decade, both creator and creation flitted to different destinations: Swift back and forth between Ireland and England, Gulliver, in the remainder of the third part of his *Travels*, to Luggnagg, and even as far away as Japan, despite the Emperor's pronounced distrust of Europeans. The 1710s were no less restless for Gulliver, who, within five months of returning to England, took his fourth and most shocking voyage. After being marooned by his mutinous crew, he eventually arrived in Houyhnhnm-land on 9 May 1711, where he encounters rational horses and is himself categorized as a Yahoo, one of the bestial humanoid creatures that the Houyhnhnms have struggled to domesticate (and which they consider exterminating). In the real world, Swift was working as a propagandist for the government of Robert Harley, who was ennobled as the Earl of Oxford and made Lord Treasurer on 23 May 1711. Swift revelled in the role until the ignominious fall of the leader and the death of Queen Anne in August 1714. Before then, Swift batted away Harley's enemies in vicious prose and verse satires, and even foiled the Bandbox Plot, an attempted assassination of the Lord Treasurer. Gulliver during this time had become a self-loathing disciple of the Houyhnhnms. Even though they dubbed him a 'gentle' Yahoo in recognition of his apparent advantages over the native species, the Houyhnhnms ultimately dismiss Gulliver from their austere utopia on 31 December 1714. Gulliver's long, celebratory accounts of military conflict, the nefarious practices of the legal profession, and other mainstays of European society had proven too much for an intelligent if unimaginative race for whom lying does not exist (*the thing which was not*). Swift sailed for Dublin in August 1714, before the Hanoverian King George I arrived from Germany, and commenced a six-year abstinence from publishing.

Gulliver was back in England by December 1715, just after the surrender at Preston of Jacobite rebels, whose uprising sought to restore the House of Stuart. Unable to settle among his own kind, Gulliver spent the rest of the decade penning his account, evidently changed by his extraordinary experiences and yet reluctant to concede his own monstrosity. After all, to the Lilliputians he is a murderous giant akin to a one-man plague, to the Brobdingnagians he is vermin, and to the Houyhnhnms he may be worse than a Yahoo. The Houyhnhnm-land Yahoos do not hide their nakedness, for one thing, and a smidgen of rationality could prove dangerous were the interloper to incite an uprising. Circumstances had taken Gulliver the

English sea captain and Swift the Irish churchman in vastly different directions. Swift had in June 1713 been installed as Dean of St Patrick's Cathedral, putting an end to any lingering hopes of securing a position in the Church of England. Apart from occasional trips back to England, including the trip to deliver the manuscript of *Gulliver's Travels*, Dean Swift spent the rest of his life in Dublin, reinventing himself as a Hibernian patriot through a series of potent political pamphlets and economic satires. Politics *always* mattered to Swift. As the Dean, though, his satire became even sharper, less guarded, and more socially driven. A court favourite of sorts under Queen Anne, he faced a much riskier future under George I. His reputed authorship of a potentially blasphemous satire, *A Tale of a Tub* (1704), caused hushed alarm among religious figures, and even the queen. A decade later, his attack on the Whig opposition, *The Public Spirit of the Whigs* (1714), was declared seditious and libellous because of some animadversions on Scotland, and rendered him *persona non grata* when the Whigs swept to power in 1715. Some commentators even implicated Swift in various Jacobite plots against the state. The treatment of Swift's friend Bishop Francis Atterbury, who was put on trial and exiled in 1722–3, offered a chastening example of how Tory churchmen might fare in the new Hanoverian regime.

That political uncertainty did not hinder Swift's increased attention to Irish affairs. In 1724–5, while finishing his first draft of *Gulliver's Travels*, he composed and published (at his own expense, for a wider circulation) *The Drapier's Letters*. Across five epistolary commentaries on Irish manufacture – the Wood coinage scandal, among other things – Swift as M. B. Drapier attacked the British government's abuse of the people of Ireland. A bounty of £300 (the same as for *The Publick Spirit of the Whigs* a decade earlier) was offered to anyone who could expose the identity of the Drapier. Swift's authorship of the *Letters* had become an open secret, but few, if any, dared to name and shame the Dean. Created a freeman of the City of Dublin the following April, Swift enjoyed greater local esteem than ever before. While keeping up with his day job and other writing tasks, Swift worked quickly and with renewed vigour in Dublin. He had completed Part IV of *Gulliver's Travels* by January 1724, before turning to Part III. The full manuscript appears to have been finished by 14 August 1725.[2] Corrections kept the author occupied over the next few weeks: 'I have employd my time (besides ditching) in finishing correcting, amending, and Transcribing my Travells, in four parts Compleat newly Augmented, and intended for the

[2] Swift to Charles Ford, 14 August 1725, *Correspondence*, II, 586.

press when the world shall deserve them, or rather when a Printer shall be found brave enough to venture his Eares'.[3] That brave publisher would be the thirty-two-year-old Benjamin Motte Jr, who was quietly enlisted to the project by Swift's friends in London during August 1726. Roughly two and a half months after receiving the full manuscript, Motte and a team operating independently across five different printing houses produced the book on 28 October in two standard-sized, octavo volumes, at the hefty price of eight shillings and sixpence.[4] It quickly sold out.

Two more octavo editions followed within the next two months. In December, John Hyde brought out a Dublin edition in duodecimo (a smaller, cheaper format) that introduced minor alterations supplied by Swift. Back in London, in 1727, Motte hurriedly issued another two editions, one referred to as the 'Second' edition on the title page, in the usual octavo size, and one in duodecimo. Evidently, Motte was not afraid of losing his ears over sedition – but he did want to cut the text. The Reverend Andrew Tooke, a schoolteacher with a financial interest in the business, advised the publisher to censor overt criticisms of the government and to insert a new passage praising the late queen.[5] Resetting the text, Motte's team corrected numerous errors identified by Swift and his circle but retained many of Tooke's alterations. With Charles Ford's help, Swift took the opportunity to update the work yet more substantially for George Faulkner's 1735 *Works of J. S, D.D, D.S.P.D.*, the 'official' multivolume edition of Swift's writings printed in Dublin. Faulkner probably used the first 1726 edition as his basic copy text for *Gulliver's Travels*, but the new version looks markedly different, not just typographically; even the portrait of Gulliver and the maps were redrawn. Faulkner issued a revised edition in 1738.

Modern editors (and commentators) typically use the 1735 Faulkner edition, as Swift seems to have had greater involvement in its production. 'Authoritative' implies singularity, even finality, but the Faulkner publication presents a version of the work that relied on multiple sources. (Amid the hustle and bustle of the printer's workshop, the team also endorsed old slips, or introduced new ones.) Reversing Tooke's censorship, in any case, would remove only in part, and messily, material consumed by many readers.[6]

---

[3] Swift to Alexander Pope, 29 September 1725, *Correspondence*, II, 606.

[4] Michael Treadwell, 'Observations on the Printing of Motte's Octavo Editions of *Gulliver's Travels*', in *Münster* 3, 157–77.

[5] Michael Treadwell, 'Benjamin Motte, Andrew Tooke and *Gulliver's Travels*', in *Münster* 1, 287–304.

[6] On Motte and Tooke's alterations, and other textual matters, see James McLaverty, 'The Revision of the First Edition of *Gulliver's Travels*: Book-Trade Context, Interleaving, Two Cancels, and a Failure to Catch', *The Papers of the Bibliographical Society of America*, 106 (2012), 5–35.

Regardless of Swift's role, Faulkner would have had to make quick adjust-
ments using the materials and tools available to him. Literature might be
written for a target audience, or for the ages, but books are produced for
a marketplace under specific conditions. Far less squeamish than Motte and
Tooke, the Dublin-based bookseller sensibly kept the Lindalino Rebellion
(II, iii) and other passages off the page. Swift may have had an ideal version of
Gulliver's Travels in mind during the overlapping periods of composition
and production and reproduction, over thirteen years or more, but so did
Faulkner and the other agents of the book trade who worked on it. Tellingly,
Swift took pains to locate Ford's interleaved copy as late as October 1733,
suggesting the author felt the amendments still had significant editorial value
at the time.

Ostensibly an aggravated justification for the new version of the text,
Swift added in 1735 an 'Advertisement' and 'A Letter from Capt. Gulliver,
to his Cousin Sympson', both of which include famous in-character attacks
on Motte's treatment of the manuscript, as well as a commentary on
Gulliver's Travels as a print event. Gulliver draws attention to unofficial
sequels and extensions, even while disavowing their authorship. Criticising
the 'mangled' Motte version, along with the derivatives proliferating across
the marketplace, is all part of the same textual game. Throughout the book
itself, our narrator keeps alluding to unwritten memoirs and treatises, as
well as passages cut short (for now, at least). The new prefatory materials
also alter our view of Gulliver the character. Can the man tortured in
Lilliput and Brobdingnag ever be in his right mind again? Perhaps his
account of all the voyages becomes increasingly compromised by the
misanthropy developed by the end; or perhaps the whole book is the
product of a delusional scribbler? In real life the experienced author
certainly shrouded the origins of the book in mystery, arranging for
intermediaries to transcribe and drop off the manuscript in London after
he had retreated to Dublin, and using the alter ego Richard Sympson in
correspondence.[7] There was method in the madness.

An at turns humorous and harrowing indictment of human behaviour,
Gulliver's Travels has been reinterpreted in many different ways. Divided
into four parts (appropriately enough, after the structure of *Gulliver's Travels*
itself), this collection maps out a range of intellectual and generic contexts,
examines pertinent passages in each of the four parts of Swift's text, and

---

[7] See Stephen Karian, 'The Texts of *Gulliver's Travels*', in *Les voyages de Gulliver: Mondes lontains ou
mondes proches*, ed. Daniel Carey and François Boulaire (Caen: Presses Universitaires de Caen, 2002),
35–50.

explores the work's critical and creative receptions. Part I, 'Contexts', comprises four chapters. Joseph Hone demonstrates that contemporary political controversies over the nature and conduct of government run through the text. Ian Higgins attends to the subtleties of contemporary religio-political controversy that seeped into the satirist's thinking over the years, as evident in the many biblical analogies, allusions, and phrases that pervade the book, despite Gulliver's apparent lack of faith in God's mercy. Liz Bellamy addresses Swift's portrayal of bodies and gender, including Gulliver's monstrous maleness in Lilliput and the grotesqueness of the Brobdingnagian women. And Gregory Lynall considers the range of scientific writings with which Swift engaged, often abrasively, here and elsewhere, teasing out positions Swift takes on empiricism and empire.

Part II, 'Genres', places the text within several generic contexts. Addressing the ongoing concern about the validity of classifying *Gulliver's Travels* as a 'novel', J. A. Downie draws on contemporary works by Daniel Defoe and Mary Davys, among others, to reveal common narrative strategies to which readers would have been alert. Reading *Gulliver's Travels* within an expanded purview of imaginary voyages, most notably Lucian's *True History* and its many modern imitations, does not detract from its fictionality. On the contrary, such a purview enhances Swift's complex gamesmanship. Pat Rogers stabilises our understanding of the different satirical models at play while unlocking the sheer pervasiveness of it in the book's form, plotlines, narrative style, language, allusions and, above all, its purposeful humour. Paddy Bullard makes the case for reading *Gulliver's Travels* as a philosophical tale. Beyond the farcical physics or absurd humour, each voyage raises profound questions about how we perceive and understand the world. Such explorations, as Bullard shows, even trouble our everyday assumptions about what is hugely significant or minutely trivial within it. Dirk F. Passmann grounds the book among a proliferation of sincere and fantastical travel writing in the period. After all, Swift had been interested in travel literature since at least 1696. Tales of difficult journeys, savage nations, hardships, and tempests evidently stayed with him, and coalesced around his insistently satirical mind.

After two parts that refresh significant historical and literary contexts, Part III, 'Reading *Gulliver's Travels*', shifts the focus to controversial, famous, or otherwise important episodes in each of the four voyages. Before this, Brean Hammond demonstrates the importance of considering the prefatory matter alongside the text proper in any comprehensive understanding of Swift's project, particularly for its playfulness with fictionality and truth. 'A Voyage to Lilliput', the subject of Melinda Alliker Rabb's chapter, establishes the vexing narrative strategies Swift uses throughout *Gulliver's Travels*. At the same time, Lilliput, like each of the worlds, is utterly unique. In Lilliput the charm of the miniature proves deceptive, as Rabb has it. Nicholas Seager's chapter on 'A Voyage to Brobdingnag' shows that this part of the narrative radically unsettles notions of human superiority in both physical and moral terms. Barbara M. Benedict ranges over the most miscellaneous part of *Gulliver's Travels*, 'A Voyage to Laputa, Balnibarbi, Luggnagg, &c'. This part of the story offers a comprehensive yet compressed satire on the abuses of Modern learning, as Benedict demonstrates, as well as excoriating political corruption and illustrating the vanity of human wishes. In the final chapter in this section, Judith Hawley identifies significant moments in 'A Voyage to the Land of the Houyhnhnms'. One critical school of thought, which emerged among Swift's own circle, viewed the rational Houyhnhnms as an embodiment of Swift's ideal view of humanity, and the Yahoos our baseness. A coterminous school found the Houyhnhnms cold and insipid, and therefore dismissed the ideal as false. Houyhnhnms or Yahoos or neither: Swift's vision of humans, especially of eighteenth-century Europe, is far from flattering. For some, it amounts to blasphemy. The chapters addressing each of the book's voyages also tackle the debated question about the overall coherence of *Gulliver's Travels*: is Swift's work a collection of four separable episodes or a cogent whole?

Part IV, 'Afterlives', explores what critics and artists have done with *Gulliver's Travels* in the time since it was published. Jack Lynch digests the extensive body of scholarship produced all the way from the dominant eighteenth-century man of letters Samuel Johnson and his peers, up to the present day. This includes a highly useful account of significant debates such as the 'hard' and 'soft' schools of interpretation. Daniel Cook considers the difference between Gulliveriana and the Gulliveriad, amid discussions of fictional clones, sequels, spin-offs, and other creative engagements that appeared within weeks of the first publication of *Gulliver's Travels*, and which show no sign of abating even now. Ruth Menzies explores the extraordinary breadth of visual reworkings of Swift's materials, in satirical cartoons, paintings, comics, and other diverse media. Addressing filmic reworkings of *Gulliver's Travels*, Emrys Jones takes stock of perhaps the most prominent modern engagements with Swift's text in the public consciousness.

Collectively, the seventeen chapters that make up this *Companion* address anew longstanding debates that have circled around, and often invaded, the world of *Gulliver's Travels*. Even as we near the 300th anniversary of the first appearance of Swift's satirical masterpiece, its impact continues to pinch.

PART I

Contexts

CHAPTER I

Politics

Joseph Hone

In the summer of 1726, a manuscript was delivered to Benjamin Motte under mysterious circumstances. On 8 August, the London bookseller had received a letter from a gentleman calling himself Richard Sympson regarding the memoirs of his cousin, Captain Lemuel Gulliver. The letter explained that Captain Gulliver had entrusted Sympson to arrange the publication of these memoirs. Sympson had enclosed the first volume with his letter, as a sample to entice the bookseller. 'And although some parts of this and the following Volumes may be thought in one or two places to be a little Satyrical', he explained, 'in that you must Judge for your self, and take the Advice of your Friends' (*Correspondence*, III, 9). If this was a tacit warning for Motte to be on the lookout for sensitive material, the bookseller was undeterred by what he read and agreed to Sympson's terms. Within a fortnight of his receiving the original letter, the complete manuscript was 'dropp'd at his house in the dark, from a Hackney-coach' by persons unknown (*Correspondence*, III, 52).

'Richard Sympson' was Jonathan Swift and the book was *Gulliver's Travels*. Swift often enjoyed playing elaborate games with his publishers, but in this case his concern for anonymity was no mere ruse. By the time his manuscript landed on Motte's doorstep, the author had already fled the country; even if the bookseller had guessed Swift's involvement, he would have been able to prove nothing, for neither manuscript nor letters were in the author's handwriting. Swift's circumspect dealings with his publisher suggest the degree to which he thought the *Travels* engaged with the political controversies of its moment. From his previous experiences with government surveillance and censorship, Swift understood that transgressive satire could land authors and their publishers in a dangerous position. While preparing the draft of the *Travels*, he had joked that the book was 'intended for the press' only once 'a Printer shall be found brave enough to venture his Eares' (*Correspondence*, II, 606). The slitting of ears was, as Thomas Keymer points out, an outdated punishment for the crime of

seditious libel, for which the dreaded penalty in Swift's day was the pillory.[1]
Beneath the jest lurked a very real fear of prosecution.

When the *Travels* finally appeared in late October, Swift's enemies in
Grub Street were outraged by the book. One early reader expressed his
desire 'to bring the Author, and those concerned with him to exemplary
Punishment', frustrated only by the author being 'so much upon his
Guard, that no Forms of Law can touch him'.[2] Although claiming to
have 'no Design to prove Mr. GULLIVER a *Traitor*', another government
hack reported how 'every Body says that he is disaffected'.[3] And yet, despite
the best efforts of 'Exasperated Pettyfoggers' combing through the text for
actionable material, Swift's friends in London reported the generally held
view that the book was 'free from particular reflections' (*Correspondence*,
III, 60–1, 47–8). Alexander Pope, who knew all about Swift's covert
arrangements with Motte, even remarked that his friend 'needed not to
have been so secret' with the publisher, for 'I find no considerable man very
angry at the book: some indeed think it rather too bold, and too general
a Satire: but none that I hear of accuse it of particular reflections'
(*Correspondence*, III, 52).

What prompted some readers of this 'general' satire to accuse its author
of criminal sedition, despite the apparent absence of 'particular reflections'? What features of the book compelled Swift to arrange its publication in a surreptitious manner? Contending parties, kings and queens,
venal courtiers, and scheming ministers parade through Swift's narrative,
though the degree to which Gulliver's voyages constitute a sustained exercise in political allegory, a series of opportunistic satiric potshots, or
a general burlesque on human vice remains a vexatious question. In recent
scholarship, the nature of Swift's political satire is constantly 'elusive' or
even incoherent.[4] My aim in this chapter is not simply to revisit old debates
about matters of allegory and allusion, which focus overwhelmingly on
Gulliver's early adventures in Lilliput. Rather, I want to situate the *Travels*
in the political conflicts of its moment. In doing so, it will become clear
that Swift's 'general' satire, far from abstract political moralising, made

---

[1] Thomas Keymer, *Poetics of the Pillory: English Literature and Seditious Libel, 1660–1820* (Oxford: Oxford University Press, 2019), 102.
[2] *A Letter from a Clergyman to His Friend, with an Account of the Travels of Capt. Lemuel Gulliver* (1726), 9–10.
[3] *Gulliver Decypher'd* [1727], xii.
[4] David Oakleaf, *A Political Biography of Jonathan Swift* (London: Pickering and Chatto, 2008), 188; Ashley Marshall, *The Practice of Satire in England, 1658–1770* (Baltimore: Johns Hopkins University Press, 2013), 225.

a very particular and coherent intervention in contemporary debates about latent vulnerabilities in the English system of politics.

The subject of England's political institutions had long interested Swift. His debut pamphlet, *A Discourse of the Contests and Dissentions between the Nobles and the Commons in Athens and Rome* (1701), had argued for the primacy of England's 'ancient constitution', which balanced the three classical forms of government – monarchy, aristocracy, and democracy – in the legislative relationship between the king, the lords, and the commons. Each branch of government held the others in check, thus enshrining liberty and law against tyranny.[5] This English system followed what Swift called the 'eternal Rule in Politicks among every free People': that the powers of each branch of government must be kept in balance. For when 'the Balance is broke', those powers 'will never continue long in equal Division between the two remaining Parties' but will 'run entirely into one'. Such 'breaking of the Balance by whatever Hand, and leaving the Power wholly in one Scale' was, Swift argued, 'the truest account' of tyranny.[6] Such tyranny could take several forms. Many nations had unwittingly surrendered balanced government for monarchical despotism. Reserving special contempt for populist forms of government, Swift was more apprehensive of the '*Tyranny of the Commons*', which he feared could be one outcome of the parliamentary manoeuvres of 1701.[7]

Following the tyrannical encroachments of the Stuart kings over parliament, orthodox Whig polemicists were convinced the Revolution of 1688 had rebalanced the constitution to its original harmony. But for Swift the heyday of constitutional balance would not arrive until the final years of the reign of Queen Anne, when he was in London working as a propagandist for the Tory ministry led by Robert Harley, Earl of Oxford, through whom he enjoyed access to the corridors of power and was on intimate terms with some of the most celebrated men of his age, notably Harley's deputy Henry St John, Viscount Bolingbroke. Under Harley's leadership, Swift believed, 'successful Endeavours' were being made to restore the constitution 'in every Branch to its antient Form, from the languishing Condition it hath long lain in'.[8] This encouraging

---

[5] Mark Goldie, 'The English System of Liberty', in *The Cambridge History of Eighteenth-Century Political Thought*, ed. Mark Goldie and Robert Wokler (Cambridge: Cambridge University Press, 2006), 40–78.

[6] [Jonathan Swift], *A Discourse of the Contests and Dissensions between the Nobles and the Commons in Athens and Rome* (1701), 6.

[7] Mark Goldie, 'Situating Swift's Politics in 1701', in *Politics and Literature in the Age of Swift: English and Irish Perspectives*, ed. Claude Rawson (Cambridge: Cambridge University Press, 2010), 31–51.

[8] *The Examiner*, 22 (28 December 1710).

state of affairs was not to last. Even while Harley was bringing the costly War of the Spanish Succession to a close, he was being challenged by Whig politicians who sought, in Swift's words, 'to alter and adjust the constitution to their own pernicious principles'.[9] Soon after Anne's death in the summer of 1714, with Swift already having quit London for Dublin and the deanery of St Patrick's, the Whigs made their move. The new king, George I, took them to his bosom and entrusted the ambitious rising star of the party Robert Walpole with the task of hunting down evidence of treason among the Tories, as chairman of the new 'Committee of Secrecy'. In the following July, Walpole's committee presented sixteen articles of impeachment against Harley and Bolingbroke, concerning their alleged misconduct during the peace negotiations. Bolingbroke fled to France before he could be questioned, seeking refuge among the exiled Jacobites. Harley chose to remain in London and was imprisoned for two years in the Tower, until he was finally acquitted in June 1717.

By the time Swift returned to England with the draft of the *Travels* in the spring of 1726, the constitution was widely believed to be in crisis. The passage of the Septennial Act ten years earlier ensured that parliamentary elections would be held only every seven years, propping up the incumbent Whig administration. Tories opposed the bill on grounds that it made a mockery of parliamentary independence, shattering the constitutional scales, an assessment with which Swift agreed wholeheartedly.[10] Walpole had used the opportunity to consolidate his grip on power, accumulating vast personal wealth after 1721 through his offices as first lord of the treasury and chancellor of the exchequer. There was growing discomfort in opposition circles about the degree to which Walpole, as 'prime minister', had centralised government in his own hands, moving ever further away from proper constitutional balance. Bolingbroke's return from exile in the summer of 1725 breathed life into the opposition, which campaigned on the basis that Walpole had replaced the English system of liberty with his own corrupt 'Robinocracy'. Through its chief propaganda organ, *The Craftsman*, which launched a mere six weeks after the publication of *Gulliver's Travels*, the opposition portrayed Walpole as the embodiment of tyranny, a minister whose influence over the king and subornation of

[9] *The Examiner*, 32 (8 March 1711).
[10] Max Skjönsberg, 'Ancient Constitutionalism, Fundamental Law and Eighteenth-Century Toryism in the Septennial Act (1716) Debates', *History of Political Thought*, 40 (2019), 270–301; Ashley Marshall, *Swift and History: Politics and the English Past* (Cambridge: Cambridge University Press, 2015), 38–40.

parliament endangered the constitution and subverted the liberty of the people.[11]

The corruption of political institutions is a core theme of the *Travels*. This general motif is localised when Gulliver is summoned by the King of Brobdingnag to elucidate the English system of government. He proudly explains the constitutional position of the crown, the duties of the lords as 'Counsellors born to the King and Kingdom', and the role of the commons, 'who were all principal Gentlemen, *freely* picked and culled out by the People themselves, for their great Abilities, and Love of their Country' (II, vi, 180–1). These are the conventional shibboleths of English liberty, familiar from Swift's own polemical writings and, with the exception of a Jacobite fringe who maintained the doctrine of divine monarchy, widely accepted across the political spectrum. And yet, following Gulliver's lengthy account of the English system, the king bombards him with questions and doubts. 'What Qualifications were necessary in those who were to be created new Lords', he asks. He wants to know whether the 'Humour of the Prince, a Sum of Money to a Court-Lady, or a Prime Minister; or a Design of strengthening a Party opposite to the publick Interest, ever happened to be Motives in those Advancements', and whether the lords 'were always so free from Avarice, Partialities, or Want, that a Bribe, or some other sinister View, could have no Place among them'. Turning to the commons, the king asks 'what Arts were practiced in electing those whom I called Commoners. Whether, a Stranger with a strong Purse might not influence the vulgar Voters to chuse him before their own Landlord, or the most considerable Gentleman in the Neighbourhood', a query anticipated by the suggestive italics in Gulliver's description of members of parliament as '*freely* picked' from the people. And having been elected to parliament, what measures existed to prevent 'such zealous Gentlemen' from 'refunding themselves for the Charges and Trouble they were at, by sacrificing the publick Good to the Designs of a weak and vicious Prince, in Conjunction with a corrupted Ministry' (II, vi, 184)?

Gulliver has no response to these questions, which remain pointedly unanswered. Though his questions are voiced in general terms, by highlighting the vulnerability of a mixed constitution to forms of corruption, the King ventriloquises the core argument of the opposition to Walpole: that he had replaced the English system of liberty with a system of

---

[11] On the *Travels* and the opposition campaign, see Bertrand A. Goldgar, *Walpole and the Wits: The Relation of Politics to Literature, 1722–1742* (Lincoln: University of Nebraska Press, 1976), 49–63.

corruption. Walpole had achieved this by three means. Firstly, by rigging elections. To secure their seats, candidates relied on the ministry's financial support and thus, once elected to parliament, could not be trusted to vote independently or for the public good. In one of his most outspoken essays for *The Craftsman*, published in 1728, Bolingbroke explained that the choice of a member of parliament 'ought always to be at the *free* Election of the People, and not at the Appointment of *Great Men*', for 'if we take Money, we must expect it is for something; and if we feel a Burthen on our Shoulders, we have the Wages in our Pockets'. It would be in the private interest of these recipients of '*Election Money*' to 'vote any Sum demanded for *Secret Service*, by so honourable and *bountiful* a Distributer of it' and so funnel public money from the treasury into their own pockets.[12] When the King of Brobdingnag asks whether 'a Stranger with a strong Purse' might influence elections and whether members of parliament would vote in the interest of 'refunding themselves', he precisely anticipates Bolingbroke's line of attack against Walpole and his minions.

Secondly, and relatedly, Walpole planted servile 'placemen' in parliament: men who held pensions or salaried government positions and whose votes could be swayed by the offer or retraction of such posts. Potential critics of the administration could be bought off or silenced with pensions and lucrative offices of state. Suppose such a minister should act against the public interest, Bolingbroke asked, 'what Redress could we expect from an *adulterated Parliament*; who, instead of punishing the *Minister*, would support and avow the Fact, and so justifying him in the Eye of his Prince?' It was in the nature of these '*obsequious Pensioners*' to 'lavish all the People's Treasure' on their minister, who would in turn use that money to buy the compliance of parliament. 'From such Measures', wrote Bolingbroke, 'would naturally result a Necessity for a *standing Army*; for the Hatred of the People at Home against such an *over grown Minister*' would grow to such a point that the minister may need to deploy an army against his own people 'to silence their Murmurings, and choak up their just Complaints'.[13]

Here was Walpole's third pillar of corruption: the maintenance by the state of a standing army. There was a strong vein of polemical literature arguing that such professional armies posed a menace to liberty and free government, ranging from the recent essays of the commonwealthmen

---

[12] Henry St John, Lord Bolingbroke, *Contributions to the Craftsman*, ed. Simon Varey (Oxford: Oxford University Press, 1982), 61–2.

[13] Bolingbroke, *Contributions*, 62.

John Trenchard and Thomas Gordon to those by disaffected Jacobites.[14] Swift himself had earlier scoffed that 'Mercenary Troops are only *Servants armed*', loyal to the whims of their paymaster and not to the public good (*Prose Writings*, III, 41). So long as Walpole continued to amass personal wealth at the expense of the nation, he would be able to control this army much like his placemen in parliament. The overarching fear was that such a force could be used by one branch of government against the others, destroying the balance of the constitution. Walpole could not be trusted with such power. As Bolingbroke phrased it in *The Craftsman*, 'how dangerous such a Weapon might be in the Hands of a *wicked Minister*, every *Englishman* can judge'.[15] Once again the King of Brobdingnag precisely anticipates Bolingbroke's argument against the prime minister, for, Gulliver reports, 'Above all, he was amazed to hear me talk of a mercenary standing Army in the Midst of Peace, and among a free People. He said, if we were governed by our own Consent in the Persons of our Representatives, he could not imagine of whom we were afraid, or against whom we were to fight' (II, vi, 186). His implication was that this army would be used by the prime minister against the state.

Although the King of Brobdingnag's questions are couched in general terms, the degree to which his grievances overlap with those of the campaign against Walpole underscores how the general could become particular. The opposition propagandist Nicholas Amherst gestured to the importance of this interplay between the general and the particular, explaining that his columns in *The Craftsman* 'are written against *Vice* and *Corruption*, and *bad Ministers* in general; though I do not think myself obliged to declare, that I never had any *particular Persons* in my Eye'. So long as he confined himself to '*general Expressions*' or disguised his 'Invectives against Vice in *Dreams*, *Fables*, *Parallels*, and *Allegories*', he believed he was safe from legal action.[16] In Amherst's formulation, general satire could have a very specific target. This was a lesson Swift understood, but which several of his modern readers have failed to grasp. It has become a truism that Swift's satirical target was not Walpole or the political squabbles of his moment, but rather, in the influential phrasing of F. P. Lock, the 'perennial disease' of which Walpole was only a 'contemporary manifestation'.[17] But equally, the King of Brobdingnag's

[14] Lois Schwoerer, *No Standing Armies! The Antiarmy Ideology in Seventeenth-Century England* (Baltimore: Johns Hopkins University Press, 1974), 188–200; Ian Higgins, *Swift's Politics: A Study in Disaffection* (Cambridge: Cambridge University Press, 1994), 180–2. For an overview and selection of primary texts, see *Writings on Standing Armies*, ed. David Womersley (Indianapolis: Liberty Fund, 2020).
[15] Bolingbroke, *Contributions*, 63. [16] *The Craftsman*, 88 (9 March 1728).
[17] F. P. Lock, *The Politics of Gulliver's Travels* (Oxford: Clarendon Press, 1980), 2.

questions suggest that the debasement of England's political institutions was symptomatic of Walpole's rotten influence. The king discerns in Gulliver's explanation of the English system 'some Lines of an Institution, which in its Original might have been tolerable', but which has been 'half erased, and the rest wholly blurred and blotted by Corruptions' (II, vi, 188). Likewise, in the technologically advanced nation of Glubbdubdrib, when Gulliver tires of raising celebrated historical leaders from the dead, he is tempted to summon 'some *English* Yeomen of the old Stamp', famous 'for their true Spirit of Liberty', before considering how disappointed they will be to see how their 'pure native Virtues were prostituted for a Piece of Money by their Grand-children; who in selling their Votes, and managing at Elections have acquired every Vice and Corruption that can possibly be learned' (III, viii, 303–4). Here corruption is a modern accretion, not some perennial disease. Beneath layers of vice, the outlines of an ancient constitution can still be glimpsed. The question is whether it is too late for them to be recovered.

Readers of *The Craftsman* would have been heartened to learn that, although the ancient constitution 'hath been often interrupted' by periods of corruption, 'the *Stamina* of it have been still preserved, and transmitted down to us thro' all Ages and Changes of Government'.[18] Through vigorous opposition activity, England's political institutions could still be returned to their former glory. It is far from certain that Swift agreed with this assessment. In Brobdingnag it is revealed that their now virtuous nation was once 'troubled with the same Disease, to which the whole Race of Mankind is Subject; the Nobility often contending for Power, the People for Liberty, and the King for absolute Dominion' (II, vii, 200–1). The only means by which this conflict between the branches of government could be tempered was through enforcing the constitution. And yet Brobdingnag is the exception. As he continues his voyages, Gulliver is repeatedly prompted to consider 'How many innocent and excellent Persons had been condemned to Death or Banishment, by the practising of great Ministers upon the Corruption of Judges' (III, viii, 298–9); and to reckon with 'the Corruption of Ministers, who engage their Master in a War in order to stifle or divert the Clamour of the Subjects against their evil Administration' (IV, v, 363). In Glubbdubdrib he is even assured that no nation could 'be supported without Corruption' because virtuous behaviour 'was a perpetual Clog to publick Business' (III, viii, 300). Most of the societies that Gulliver encounters on his travels are in terminal decline resulting from political maladministration.

[18] *The Craftsman*, 405 (6 April 1734).

In a neat parallel of his earlier debate with the King of Brobdingnag, when Gulliver reaches the land of the Houyhnhnms, he is once more asked about 'the Nature of *Government* in general, and particularly of our own *excellent Constitution*' (IV, vi, 382). Whereas his previous discussion had centred on the balance of powers, only to be disrupted by the king's questions about the weakness of the English system to forms of ministerial corruption, this time Gulliver launches into a vicious tirade against that breed of ministers who possess 'no other Passions but a violent Desire of Wealth, Power, and Titles' (IV, vi, 382). He explains to his Houyhnhnm master both the underhand 'Methods by which a Man may rise to be Chief Minister' and the means by which they 'preserve themselves in Power', which include 'bribing the Majority of a Senate or great Council' with 'all Employments at their Disposal', reiterating the opposition's familiar complaints about 'placemen' in parliament. Through imitating their leader, a prime minister's servants 'learn to excel in the three principal *Ingredients*, of *Insolence*, *Lying*, and *Bribery*'. And when the time comes to retire from public life, a prime minister will introduce legislation designed to 'secure themselves from After-reckonings' and so retire to their country homes 'laden with the Spoils of the Nation' (IV, vi, 383–4). In response, Gulliver's master agrees that 'in most Herds there was a Sort of ruling *Yahoo*' who was 'always more *deformed* in Body, and *mischievous in Disposition*, than any of the rest'. 'But how far this might be applicable to our *Courts* and *Favourites*, and *Ministers of State*', Gulliver adds, 'my Master said I could best determine' (IV, vii, 395).

Here Swift sailed too close to the wind, for this savage description of an avaricious prime minister accumulating personal wealth at the expense of the nation was transparently a portrait of Walpole. Because of Swift's warning that the *Travels* may 'in one or two places' be 'a little Satyrical', Motte was on the lookout for potentially sensitive material (*Correspondence*, III, 9). As publisher of the book, he was legally responsible for its contents.[19] Although Swift had learned to wrap up his 'Invectives against Vice in *Dreams*, *Fables*, *Parallels*, and *Allegories*', like the authors of *The Craftsman*, the anti-ministerial hostility of the final voyage alarmed Motte. He instructed his business partner, Andrew Tooke, to cut suggestive phrases from the text, particularly where they concerned ministers, standing armies, or the royal family. But he could not erase this particular attack without gutting the entire chapter, so instead added a paragraph reminding the reader that Gulliver is speaking during the reign of Queen

[19] Joseph Hone, 'Legal Constraints, Libellous Evasions', in *The Oxford Handbook of Eighteenth-Century Satire*, ed. Paddy Bullard (Oxford: Oxford University Press, 2019), 525–41.

Anne and that he is concerned only with ministers employed by the princes of Europe. As James McLaverty has argued, this intervention underscores that Gulliver is speaking long before Walpole's rise to power and that he is concerned only with 'former Reigns' and foreign courts.[20] Though clumsily done, the insertion insists that Gulliver could not have been reflecting on contemporary English politics.

When news of the publisher's mutilations reached Swift in Dublin, he fired a letter to Pope complaining of 'several passages which appear to be patch'd and altered, and the style of a different sort' (*Correspondence*, III, 56). He was particularly incensed by the inserted paragraph suggesting that Queen Anne 'directs her own Actions to the Good of her People' and thus had no need to rely on ministers (*GT*, 710). His friend Charles Ford was tasked with contacting Motte about the changes: 'it is plainly false in Fact', he explained to the publisher, 'since all the World knows that the Queen during her whole Reign governed by one first Minister or other' (*Correspondence*, III, 66). The question of why Swift was so annoyed by this specific interpolation brings us to the subject of political allusion in Lilliput. Although the tradition of finding consistent or 'foolproof' patterns of allegory in Gulliver's first voyage has been discredited by scholars such as J. A. Downie, it is impossible to ignore the volume of allusions to events surrounding the Hanoverian succession.[21] When Gulliver is shackled in an 'ancient Temple' which had 'been polluted some Years before by an unnatural Murder', Swift seems to gesture at Harley's imprisonment in the Tower of London. Gulliver's flight across the water to Blefuscu, pre-emptively escaping the articles of impeachment drawn up against him, calls to mind the departure of Bolingbroke to France. The inelegant means by which Gulliver extinguishes the fire in the royal palace, leading to his impeachment, nods to the ministry's hurried efforts to draw the War of the Spanish Succession to a close. Skyresh Bolgolam appears to be a composite of Harley's political enemies in those years, while Flimnap, the nimble Lord High Treasurer who manufactures evidence of treason against Gulliver, embodies much of Walpole without ever being a direct match.[22]

[20] James McLaverty, 'The Revision of the First Edition of *Gulliver's Travels*: Book-Trade Context, Interleaving, Two Cancels, and a Failure to Catch', *The Papers of the Bibliographical Society of America*, 106 (2012), 5–35 (19–20).

[21] J. A. Downie, 'Political Characterization in *Gulliver's Travels*', *The Yearbook of English Studies*, 7 (1977), 108–20 (108).

[22] Downie, 'Political Characterization'; Simon Varey, 'Exemplary History and the Political Satire of *Gulliver's Travels*', in *The Genres of Gulliver's Travels*, ed. Frederik N. Smith (Newark: University of Delaware Press, 1990), 39–55. On Flimnap as Walpole, see Paul Langford, 'Swift and Walpole', in *Politics and Literature*, ed. Rawson, 52–78 (70–4).

Why, in a satire on the corruptions of the Walpole administration, would Swift focus a quarter of his narrative on the years surrounding the death of Anne? And why did he react so negatively to what he viewed as a misrepresentation of her mode of governing? Writing to Bolingbroke in 1719, Swift claimed 'there was never a more important' time in England 'than that which made up the four last years of the late Queen' (*Correspondence*, II, 299). Under Harley's leadership, the constitution was being restored 'to its antient Form'.[23] The sudden reversal of fortunes after Anne's death was thus a key moment in Swift's timeline of English political corruption.[24] 'Here ended all our golden Dreams', he moaned in *Verses on the Death of Dr. Swift* (1731), with Walpole and his cronies proceeding to 'Pervert the Law, disgrace the Gown, / Corrupt the Senate, rob the Crown' (*Poems*, II, 567). Far from a perennial disease, the corruption of the ancient constitution under Walpole could be traced back to this very moment: to the end of Anne's reign, the baseless persecution of Harley and Bolingbroke, the suppression of the Tory opposition, and the act establishing seven-year parliaments.[25] These modern deviations from the constitution find their analogues in the activities of Gulliver's enemies in Lilliput. Here for 'the first time' Gulliver 'began to conceive some imperfect Idea of Courts and Ministers' (I, v, 78). By the time he reaches the land of the Houyhnhnms, Gulliver's 'imperfect' view of ministers is thoroughly entrenched. The specificity of political allusion in Lilliput underscores the significance of this fraught period in Swift's narrative of English political corruption. It also explains why Swift was so frustrated by his publisher's false assertion that Anne did not govern by ministers: in Swift's eyes that queen's relationship with Harley exemplified the correct balance of power between monarch and minister, a balance that Walpole had tipped in his favour under George I.

Swift revered the traditional English system of balanced monarchical government. He was disgusted by what he viewed as a perfect storm of infrequent and corrupted elections, a standing army, parliamentary bribery, and a weak king overruled by a crafty minister. *Gulliver's Travels* is imbued with the sense that England was moving ever further from the proper constitutional balance last achieved under Queen Anne. By the time Gulliver arrives back in England in December 1715, the queen lies

---

[23] *The Examiner*, 22 (28 December 1710).
[24] Ashley Marshall, '"*fuimus Torys*": Swift and Regime Change, 1714–1718', *SP*, 112 (2015), 537–74.
[25] Swift made no complaints about Walpole's conduct until his involvement in the impeachment of Harley and Bolingbroke: see Langford, 'Swift and Walpole', 54–6.

dead; Walpole has already presented his articles of impeachment to parliament; Harley is imprisoned in the Tower; Bolingbroke has fled to the continent. In the final chapter Gulliver reflects that 'it would be our Happiness to observe' the King of Brobdingnag's 'wise Maxims in Morality and Government', but concedes this seems unlikely (IV, xii, 438). The visceral 'Hatred, Disgust, and Contempt' he experiences towards his family appear to confirm the king's assessment of modern Englishmen as 'the most pernicious Race of little odious Vermin that Nature ever suffered to crawl upon the Surface of the Earth' (II, vi, 189).

When Gulliver claimed in the final chapter of the *Travels* to 'meddle not the least with any *Party*' and to 'write without Passion, Prejudice, or Ill-will against any Man', his author was lying (IV, xii, 438). The *Travels* is a deeply partisan book. Swift was nervous about publishing it and rightly so. By describing the vulnerabilities of the ancient constitution to forms of ministerial corruption, Swift was contributing to debates initiated by the opposition to Walpole. His general satire against debased political institutions was aimed at a specific target: the men who debased them. Walpole was the criminal-in-chief, though his lackeys in parliament were equally culpable for tarnishing the body politic. Swift offers no cure with his diagnosis. His book is a fantastical tale, not a straight-shooting party pamphlet. There is no sense that he shared Bolingbroke's confidence that a vigorous opposition could restore the constitution to its rightful balance. 'I fear I might outlive liberty in England', Swift later wrote (*Correspondence*, IV, 103). The political universe of the *Travels* is governed by much the same fear.

Religion

Ian Higgins

The frontispiece portrait of Lemuel Gulliver in *Gulliver's Travels* published as volume three of George Faulkner's four-volume octavo edition of Swift's *Works* in 1735 (Figure 9.1) strongly resembles the edition's frontispiece portrait of the Reverend Dr Jonathan Swift. Swift's formal wig has been removed and his clerical collar replaced with a raffish kerchief for his incognito appearance as Gulliver.[1] *Gulliver's Travels*, supposedly written by a layman, Lemuel Gulliver, is predominantly secular in its focus on society and governance, but its political and historical perspectives and view of human nature are refracted by Swift's religious confession.

Swift was Dean of St Patrick's, Dublin in the (Anglican) Church of Ireland. His public and private piety and devotion in ministering his spiritual office as Dean in his cathedral and as a priest in his household are attested by contemporary witnesses who knew him well. His homiletic and polemical writings are militant in defence of the episcopal Church of England as the true orthodox Catholic and Apostolic Church, reformed from the corruptions of Rome, but whose doctrinal integrity, rights, powers and privileges, status and influence were being threatened by Presbyterian and sectarian Protestantism, Whig monarchs and parliaments, anti-clericalism, and 'free-thinking'. At the beginning of Queen Anne's reign, Swift 'confessed myself to be an High-churchman, and that I did not conceive how any one, who wore the habit of a clergyman, could be otherwise'.[2] In 1726, the year of *Gulliver's* publication, he implied that he was on principle among the 'Rank Toryes' in the Church.[3] Gulliver, however, displays no Christian devotion, in private or in a Church. Christian religious reference is conspicuously absent from what is shown

---

[1] See *GT*, 2 and 570 for the frontispiece portraits. Swift's correspondence relating to *Gulliver's Travels* is also quoted from this edition.

[2] Swift, 'Memoirs, Relating to That Change Which Happened in the Queen's Ministry in the Year 1710', in *Prose Writings*, VIII, 120.

[3] Swift to Thomas Tickell, 7 July 1726, *Correspondence*, II, 650.

of Gulliver's mental and emotional world, such as it is. Gulliver attributes his life experiences to his 'Fortune', 'Nature', 'Destiny' and 'Fate', never to Providence or the Will of God. In crises he never appeals to God in prayer. He trusts himself to the 'Mercy of the Waves', not to God's mercy. Gulliver is largely silent about the established Church of his country. However, *Gulliver's Travels* contains biblical analogies, allusions and phrases and religio-political satire. It presupposes a largely Christian readership with secure moral categories of good and evil, virtue and vice, and an assumption of human superiority over animals. A readership therefore likely to be confronted and challenged by the satire's relentless account of human turpitude, endemic individual and institutional corruption, and of human brutality infinitely worse than beasts. In Gulliver's voyages to remote nations of the world, the reader is to learn some home truths about Christian Europe.

Gulliver's family and education are suggestive of a Puritan background – Gulliver's ancestors are buried in Banbury, a town associated by Swift and his contemporaries with sectarian Puritan fanaticism; he studied at Emmanuel College, Cambridge, a college of Puritan foundation, and at Leyden, a preferred continental educational destination of dissenting Protestants in England and a town notorious as the birthplace of the Anabaptist leader, 'Jack of Leyden', satirised in Swift's *A Tale of a Tub* and *A Mechanical Operation of the Spirit*. 'Lemuel' is a biblical name and means 'dedicated to God' in Hebrew. Gulliver, however, displays no Puritan idiom or religiosity, religious emotion or personal Christian reference. Ironically, he perhaps undergoes a kind of Puritan conversion experience in Part IV, as he becomes enlightened by and a proselyte for a rational and natural order of prelapsarian equine arcadians. He has little or nothing to say about religion or the priesthood in the countries he visits. There is no interest in comparative religion. Gulliver indeed says that his 'Story' will be without the descriptions of 'the barbarous Customs and Idolatry of savage People, with which most Writers abound' (II, viii, 211). What he does describe of religious customs is derisive. In the 'Voyage to Lilliput', for example, Swift recycles voyage literature accounts of upright burials in ridiculing the absurd literalism of Lilliputian burial customs: 'They bury their Dead with their Heads directly downwards; because they hold an Opinion, that in eleven Thousand Moons they are all to rise again; in which Period, the Earth (which they conceive to be flat) will turn upside down, and by this Means they shall, at their Resurrection, be found ready standing on their Feet' (I, vi, 83).

While Gulliver is reticent on religion, his Christianity is simply assumed in the narrative. It is memorably activated just once by Swift in order to satirise the Calvinist Protestant Dutch as infidels. On his return to England via Japan at the end of Part III, Gulliver, who is pretending to be a Dutchman, petitions to be excused from '*trampling upon the Crucifix*', the ceremony of *Yefumi* imposed by the Japanese in order to detect Christians who were forbidden in Japan. The Emperor of Japan is surprised by Gulliver's '*singularity*' in requesting to be excused from the test, 'and said, he believed I was the first of my Countrymen who ever made any Scruple in this Point; and that he began to doubt whether I were a real *Hollander* or no; but rather suspected I must be a CHRISTIAN' (III, xi, 324). In a letter to Alexander Pope about *Gulliver's Travels* Swift described his worldview:

> I have ever hated all Nations professions and Communityes and all my love is towards individuals for instance I hate the tribe of Lawyers, but I love Councellor such a one, Judge such a one for so with Physicians (I will not Speak of my own Trade) Soldiers, English, Scotch, French; and the rest but principally I hate and detest that animal called man, although I hartily love, John, Peter, Thomas and so forth. ('Swift to Alexander Pope, 29 September 1725' in *GT*, 592)

Except for a passage in Part II, Swift does not speak about the Anglican priesthood in this satire. The anti-clerical, sceptical philosopher David Hume noted Swift's silence about his profession:

> I have frequently had it in my Intentions to write a Supplement to *Gulliver*, containing the Ridicule of Priests. Twas certainly a Pity that Swift was a Parson. Had he been a Lawyer or Physician, we had nevertheless been entertain'd at the Expense of these Professions. But Priests are so jealous, that they cannot bear to be touch'd on that Head; and for a plain Reason: Because they are conscious they are really ridiculous.[4]

The book's one extended reference to the ecclesiastical order in England occurs during Gulliver's patriotic eulogy of the English Constitution in his conversation with the King of Brobdingnag. Gulliver describes exemplary bishops in the House of Lords:

> [...] holy Persons [...] under the Title of Bishops; whose peculiar Business it is, to take care of Religion, and of those who instruct the People therein. These were searched and sought out through the whole Nation, by the

---

[4] Hume to Gilbert Elliot, 18 February 1751, *The Letters of David Hume*, ed. J. Y. T. Greig, 2 vols. (Oxford: Clarendon Press, 1932), I, 153; quoted in *GT*, 83.

Prince and wisest Counsellors, among such of the Priesthood, as were
deservedly distinguished by the Sanctity of their Lives, and the Depth of
their Erudition; who were indeed the spiritual Fathers of the Clergy and the
People. (II, vi, 181)

As a High Churchman, Swift regarded church government by bishops
(episcopacy) as an Apostolic institution, one deriving from Christ's early
followers. A prime function of the episcopate was to protect the Church
from heresy and Schism (religious division or separation that breaks the
unity of the Church). Swift defended episcopacy but was a scathing critic
of particular bishops. Unlike Gulliver, Swift was highly critical of the
current bench of bishops in England and Ireland, many of whom were
Williamite and Hanoverian appointments perceived by High Churchmen
like Swift to be heterodox, timeserving supporters of the Whig government, and sympathetic to Whig and Dissenting aspirations and legislative
attempts to remove the civil disabilities placed upon non-Anglican
Protestants. In the words of one of Swift's correspondents, the established
Church's 'hierarchy is in heterodox hands [...] Presbytery is become
episcopal; and she is reduced, in regard of her authority and livings, to
be only presbyterian'.[5] Swift's own views about several individual Whig
bishops are precisely articulated in the King of Brobdingnag's acute query
put to Gulliver after his panegyric of them: 'Whether those holy Lords
[...] had never been Compliers with the Times, while they were common
Priests; or slavish prostitute Chaplains to some Nobleman, whose opinions
they continued servilely to follow' in the House of Lords. The King's
damning conclusion is that priests were not advanced to bishoprics 'for
their Piety or Learning' (II, vi, 183, 189).

    As an author and priest, Swift had a scandalous aura as the suspected
author of the anonymously published *A Tale of a Tub* of 1704 which had
attracted charges of irreligion and blasphemy. As the same charges would
be levelled again at *Gulliver's Travels*, it is germane to consider briefly what
was considered scandalous about the treatment of religion in Swift's earlier
book. *A Tale of a Tub* is a satire on corruptions in religion and learning.
The religious satire is conducted mainly through an allegorical tale of three
brothers Peter (Roman Catholicism), Martin (the moderate Protestant
Reformation and Anglicanism), and Jack (the Radical Reformation,
Puritan Nonconformity and Protestant Dissent). Swift never publicly
acknowledged his authorship of the work. In the revised fifth edition of

---

[5] Charles Wogan's epistle to Swift in 1733, in *Miscellaneous Pieces. In Prose and Verse. By the Rev.
Dr. Jonathan Swift, Dean of St. Patrick's, Dublin* (1789), 63.

the volume published in 1710, Swift affixed an 'Apology' in which he asked: *'Why should any Clergyman of our Church be angry to see the Follies of Fanaticism and Superstition exposed, tho' in the most ridiculous Manner? since that is perhaps the most probable way to cure them, or at least hinder them from farther spreading'*. He claimed his book *'Celebrates the Church of* England *as the most perfect of all others in Discipline and Doctrine, it advances no Opinion they reject, nor condemns any they receive' (Tale,* 6). But the profane mockery and extremism of the satiric ridicule, especially against Protestant Dissenters, provoked contemporary readers. The linguist and cleric William Wotton in his 'Observations upon The *Tale of a Tub*' was appalled. The book 'is of so irreligious a nature, is so crude a Banter upon all that is esteemed as Sacred among all Sects and Religions'. It is 'one of the Prophanest Banters upon the Religion of *Jesus Christ*, as such, that ever yet appeared [. . .] whilst the Protestant Dissenters are, to outward appearance, the most directly levelled at'.[6] The High Churchman Francis Atterbury, dean of Carlisle and later bishop of Rochester, was an admirer of the book and seems to have identified Swift as its author. But he confided to a correspondent: 'The author of "A Tale of a Tub" will not as yet be known; and if it be the man I guess, he hath reason to conceal himself, because of the prophane strokes in that piece, which would do his reputation and interest in the world more harm than the wit can do him good'.[7] Two instances of the profane strokes in the religious satire may suffice here. In the ridicule of the Roman Catholic doctrine of transubstantiation in Section IV, Peter at a formal dinner passes off a crust of bread to his brothers saying it is a feast of '*Mutton*'. Jesus Christ, known to Christians as the 'Lamb of God', is equated with old sheep meat (*Tale*, 76). In Section XI of the *Tale*, Swift parodies Calvinist Predestination by having Jack 'shut his Eyes as he walked along the Streets' and break his nose against a post, '*a Rencounter*', Jack says, that was '*ordained . . . before the Creation*' and allowed to happen by '*Providence*' (*Tale*, 125). Wotton remarked: 'This is a direct Prophanation of the Majesty of God' (Wotton, 'Observations', *Tale*, 226), an imputation of impiety that Swift as priest felt he needed particularly to address. In the revised fifth edition of *A Tale of a Tub*, references to '*Providence*' in the passage were altered to '*Nature*' and '*Fortune*' (*Tale*, 125, 303). Swift seems especially careful not to be profane about Providence in *Gulliver's Travels*. Gulliver is 'condemned by Nature

---

[6] 'William Wotton's Observations upon the *Tale of a Tub*', in *Tale*, 218, 227.

[7] *The Epistolary Correspondence, Visitation Charges, Speeches and Miscellanies of the Right Reverend Francis Atterbury, D. D., Lord Bishop of Rochester*, ed. John Nichols, 4 vols. (1783–7), III, 218.

and Fortune to an active and restless Life' (II, i, 117) and throughout the
Travels Gulliver refers to 'Nature' and 'Fortune' rather than 'Providence'.
Pointedly, an admirable original institution of Lilliput is that 'the Disbelief
of a Divine Providence renders a Man uncapable of holding any publick
Station' (I, vi, 87). As a priest, Swift regarded himself as on combat duty for
Providence. One of his 'Thoughts on Religion' states: 'I look upon myself,
in the capacity of a clergyman, to be one appointed by providence for
defending a post assigned me, and for gaining over as many enemies as
I can. Although I think my cause is just, yet one great motion is my
submitting to the pleasure of Providence, and to the laws of my country'
(*Prose Writings*, IX, 262).

Swift was an ardent advocate for the confessional state. It is a reiterated
religio-political positive in *Gulliver's Travels*. Swift distinguished between
an individual's private liberty of conscience, which was to be tolerated, and
the public expression of conscience which was to be regulated by the
magistrate. Swift believed that for the peace and safety of the Church
and State there must always be public conformity to the state religion as
established by 'the laws of my country', which in Britain and Ireland was
Anglican. The non-Anglican religious confessions presented a security risk
to the establishment in Church and State. Roman Catholics owed their
first allegiance to a foreign power, the Pope in Rome. Presbyterians and
Independents, when they had power in the 1640s and 1650s, had abolished
monarchy and episcopacy and imposed military government. The Test
Acts of 1673 and 1678, and the 'Test Clause' of 1704 in Ireland, were the
legislative means to coerce public conformity to the Church of England
and the Church of Ireland and to exclude non-Anglicans from civil power.
The Sacramental Test required holders of public office to receive the
Sacrament according to the rites of the Church of England. This law was
defended by Swift, almost as an act of faith. He was profoundly hostile to
those Protestants who had separated from the established Church and so
had divided the Protestant body of worshippers.

As a High Churchman Swift regarded Schism with gravity. Responding
to arguments by an anti-clerical Whig and Deist, Matthew Tindal, for
unlimited liberty of conscience and the removal of the statutes excluding
Protestant Dissenters from public offices, Swift wrote: 'The Scripture is full
against Schism. *Tindall* promoteth it, and placeth in it all the present and
future Happiness of Man'. What 'hath corrupted Religion, is the Liberty
unlimited of professing all Opinions' (*Prose Writings*, II, 94, 96). Tindall
does not consider 'that most religious Wars have been caused by Schisms,
when the dissenting Parties were ready to join with any ambitious

discontented Men' (*Prose Writings*, II, 100). In his position statement 'The Sentiments of a Church-of-England Man', '*Schism*' is a 'Spiritual Evil' and also 'a Temporal one': 'And I think it clear, that any great Separation from the established Worship, although to a new one that is more pure and perfect, may be an Occasion of endangering the publick Peace' (*Prose Writings*, II, 11). Swift anathematised schism in religion and was particularly antipathetic to the Puritans, whom he blames for the Civil War which destroyed 'the Constitution, both of Religion and Government' (*Prose Writings*, II, 12), and to contemporary Protestant Dissenters as their schismatical heirs. The gravity of schism is stressed in Section VI of *A Tale of a Tub* when moderate Martin counsels zealot Jack on reformation:

> That *it was true, the Testament of their good Father was very exact in what related to* [the Doctrine and Faith of Christianity]; *yet was it no less penal and strict in prescribing Agreement, and Friendship, and Affection between them. And therefore, if straining a Point were at all dispensable, it would certainly be so, rather to the Advance of Unity, than Increase of Contradiction.* (*Tale*, 93)

The opposition to Schism expressed in Swift's polemic and imaginatively in *A Tale of a Tub* is reprised in *Gulliver's Travels* and the solution to it rendered with increasing extremism.

In Lilliput there is a violent religious and civil dispute over which end of an egg to break in order to eat it. A regal change to the primitive way of breaking an egg has occasioned rebellions, executions, regicide, deposition and abdication, and war. The history of this Lilliputian dispute bears an obvious close analogy with the history of religio-political conflict in England since the Reformation (I, iv, 70–2). The satire's primary point is that a 'Schism in Religion' has been made out of '*straining a Point*', a difference of opinion over something not doctrinally significant (the technical theological term is 'adiaphora'). Gulliver reports that the controversy derives from 'a meer Strain upon the Text' in a chapter of their Holy Book: 'For the Words are these: *That all true Believers shall break their Eggs at the convenient End*'. Gulliver opines that the 'convenient End' should 'be left to every Man's Conscience, or at least in the Power of the chief Magistrate to determine' (I, iv, 71–2). The analogy of the Lilliputian religious history with English history does seem to raise the question as to whether Swift is implying that the momentous Reformation religious disputes were actually just differences of opinion over adiaphora which should not have led to divisions in the religious body. In Part II the King of Brobdingnag gives Gulliver his opinion (it is also Swift's) on 'the several

Sects among us in Religion and Politicks'. It is now different private opinions that are toxic and their expression is to be suppressed: 'He said, he knew no Reason, why those who entertain Opinions prejudicial to the Publick, should be obliged to change, or should not be obliged to conceal them [...] For, a Man may be allowed to keep Poisons in his Closet, but not to vend them about as Cordials' (II, vi, 187). Poisons are Swift's trope for sectarian opinions in his tracts defending the Test Acts.[8] In Part IV, Gulliver gives the Houyhnhnm master a reductive summary account of the causes of horrific religious wars in Christian Europe:

> Difference in Opinions hath cost many Millions of Lives: For Instance, whether *Flesh* be *Bread*, or *Bread* be *Flesh*: Whether the Juice of a certain Berry be *Blood* or *Wine*: Whether *Whistling* be a Vice or a Virtue: Whether it be better to *kiss a Post*, or throw it into the Fire: What is the best Colour for a *Coat*, whether *Black*, *White*, *Red* or *Grey*; and whether it should be *long* or *short*, *narrow* or *wide*, *dirty* or *clean*; with many more. Neither are any Wars so furious and bloody, or of so long Continuance, as those occasioned by Difference in Opinion, especially if it be in things indifferent. (IV, v, 363)

Swift's satiric technique here is absurdist: the opinions and actions described are deprived of the substance and context that would make them intelligible. The material sign or symbol, emptied of explanatory religious significance, becomes in Gulliver's account the literal subject of the dispute, and an inexplicably ridiculous or trivial cause of war. The Reformation religious divisions over the Roman Catholic doctrine of transubstantiation, Romanist image worship and Puritan iconoclasm, vestment controversies, and so on are presented by Swift as 'things indifferent', non-essential points of no doctrinal significance. Swift's burlesque seems to treat some fundamental differences in sacred belief among Christians as adiaphora, as points dispensable in the interest of unity and peace.

The utopian Houyhnhnms have no difference in opinion, or at least no unregulated public disagreement. There are no wars in Houyhnhnm-land. Their island agrarian economy has a pest problem, but is otherwise at peace. The Houyhnhnms' only subject of debate is 'Whether the Yahoos should be exterminated from the Face of the Earth' (IV, ix, 408, an echo of Genesis 6:7). (We only hear of arguments for the affirmative.) The Yahoos are a humanoid species in the fable of Part IV, odious and unreasoning, intractable and unruly. There is a Houyhnhnm tradition that they are not '*Aborigines*' of the island but are the engendered brood of two brutes that appeared on a mountain, a kind of Yahoo Adam and Eve (IV, ix, 409). The

---

[8] See *Prose Writings*, XII, 246, 257.

Yahoos derive from an amalgam of sources available to Swift. But Swift's phobic vitriol and genocidal utterances against 'cursed', 'damned' rebellious Scots and 'Scots Irish' Presbyterians are certainly echoed in the account of the Yahoos, and of Houyhnhnm actions and intentions against them. The noisome Yahoos are odiously shaped, nasty and greedy, seize and destroy cattle, and cause '*Civil War* among themselves' (see IV, vii, 390–1, 421–2). The Presbyterian Scots are depicted as 'stinking' and 'ill-shaped', stealing cattle, and causing civil war in Swift's allegory of them in *The Story of the Injured Lady. Being a True Picture of Scotch Perfidy, Irish Poverty, and English Partiality* written at the time of the Act of Union in 1707 (*Prose Writings*, IX, 3–4). There have been killing times in Houyhnhnm-land in the past (when the Yahoos were hunted down), as there had been in Scotland when the Scots Presbyterians would not conform to the episcopal established religion under the restored Stuart monarchy. The Houyhnhnms want to extirpate the Yahoos from their island, 'to get rid of this Evil', to have the Yahoos 'rooted out' (IV, ix, 409). Swift used such language in his Test Act tracts against Ulster Scots Presbyterians who 'never are rooted out where they once fix' (*Prose Writings*, II, 116). Swift approved the resolution of his hero, the Earl of Strafford, when on coming from Ireland, he allegedly said that 'if he ever return'd to that Sword again, he would not leave a *Scotish*-man in that Kingdom' (*Prose Writings*, V, 298). Swift's abusive marginalia against the Presbyterian Scots in his copy of the Earl of Clarendon's *History of the Rebellion* (1702–4) culminates at one point with the wish that 'the whole Nation to a Man' were hanged (*Prose Writings*, V, 317).

The King of Brobdingnag's verdict to Gulliver concludes 'the Bulk of your Natives, to be the most pernicious Race of little odious Vermin that Nature ever suffered to crawl upon the Surface of the Earth' (II, vi, 189). But Gulliver's Fourth Voyage takes Swift's satire on the 'animal called man' to a new level of extremity. Swift was explicit about the intentional misanthropic project of his satire. Swift's correspondence relating to the satiric purpose of *Gulliver's Travels*, and the view of human nature insisted upon throughout the book, imply Swift's strong Augustinian sense of humankind as flawed by Original Sin. In the letter to Alexander Pope of 29 September 1725, Swift wrote that his 'Travells' are erected on a 'great foundation of Misanthropy' (*GT*, 592). Pope saw the book's misanthropic project as religious in intention, telling Swift: 'But I find you would rather be employ'd as an Avenging Angel of wrath, to break your Vial of Indignation over the heads of the wretched pityful creatures of this World' (*GT*, 593). 'Drown the World', Swift wrote in his letter of reply, recalling the biblical judgement of God on a fallen humankind (*Correspondence*, II, 623). On 7 November 1726 John Gay and Alexander Pope reported reader responses to Gulliver's misanthropy: 'Those of them who frequent the Church, say, his design is impious, and that it is an insult on Providence, by depreciating the works of the Creator' (*GT*, 598). They are allegations that Gulliver unapologetically acknowledges in 'A Letter from Capt. Gulliver, to his Cousin Sympson' affixed to the 1735 edition of the book: 'I see myself accused [. . .] of degrading human Nature, (for so they have still the Confidence to stile it)' (*GT*, 11).

There continues to be scholarly controversy about the possible religious implications or overtones of what seems to be primarily a secular philosophical fable in Part IV. In Houyhnhnm-land, Gulliver encounters two mythic species, rational horses and unreasoning brutes, with Gulliver and his kind compared to, conflated with, and generally shown to be worse than the bestial humanoid Yahoos. The Yahoos are not solely identified with any one particular human group, whether English, Irish, 'Scots Irish', Jews, natives of Africa, Australia, the Americas, or the helots of ancient Sparta, though they have some resemblances with each of them, as well as with voyage literature accounts of monkeys and apes. The pariah Yahoo species in the fable rather functions as the repellent image for all humankind when acting without reason and virtue. The Houyhnhnms have been associated with Deists and Atheists by some scholars. But, obviously, the Houyhnhnms are pre-Christian. Their society is modelled on Lycurgan Sparta, the utopias of Plato's *Republic* and Thomas More's *Utopia*, and accounts of a primitivist Golden Age. The Houyhnhnms seem hypothetical embodiments of the stoic-influenced state of nature described in the 'Prolegomena' of Hugo Grotius's *De Jure Belli ac Pacis* (*The Law of War and Peace*) where there is conformity to natural law without the necessity of divine injunction. Swift has enabled readers to view the Houyhnhnms as pre-Christian Ancients in an austere but admirable arcadia. They do not reject the Christian revelation, like a Deist or an Atheist, it is just that they have never heard of it, and Gulliver is no Christian missionary intending to convert them. The Houyhnhnms are like More's Utopians in that they follow reason and nature, and their conception of reason, and of virtue as living in accord with nature, is stoic. The vast majority of More's Utopians are said to believe in an eternal, infinite divinity diffused throughout the universe: 'Him they call their parent'.[9] Gulliver reports that the 'strongly expressive' word for

---

[9] Thomas More, *Utopia*, ed. George M. Logan, trans. Robert M. Adams, Cambridge Texts in the History of Political Thought, 3rd ed. (Cambridge: Cambridge University Press, 2016), Book II, 98.

dying among the Houyhnhnms means '*to retire to his first Mother*' (IV, ix, 414). The communism of Swift's Houyhnhnms, like that of More's Utopians, may be recalling the communistic practices of the early Christians, as well as those of classical utopias. But there is no mention of a Houyhnhnm religion. Swift's insult, added to the satiric injury of Part IV of *Gulliver's Travels*, is that the kind of peaceful, rational, natural and virtuous social order, admired in charismatic writings of the classical humanist tradition, and absent in flagitious Christian Europe, is found in a mythic equine arcadia, an emphatically non-human world without a long list of human vices and follies, and from which a human, Gulliver, is deported.

Swift told his close friend Charles Ford in a letter of 1725 that his forthcoming 'Travells' would 'wonderfully mend the World' (*GT*, 591). But in the familiar paradox of the radical satirist, the view of the world displayed in these *Travels* sees humankind, for the most part, as incapable of amendment and too depraved to be saved. Swift did intimate how the fable of Part IV might be interpreted by readers enduring this fallen world. In another letter of 1725, Swift drew a lesson from his forthcoming work for his close friend, the Irish High Church clergyman Thomas Sheridan, described by Swift as 'having been famous for a high Tory, and suspected as a Jacobite' (*Prose Writings*, V, 223). Sheridan had preached a sermon in Cork on 1 August 1725, the anniversary of the Hanoverian King George I's succession, on the Gospel text (St. Matthew 6: 34): 'Sufficient unto the day is the evil thereof'. A Whig informer in the congregation reported him. Sheridan was promptly struck from the list of chaplains to the Lord Lieutenant of Ireland. Swift offered his proscribed friend the following counsel: 'expect no more from Man than such an Animal is capable of, and you will every day find my Description of *Yahoes* more resembling. You should think and deal with every Man as a Villain, without calling him so, or flying from him, or valuing him less. This is an old true Lesson' (*GT*, 591–2).

CHAPTER 3

Bodies and Gender

Liz Bellamy

During his sojourn in Lilliput, when Gulliver is still in favour with the court, he participates in a curious performance. He stands with legs apart, 'like a *Colossus*', while 3,000 infantry and 1,000 cavalry march beneath, 'with Drums beating, Colours flying, and Pikes advanced'. Despite being ordered to 'observe the strictest Decency', some of the 'younger Officers' are tempted to look up, and Gulliver remarks that his 'Breeches were at that Time in so ill a Condition, that they afforded some Opportunities for Laughter and Admiration' (I, iii, 61–2). The *OED* defines the principal meaning of 'Admiration' in this period as 'wonder, astonishment, surprise', and Gulliver deploys all these synonyms to describe the reactions of the Lilliputians not just to his giant genitals, but to his entire body. The first inhabitant to see his face raises 'his Hands and Eyes' in a gesture that Gulliver interprets as 'by way of Admiration' (I, i, 34); the consumption of his first meal elicits 'a thousand Marks of Wonder and Astonishment' from the assembled crowd, who 'shouted for Joy, and danced upon [his] Breast' when he had 'performed these Wonders' (I, i, 36–7), while the sight of his scimitar and his entertainment of the Blefuscudian ambassadors are both subsequently described as causing 'surprise'. Gulliver's prodigious consumption of wine on first arrival in Lilliput is followed by an equally dramatic discharge, as he makes water 'very plentifully', in a 'Torrent', 'to the great Astonishment of the People' (I, i, 38).

Later, 'pressed by the Necessities of Nature', Gulliver creeps into his 'House' to discharge his 'uneasy Load'. He refers to the 'Shame' of this 'uncleanly [...] Action', but while it is not a public display to the people of Lilliput in the manner of his earlier urination, the detail with which this evacuation is described renders it performative to 'the candid reader'. The reader is enjoined to consider it 'maturely and impartially', although the sympathies of modern readers are probably less for Gulliver than for the servants employed to remove the 'offensive Matter [...] in Wheel-barrows' each day (I, ii, 43–4). The meditation on defecation concludes with a reference to 'When this Adventure was at an End' (I, ii, 44). Adventure may be used here in the sense of 'a chance occurrence or event', but the *OED* suggests that this meaning can be difficult to distinguish from 'A remarkable or unexpected event, [. . .] a novel or exciting experience'. Developing from the idea that Gulliver's toilet arrangements may be remarkable and exciting, this essay will explore the significance of bodies within *Gulliver's Travels*. Critics have frequently characterised the narrative as misogynistic and stressed its negative representation of female physicality, but this reading will highlight the importance of both male and female forms in the construction of gender relationships. It will conclude by suggesting that the text needs to be read alongside contemporary drama to get a sense of its domestic ideology and concept of gender identity.

Gulliver's Monstrous Masculinity

Many early readers took the excremental allusions in Swift's writings as evidence that he was unhealthily obsessed, citing poems such as *The Lady's Dressing Room* (1732), in which the protagonist is shocked by the realisation that 'Celia, Celia, Celia shits'. More recently, the critical consensus has moved away from what Paul-Gabriel Boucé describes as 'the recurrent and tiresomely systematic confusion of Swift and his fictive persona', emphasising the distinction between Swift and Gulliver, and the importance of the literary and historical, rather than biographical, contexts of the *Travels*.[1] The scatological references should be read within a long tradition of comic writing about bodily functions. Gulliver's body positivity in Lilliput invokes the festive comedy of François Rabelais, whose stories celebrate the excessive consumption and evacuation of the giants Gargantua and Pantagruel, but there are also echoes of Joseph Hall's mock voyage narrative, *Mundus Alter et Idem* (1605).[2] Hall's hero, Mercurius Britannicus, visits Crapulia, the land of gluttons, where political power is proportionate to girth, and readers are invited to condemn a society based on greed.[3] Gulliver deploys Rabelaisian comedy in presenting his body as a wonder and a spectacle, but this is undercut by intimations that the Lilliputians may experience some of the disgust of the British Mercury in relation to his

---

[1] Paul-Gabriel Boucé, 'Gulliver Phallophorus and the Maids of Honour in Brobdingnag', *Bulletin de la société d'études anglo-américaines des XVIIe et XVIIIe siècles*, 53 (2001), 81–98 (84).
[2] François Rabelais, *Gargantua and Pantagruel*, trans. M. A. Screech (London: Penguin, 2006); Joseph Hall, *Another World and Yet the Same: Bishop Joseph Hall's Mundus Alter et Idem*, trans. John Millar Wands (London: Yale University Press, 1981).
[3] Hall, *Mundus Alter*, 26–9.

monstrous form. For example, while Gulliver represents his action in extinguishing the palace fire as a 'very eminent Piece of Service', readers may understand her Majesty's 'Abhorrence' at the deed, sympathising with her decision to remove 'to the most distant Side of the Court', and her resolution 'that those Buildings should never be repaired for her Use' (I, v, 80–1).

The royal distaste at Gulliver's micturition is accompanied by anxieties over his appetite. Maintaining the complacence manifested on his first arrival, Gulliver boasts of the hundreds of Lilliputians employed to sustain his 'Domestick' (I, vi, 92). Eighteenth-century readers would recognise the strain this placed on the public purse through echoes of contemporary debates on the costs of maintaining the army, yet Gulliver remains curiously oblivious to the financial consequences of his presence within Lilliput. So obtuse is he that, when entertaining the Emperor and his family, he resolves to 'eat more than usual, in Honour to my dear Country, as well as to fill the Court with Admiration' (I, vi, 94). This preoccupation with conspicuous consumption is contrasted with the fiscal pragmatism of Flimnap, the Lord High Treasurer, who:

> Represented to the Emperor the low Condition of his Treasury; that he was forced to take up Money at a great Discount; that Exchequer Bills would not circulate under nine *per Cent.* below Par; that I had cost his Majesty above a Million and a half of *Sprugs*, [. . .] and [. . .] that it would be adviseable in the Emperor to take the first fair Occasion of dismissing me. (I, vi, 94)

The reader can see that far from being the social call that Gulliver assumes, the visit from the court is politically motivated, to assess the impact of his appetite. Yet Gulliver persists in attributing the enmity of Flimnap to private jealousy and 'the Moroseness of his Nature' (I, vi, 94), rather than legitimate economic concern, citing gossip about his wife to validate this view. The ludic Rabelaisian comedy of the suggestion that Gulliver had a sexual relationship with a six-inch woman is reinforced by his protracted and pompous rebuttal of rumours that he himself has raised, signalling that he is not a reliable guide to individual or political bodies.

Gulliver attributes his fall from favour to his virtuous refusal to gratify the passions of his Imperial Majesty and destroy the Blefuscudian fleet (I, v, 76). This is cited in the Articles of Impeachment, alongside desecration of the Royal Palace, entertainment of the Blefuscudian ambassador and the planned visit to Blefuscu (I, vii, 98–9). Yet the debates in the Committees of Council suggest that the principal concern is not with the treasonable actions of the past but with the physical and economic dangers posed by

Gulliver's monstrous body. There is anxiety that he could 'drown the whole Palace' with a 'discharge of Urine', but the main worry is the financial strain imposed by the appetite on which Gulliver so prides himself. Flimnap 'shewed to what Streights his Majesty's Revenue was reduced by the Charge of maintaining' him, arguing this 'would soon grow insupportable' (I, vii, 101). The methods discussed for Gulliver's extermination reference classical stories of treachery (I, vii, 99), but the problem is indisputably real. The final decision that Gulliver should be gradually starved, 'leaving the Skeleton as a Monument of Admiration to Posterity' (I, vii, 102), is ironically consonant with Gulliver's construction of himself as an object of public wonder.

Gulliver's Rabelaisian pride in the functions of his monstrous body is therefore juxtaposed with the Lilliputian state's identification of this body as a political problem. As readers of Hall's narrative are invited to judge the gustatory excesses of the inhabitants of Crapulia, so Swift's readers can see what Gulliver fails to notice – the strain his maintenance places on the people of Lilliput and the public rather than personal imperative for his removal. This is reinforced when Gulliver escapes to Blefuscu, for although the Emperor welcomes him, there is general relief within the court when he announces his departure and the country is, as the Emperor puts it to his Lilliputian counterpart, 'freed from so insupportable an Incumbrance' (I, viii, 109). Gulliver's celebration of his body within Lilliput suggests a dominant masculinity which connotes insensitivity and lack of empathy. He does not recognise that, when he urinates in the royal apartments, his masculinity is literally toxic, and his problem of vision is signalled in the references to his spectacles (I, ii, 55; v, 74). His inability to see the needle and thread used by the tiny seamstress (I, vi, 82) is matched by his blindness to the legitimate concerns of the Lilliputian people as he continues to read their expressions as connoting admiration for his physical form rather than dismay at its capacity to consume.

Female Bodies

Gulliver's concern with his bodily functions recurs in Brobdingnag as he entertains the farmer's family (II, i, 127–8) and the Queen (II, iii, 149) by his consumption of tiny meals and again furnishes details of how he does 'more than one Thing, which another could not do for [him]' (II, i, 133), even though his evacuations no longer pose the practical problems experienced in Lilliput. When 'exposed for Money as a publick Spectacle' (II, ii, 137), he embraces the opportunity for display with a complex routine of

'Fopperies' (II, ii, 139) and while resenting the farmer's exploitation (II, iii, 142–3), he is not concerned about the 'Ignominy of being carried about for a Monster' (II, ii, 137). Although still preoccupied with performance, Gulliver now prides himself on his littleness, and this leads to a complete change in perspective and a very different concept of gender identity. The celebration of giantism that characterises the first voyage is replaced by horror at the enormous bodies he encounters in the second. This is evident from Gulliver's arrival at the farmer's house, when he expatiates on his disgust at the sight of the 'monstrous Breast' of the wet nurse (II, i, 130) and provides a description of its size, colour and shape to elicit similar reactions in the reader.

Commentators have noted Gulliver's preoccupation with breasts, and the consistently negative lexis deployed in their description has been cited to support suggestions that his perspective is inherently misogynistic.[4] This view is challenged by readings which represent Gulliver as misanthropic, disdaining not women but humanity. Claude Rawson argues that the monstrous female bodies are balanced by males such as the 'Fellow with a Wen in his Neck' and another 'with a couple of wooden Legs' (II, iv, 159).[5] Yet the description of a woman 'with a Cancer in her Breast, swelled to a monstrous Size, full of Holes' is particularly striking, not least through Gulliver's suggestion that he 'could have easily crept' in two or three of the holes and 'covered [his] whole Body' (II, iv, 159). The idea of a six-inch man entering the holes in a woman's body has inevitable sexual connotations and Louise Barnett presents a convincing argument that the female characters evoke a stronger sense of disgust than the male.[6]

The description of Gulliver's visits to the Maids of Honour is central to critical debates over Swift's constructions of gender. This was taken by early commentators as evidence of Swift's personal animus against Queen Anne's attendants[7] but is now identified as having wider cultural and historical significance. Gulliver describes how he attends the young women so that they can 'have the Pleasure of seeing and touching' him. He complains that 'they would often strip me naked from Top to Toe, and lay me at full Length in their Bosoms; wherewith I was much disgusted; because, to say the Truth, a very offensive Smell came from their Skins' (II,

---

[4] Louise Barnett, *Jonathan Swift in the Company of Women* (Oxford: Oxford University Press, 2007), 112–13.
[5] Claude Rawson, *God, Gulliver and Genocide: Barbarism and the European Imagination, 1492–1945* (Oxford: Oxford University Press, 2001), 178.
[6] Barnett, *Jonathan Swift in the Company of Women*, 111–12.
[7] John Gay to Swift, 17 November 1726, *Correspondence*, III, 183.

v, 166–7). Like the sight of the wet nurse on his first arrival, this leads Gulliver to reflect on the impact of his own body in Lilliput, where a friend was compelled to comment on his smell, reinforcing earlier suggestions that he has misread the responses of the Lilliputian people. The change in perspective is accompanied by a change in status, as Gulliver is transformed from a position of dominant masculinity to passive objectification. The sexualised language of his account, with references to pleasure, touching, stripping and nakedness, is juxtaposed with the reality of his tiny, hyper-sensitive, yet desexualised body. Men were excluded from the female quarters, so his admission confirms his emasculation, and the description of how he is 'carried' there by his 'nurse' reinforces his infantilisation. Once there, he is aggrieved that he is treated 'without any Manner of Ceremony, like a Creature who had no Sort of Consequence'. He recounts how the Maids of Honour:

> would strip themselves to the Skin, and put on their Smocks in my Presence, while I was placed on their Toylet, directly before their naked Bodies; which, I am sure, to me was very far from being a tempting Sight, or from giving me any other Motions than those of Horror and Disgust [. . .] Neither did they at all scruple while I was by, to discharge what they had drunk, to the Quantity of at least two Hogsheads, in a Vessel that held above three Tuns. The handsomest among these Maids of Honour, a pleasant frolicksome Girl of sixteen, would sometimes set me astride upon one of her Nipples; with many other Tricks, wherein the Reader will excuse me for not being over particular. (II, v, 167–8)

Gulliver's emphatic denial that he experiences any 'motions' refers to his emotions, but it may also draw on the modern sense of movement, to indicate that he has no physical stirrings at the sight of the naked bodies. Boucé expresses scepticism over Gulliver's 'virtuous protests of disgust, uneasiness and horror', pointing out that the invitations to visit the women are issued (and presumably accepted) 'often'.[8] Gulliver's claim that the giant bodies were 'far from [. . .] a tempting sight' initially works like his rebuttal of rumours concerning Flimnap's wife, exploiting the ludic comedy of physical disjunction, but it is followed by hints that he serves as a sex toy for the frolicsome girl. His horrified responses to the bodies and bodily functions of the women, and his coy reluctance to specify the nature of their 'tricks', are in notable contrast to the complacency with which he describes his own giant physique and his 'adventures' in evacuation in Lilliput.

---

[8] Boucé, 'Gulliver Phallophorus', 89.

This incident has been interpreted to support readings of *Gulliver's Travels* as misogynistic, or misanthropic, or as a satire on the tradition of misogynistic writing.[9] But while Gulliver celebrates the male body in Lilliput, and denigrates the female body in Brobdingnag, it is significant that the distinction is a juxtaposition of self and other, as much as a gendered opposition. Gulliver's positivity in Lilliput relates to his own body, rather than male bodies in general, but in Brobdingnag his sense of self is complicated and compromised by his diminutive stature, and the resultant objectification. His treatment exposes his powerlessness in the realm of the bedroom, where male agency is customarily displayed. Deborah Armintor has emphasised Gulliver's 'commodified and feminised status' in Brobdingnag, arguing that he is figured as a microscope, and specifically the kind of portable microscope that was regarded in the eighteenth century as a 'lady's instrument'. In the Maids of Honour scene, he becomes a 'human-dildo-cum-pocket microscope'.[10] The feminisation that Armintor identifies is reinforced by the contrast with the first voyage, where Gulliver constructs himself as a spectacle of masculinity and source of admiration.

Although modern readers may find the sexual politics of the narrative unsettling, the intertexts reinforce the comic implications of scenes of gender role reversal. In Book Two of *Mundus Alter et Idem*, Mercurius Britannicus visits 'Viraginia, or New Gynia', a land governed by women. The humour derives from the carnivalesque subversion of patriarchal convention, but misogynistic stereotypes are also perpetuated, as all the women in the parliament speak at once, and constantly change their minds about the laws they pass.[11] In Aphrodysia, men are comically compelled to service female lust. While Gulliver invites the reader to sympathise with his predicament, the text invites mockery of his subjection to the frolicsome girl, just as we are encouraged to scorn the men who 'are kept at stud' in the stables of Aphrodysia, and 'feasted with [. . .] Indian roots and [. . .] love potions'.[12]

The reversal highlights the established patriarchal order, but it also manifests cultural anxieties over female desire, and anticipates what Penelope Wilson has described as Gulliver's 'climactic trauma'.[13] This

[9] For a summary of these debates, see Ellen Pollak, 'Swift among the Feminists: An Approach to Teaching', *College Literature*, 19 (1992), 114–20 (115–17).

[10] Deborah Needleman Armintor, 'The Sexual Politics of Microscopy in Brobdingnag', *SEL*, 47 (2007), 619–40 (628, 620–1, 632).

[11] Hall, *Mundus Alter*, 59–60.   [12] Hall, *Mundus Alter*, 62.

[13] Penelope Wilson, 'Feminism and the Augustans: Some Readings and Problems', *Critical Quarterly*, 28 (1986), 80–92 (81).

occurs when he is bathing 'stark naked' in the river in Houyhnhnm-land and becomes the unwilling recipient of the sexual advances of a young female Yahoo who, 'inflamed by Desire', leaps into the water and embraces him 'after a most fulsome Manner' (IV, viii, 400). His roars for assistance are answered by his 'Protector the Sorrel Nag' who chases away the assailant, reinforcing Gulliver's passivity and helplessness. The incident forces Gulliver to acknowledge that he is 'a real *Yahoo*, in every Limb and Feature' but it also exposes the ambiguity of his response to human physicality (IV, viii, 400–1). He applies consistently negative adjectives to the Yahoos, repeatedly using words like 'abominable', 'filthy', and 'detestable', and his portrait of the female Yahoos is particularly unappealing. The preoccupation with breasts recurs in the description of how their 'Dugs hung between their fore Feet, and often reached almost to the Ground as they walked' (IV, i, 334). Yet Gulliver claims that the female who assaults him 'did not make an Appearance altogether so hideous as the rest of the Kind' (IV, viii, 401). Likewise, the 'frolicksome Girl' is the 'handsomest among these Maids of Honour' (II, v, 168). The portrayal of these females as comparatively alluring may represent boasting on Gulliver's part, or the latent sexual attraction that Boucé discerns, or a combination of both. But in each case, desirability is age-related; the frolicsome girl is sixteen and the female yahoo 'could not be above Eleven Years old' (IV, viii, 401), invoking misogynistic ideas of even very young females as inherently sexualised. Gulliver is enfeebled, infantilised and emasculated, unable to defend himself against the advances of a Yahoo child, and the passive plaything of a giant girl, yet he is also aware of the possibilities for desire that exist within disgust.

These erotic encounters can be contrasted with Gulliver's idealisation of his friendship with nine-year-old Glumdalclitch. When he finally escapes from Brobdingnag, he repeatedly wishes himself back with his 'dear *Glumdalclitch*' (II, viii, 206). But while this relationship is presented as asexual, it is as predicated on objectification as Gulliver's association with the Maids of Honour. Glumdalclitch sees him as a doll, or, in eighteenth-century parlance, her 'baby'. Laura Brown traces the rise of the fashion doll in the eighteenth century and argues that 'for Glumdalclitch and the contemporary reader [Gulliver] takes the place of this miniature and commodified female figure'.[14] She dresses and undresses him, puts him to bed in a doll's cradle, and holds him 'fast by Leading-strings' when they go out (II, ii, 135, 140). The *OED* defines

---

[14] Laura Brown, 'Reading Race and Gender: Jonathan Swift', *ECS*, 23 (1990), 425–43 (435).

leading strings as 'strings with which children used to be guided and
supported when learning to walk' and being in leading strings is 'to be
still a child' and 'in a state of dependence or pupilage'. Gulliver actively
encourages this state of dependence, suggesting complicity in his
own infantilisation and emasculation. He coins the soubriquet
Glumdalclitch, meaning 'little Nurse' (II, ii, 136), emphasising a role
which Carol Houlihan Flynn identifies as simultaneously nurturing and
punishing,[15] while he assumes the diminutive Grildrig or 'Mannikin'. His
boast that he did not give Glumdalclitch the trouble of dressing and
undressing him 'when she would *let me* do either my self' (II, ii, 135; my
emphasis) reinforces the extent of his subjection. The negative portrayal
of female bodies and breasts is juxtaposed with the idealisation of
a relationship in which a miniature adult male is the plaything of
a giant infant female in a comic subversion of the conventional patriarchal order.

Theatrical Bodies

Felicity Nussbaum has located Swift's writings within traditions of anti-
feminist poetry and pamphlets, suggesting that they repurpose misogynistic discourse to satirise society.[16] For many of Swift's initial readers,
however, there is a more immediate cultural context in Restoration and
eighteenth-century comedy, which was conducting its own debate over the
nature of gender relations. Although Swift's clerical calling prohibited
attendance at the theatre, he was familiar with contemporary drama and
had been childhood friends with the playwright William Congreve.[17] The
plays written in the decades after the Restoration of the monarchy in 1660,
and still part of the eighteenth-century repertoire, are characterised by
bleak visions of marriage and human nature. Relationships between men
and women are embittered and sex is about power rather than love, as men
seek power over women, and wield power over other men by cuckolding
them with their wives. Desire and disgust are complicated, as rakes seduce
women they claim to despise. Women with names like Lady Cockwood
and Lady Wishfort scheme to seduce younger men, and audiences are
invited to see sexually demanding women and foppish effeminate men as

---

[15] Carol Houlihan Flynn, *The Body in Swift and Defoe* (Cambridge: Cambridge University Press,
1990), 88.
[16] Felicity Nussbaum, *The Brink of All We Hate: English Satires on Women, 1660–1750* (Lexington:
University Press of Kentucky, 1984), 115–16.
[17] John Stubbs, *Jonathan Swift: The Reluctant Rebel* (London: Norton, 2017), 11.

legitimate subjects of mockery and humiliation.[18] The plays are characterised by conclusions which provide little sense of reformation or resolution.
At the end of William Wycherley's *The Country Wife* (1675), the deceitful
rake is undetected and unrepentant, the cuckolded husbands are unaware
that they have been duped, and the ironically named 'virtuous gang' of
wealthy women can continue their adulterous pursuits. Congreve's *The
Way of the World* (1700) ends with the union of the hero and heroine, but
the way of the world is a continuing saga of sexual exploitation and
animosity between genders.

Reading *Gulliver's Travels* in the context of Restoration comedy encourages mockery of sexually voracious females and invites laughter at Gulliver's
inadequacies and his confusion in the face of sexual assault. The invocation
of theatrical stereotypes also provides a more general critique of contemporary relationships between men and women. Book three has been recognised
as providing the most sustained satire on Swift's society, and the story of the
Laputan Prime Minister's wife, who deserts her husband and children in
order to live in poverty on the mainland with 'an old deformed Footman,
who beat her every Day', has been identified as an allusion to the marital
problems of the British Prime Minister Sir Robert Walpole (III, ii, 238).[19]
But this particular satire is also part of a wider discussion of marriage. The
women on the island do not share their husbands' interest in abstruse
knowledge, and instead 'chuse their Gallants' from visitors from the continent below (III, ii, 237). These strangers are despised by the husbands because
they lack intellectual 'Endowments', perhaps implying that they are
endowed in a manner that is more to the satisfaction of the women. The
description of how 'the Wives and Daughters lament their Confinement to
the Island' and 'long to see the World, and take the Diversions of the
Metropolis' (III, ii, 238) invokes the women of Restoration drama who are
preoccupied with schemes to ensure their residence in London, and dread
nothing more than a return to their husbands' country estates. In Laputa, as
on the contemporary stage, marriage is devoid of affection, with husbands
showing no interest in their wives, while the women seek to escape domesticity through 'diversions' or pursue sexual satisfaction in liaisons with
younger or lower-class men.

The aristocratic libertinism of Restoration comedy was increasingly
challenged from the end of the seventeenth century by the emergence of

[18] George Etherege, *She Would if She Could* (1668); William Congreve, *The Way of the World* (1700).
[19] Paul Langford, 'Swift and Walpole', in *Politics and Literature in the Age of Swift: English and Irish Perspectives*, ed. Claude Rawson (Cambridge: Cambridge University Press, 2010), 52–78 (58).

what has been described as sentimental drama. Attempted seductions, infidelities and marital disputes remain the mainstay of theatrical plots, but the plays resolve in celebrations of domesticity. Marriage increasingly connotes love and domestic harmony rather than conflict and infidelity. A key figure in the development of the new, more moralistic theatre was Colley Cibber, the hack writer satirised as chief Dunce in the 1743 version of Alexander Pope's *The Dunciad*. Cibber's plays *Love's Last Shift* (1696) and *The Careless Husband* (1704) focus on the redemption of an unfaithful husband through the exemplary virtue of his wife. This is very different from the portrayal of Gulliver's family life, which consists of perfunctory accounts of his homecoming at the end of each of the tales (I, viii, 112–13; II, viii, 213–14; III, xi, 326; IV, xi, 433–5; IV, xii, 443). Although the increasing number of young Gullivers suggests that he has some engagement with the domestic in his periodic returns, the narrative is principally concerned with his own difficulties in adjusting to family life. This culminates in the description of the 'Shame, Confusion and Horror' that he experiences on his return from Houyhnhnm-land at the thought that 'by copulating with one of the *Yahoo*-Species, I had become a Parent of more' (IV, xi, 434). This negative attitude towards family is given wider context through Gulliver's discussions of the political and educational systems of Lilliput and Houyhnhnm-land.

The Lilliputian state is initially presented as corrupt and dysfunctional, parodying British institutions in practices such as the granting of preferment for acrobatic skills (I, iii, 56–9), but the satirical tone is moderated in Gulliver's account of 'the Laws and Customs in this Empire' (I, vi, 84). The Lilliputians deny that children owe any obligation to their parents and believe that 'Parents are the last of all others to be trusted with the Education of their own Children' (I, vi, 87–8). Details follow of the 'publick Nurseries' (I, vi, 88) and the austere educational regimes implemented for the various social classes. The biannual parental visits do not last 'above an Hour'; parents 'can kiss the Child at Meeting and Parting', but cannot 'whisper, or use any fondling Expressions, or bring any Presents of Toys, Sweet-meats, and the like' (I, vi, 89).

The subversion of domestic ideology is even more overt in Houyhnhnm-land, where parents 'have no Fondness for their Colts or Foles' (IV, viii, 403), regarding them with the same benevolence that they extend to all their kind. Foals are exchanged to give all families one of each sex (IV, viii, 407), at which point, sexual relations between the parents cease (IV, viii, 404). Gulliver notes that 'Courtship, Love, Presents, Joyntures, Settlements, have no Place in their Thoughts; or Terms whereby to express them in their Language' (IV, viii, 404–5). The identification of presents, jointures, and settlements as alien concepts within Houyhnhnm-land echoes conventional satire on the materialism of marriage, but the incorporation of love and courtship into this list undermines the link with contemporary discourses celebrating affective over mercenary unions. The Houyhnhnms are equally strangers to marriage for money and marriage for love and show a lack of distress at the death of their partners which might be construed as cold-hearted (IV, ix, 413–14).

The descriptions of the social systems of Lilliput and Houyhnhnm-land draw on Plato's *Republic* and Thomas More's *Utopia*, reinforcing Gulliver's suggestions that they represent ideals. But notwithstanding these philosophical antecedents, for eighteenth-century readers, Gulliver's celebration of Lilliputian and Houyhnhnm institutions would have constituted a striking challenge to the fetishisation of domestic affections and family life which increasingly characterised moral discourses and sentimental drama and was to become central to the early novel. J. Paul Hunter has noted Swift's subversion of 'the developing novelistic mode' in the protean form and lack of realist conventions of *Gulliver's Travels*,[20] and this eschewal of the emergent genre is also discernible in the content of the work, in the portrayal of bodies, sex, and gender. The celebration of giant masculinity, anxieties over female bodies and female sexuality, rejection of the social function of the family and undermining of the polarities of disgust and desire seem less aberrant in the context of the bawdy bitterness of the Restoration stage than in that of the novel. In invoking the aristocratic rakish discourse of an earlier era, Gulliver may be making an ideological statement. His scatological and phallocentric vision could be less a manifestation of misogyny than an overt challenge to the emergence of puritanical sensibilities and reverence for domesticity which were spawning a new political climate and a new kind of literature.

---

[20] J. Paul Hunter, '*Gulliver's Travels* and the Later Writings', in *The Cambridge Companion to Jonathan Swift*, ed. Christopher Fox (Cambridge: Cambridge University Press, 2003), 216–40 (225).

CHAPTER 4

Science, Empire, and Observation

Gregory Lynall

These Insects were as large as Partridges; I took out their Stings, found them an Inch and a half long, and as sharp as Needles. I carefully preserved them all, and having since shewn them with some other Curiosities in several Parts of *Europe*; upon my Return to *England* I gave three of them to *Gresham College*, and kept the fourth for my self.

(II, iii, 155)

In the early eighteenth century, the newly formed country of Britain was seeking to establish itself as the centre of a global knowledge network and, as part of its imperial ambitions, all of nature – even in the most remote nations – was subjected to scientific scrutiny and potentially control. If his stories could be trusted, therefore, an adventurous and loquacious traveller like Lemuel Gulliver, trained in mathematics and medicine, and possessing an 'insatiable Desire of seeing foreign Countries' (I, viii, 112), would be a significant asset to institutions such as the Royal Society of London for the Improvement of Natural Knowledge, which had been granted a royal charter in 1662, and up until 1710 was based at Gresham College. Certainly, Gulliver recognises his own potential as a broker of knowledge within numerous transnational, transcultural, and trans-species encounters, padding his empirical prose with enumeration and comparison in order to convey specific information about faraway lands and peoples to 'Courteous Readers' hungry for exotic tales or looking to 'enlarge his Majesty's Dominions by [these] Discoveries' (IV, xii, 443, 440), whilst also documenting how he has sought to enrich those foreign countries with knowledge from his homeland. He is also aware of the financial and social dividends that come from such a role, and of the intellectual and cultural power of natural specimens as objects of spectacle. He had previously 'made a considerable Profit' by showing his tiny Lilliputian cattle to 'Persons of Quality' (I, iii, 112), and in Brobdingnag became an object of wonder himself. Then he toured gigantic Brobdingnagian wasp stings around Europe (perhaps visiting institutions such as the Paris Academy of Sciences), depositing some in the Royal Society's repository, and as a budding collector and natural historian kept one for himself (along with weighing, measuring and/or collecting many other natural curiosities, such as giant hailstones (II, v, 164)). The wisdom and expertise he extends to newly discovered countries do not always secure a warm reception, however: he offers knowledge of gunpowder to the King of Brobdingnag, who is disgusted at the prospect of causing such wanton destruction (II, vii, 192); his Master Houyhnhnm is similarly outraged (IV, v, 366–7). Such cosmopolitan meetings are inherently moments of epistemological crisis, countering (what Gayatri Chakravorty Spivak has called) 'epistemic violence' by revealing the partiality, contingency, and relative value of British and European knowledge, and, ultimately, undermining notions of national or racial superiority upon which visions of empire rest.[1] As this chapter will show, *Travels into Several Remote Nations of the World* (1726), which was the original title of *Gulliver's Travels*, is itself a remarkable encounter, between literature and science, and the parameters of that engagement are partly defined by the colonial project, with the seemingly objective activity of observation implicated in imperial tyranny and exploitation.

The Culture and Discourse of Science

Gulliver's story demonstrates Swift's sustained reflection upon the culture and writing of early eighteenth-century science. Swift was a reader and owner of texts which dealt with scientific topics, including Sir Isaac Newton's *Principia* (second edition, 1713), and some of his closest friends and literary collaborators, including the satirist and physician Dr John Arbuthnot (1667–1735), were practitioners or at least admirers of mathematics and natural philosophy. Swift was also acquainted with Catherine Barton (c.1680–1739), Newton's half-niece, who lived with the great mathematician for many years.[2] Generally thought to have been critical of the science of his day, Swift also found it to be a source of inspiration, constituting a vehicle as well as target of his satire.

The culture of international scientific enquiry in which Gulliver situates his natural discoveries had arisen only relatively recently. Between the

[1] Gayatri Chakravorty Spivak, 'Can the Subaltern Speak?', in *Marxism and the Interpretation of Culture*, ed. Cary Nelson and Lawrence Grossberg (Basingstoke: Macmillan, 1988), 271–313 (271).
[2] Gregory Lynall, *Swift and Science: The Satire, Politics, and Theology of Natural Knowledge, 1690–1730* (Basingstoke: Palgrave Macmillan, 2012), 13, 90–4.

Restoration and nineteenth century, the word 'science' acquired its modern meaning, referring to the physical and experimental sciences, and eventually encompassing all disciplines in which knowledge is obtained via observation and experiment; 'natural philosophy' was the term used previously in relation to understanding of the physical world. The term 'scientist', meanwhile, was probably coined in 1834.[3] Alongside these semantic changes were fundamental transformations in the organisation and practice of knowledge, although historians of science have become increasingly resistant to the notion that a 'scientific revolution' occurred in Europe sometime between the mid-fifteenth and late-seventeenth centuries. Yet many of the key scientific figures of the period asserted the novelty of their work: Johannes Kepler presented *A New Astronomy* (1609); Francis Bacon published *New Organon* (1620) to supersede Aristotle's original; Galileo wrote *Two New Sciences* (1638). Moreover, Swift considered himself to be living at a time of immense intellectual upheaval, including in natural knowledge, and documented it in parodic fashion in *The Battle of the Books* (1704), amongst other works.

As a result of these transformations, knowledge-making – focused on the establishment of 'matters of fact' – was now via the 'scientific method' pioneered by Sir Francis Bacon in *Novum Organum* (1620), involving mathematics and measurement, and inductive and empirical approaches which proceeded from observations of single experiences and artificial experiments. The mathematisation of natural philosophy culminated in the publication of Newton's *Principia* (1687), which demonstrated mathematically that the same laws of motion applied celestially and terrestrially, thereby refuting Aristotelian distinctions. With this move to mathematics, measurement consequently became important: previously, natural philosophy had been a qualitative, not quantitative enterprise, seeking to ascertain the causes of phenomena. Instead, scientists now used concepts from mechanics (shape, size, quantity, motion) to explain causation:[4] it was an approach easy for Swift to caricature in the reductionist Laputan philosophers who would describe the 'Beauty of a Woman [...]' by Rhombs, Circles, Parallelograms, Ellipses, and other Geometrical Terms' (III, ii, 233). Natural history, meanwhile, would be based in the collection, description, comparison, and classification of specimens, involving (in the

[3] Karina Williamson, '"Science" and "Knowledge" in Eighteenth-Century Britain', *Studies in Voltaire and the Eighteenth Century*, 303 (1992), 455–8; [William Whewell], 'Review of Mary Somerville, *On the Connexion of the Physical Sciences*', *The Quarterly Review*, 51 (1834), 58–61 (59).
[4] John Henry, *The Scientific Revolution and the Origins of Modern Science*, 2nd ed. (Houndmills: Palgrave, 2002), 28, 31, 69.

words of Bacon) 'hard labour, investigation and world-wide survey', with a huge increase in scientific practice in terms of geographical range, publication, and the number of expert practitioners.[5] The expansion and systematisation of natural knowledge were therefore aligned explicitly with geographical exploration and territorial acquisition (and their representation in print). Despite Thomas Sprat (1635–1713) proclaiming in *The History of the Royal Society* (1667) that 'to increase the Powers of all Mankind, and to free them from the bondage of Errors, is Greater Glory than to enlarge Empire, or to put Chains on the Necks of Conquer'd Nations', Western sciences and empires were mutually extending each other and unlocking wealth and information, often to the detriment of the environments and peoples they met.[6]

During the same period, the *practice* of 'observation' established itself as an 'epistemic genre' which described singular events witnessed first-hand and avoided conjecture, while 'experiment' came to refer to a deliberate manipulation of nature that exposes causes otherwise unreachable to the senses.[7] Collective witnessing provided the ultimate verification of knowledge, but for observations produced by the 'geographically privileged' (someone visiting, for instance, 'several remote nations'), the credibility of the source was crucial.[8] Thus Gulliver asserts his utterance of 'a faithful History' in contrast to the 'strange improbable Tales' of other explorers (IV, xii, 436). Observers provided first-person accounts, in the active voice, of discrete experiences which they observed and were also a part of. The recounting of circumstantial details surrounding an event – including information about the participants (including their social status), time, and place – seemed to encourage its veracity, with claims about natural phenomena located within specific occurrences experienced by particular people (with an honourable gentleman being the ideal witness). The observer's role was important in authenticating the credentials of an experience, and the use of the active voice served to enhance the reporter's central position within the experience itself and to convey a sense of

---

[5] Francis Bacon, *Novum Organum* (1620), 'Plan of the Work', sig. B6ᵛ, in *The Instauratio Magna Part II: Novum Organum and Associated Texts*, ed. and trans. Graham Rees with Maria Wakely (Oxford: Clarendon Press, 2004), 37.

[6] Thomas Sprat, *The History of the Royal-Society of London, for the Improving of Natural Knowledge* (1667), 'Epistle Dedicatory'.

[7] Lorraine Daston, 'The Empire of Observation, 1600–1800', in *Histories of Scientific Observation*, ed. Lorraine Daston and Elizabeth Lunbeck (Chicago: University of Chicago Press, 2011), 81–113 (81, 86).

[8] Steven Shapin, *Never Pure: Historical Studies of Science as if It Was Produced by People with Bodies, Situated in Time, Space, Culture, and Society, and Struggling for Credibility and Authority* (Baltimore: Johns Hopkins University Press, 2010), 61.

immediacy.[9] Hence, as a direct eyewitness and participant, Gulliver believes himself 'able to contradict many fabulous Accounts from [his] own Observation' (IV, xii, 437).

Generally, prose in a plain style, free from rhetorical flourish, was believed best to convey natural knowledge and encourage a spirit of co-operative enquiry. The most famous advocate of this precept was Sprat, whose *History* celebrated how Royal Society members' publications sought to reject 'swellings of style: to return back to the primitive purity and shortness, when men deliver'd so many *things*, almost in an equal number of *words*'. Fellows of the Society were instead deploying a 'naked, natural way of speaking; positive expressions; clear senses; a native easiness: bringing all things as near the Mathematical plainness as they can'.[10] Another supporter of the Royal Society, Joseph Glanvill (1636–80), advocated similarly (in a work Swift read) a '*natural* and *unaffected Eloquence*' rather than employment of '*fine Metaphors*'.[11] The 'natural', 'native' and 'naked' metaphors employed (with unconscious irony) by Sprat and Glanvill hint at how such stylistic aspirations were part of a broader ambition for scientific pursuits to return humanity to prelapsarian knowledge of nature. It is evident in numerous places that Swift was himself linguistically conservative and an advocate of plain style. Yet the *Travels* takes such linguistic simplicity to its *reductio ad absurdum*, such as with the Lagadan professors who carry about with them all they need to express (III, vi, 271–2). Moreover, Gulliver's observational passivity – in relating 'plain Matter of Fact in the simplest Manner and Style' (IV, xii, 436) – raises suspicions about the depth of intellectual insight such empiricist discourse can communicate, and the ideological assumptions in which it is enmeshed (and therefore the extent of its objectivity). The 'plain' style of observation is therefore revealed to be the vehicle of discursive distortion, full of ironic potential.

Moments of Meta-Observation

Gulliver uses the word 'observe' and its derivatives around 140 times.[12] In scientific observation, Swift found a discursive mode around which he could structure an entire prose satire whilst also probing its intellectual and

---

[9] Peter Dear, '*Totius in verba*: Rhetoric and Authority in the Early Royal Society', *Isis*, 76 (1985), 144–61 (152–4); Steven Shapin, *A Social History of Truth: Civility and Science in Seventeenth-Century England* (Chicago: University of Chicago Press, 1994), 42, 93–4.
[10] Sprat, *History*, 113.   [11] Joseph Glanvill, *Scepsis Scientifica* (1665), sig. C4ʳ.
[12] Pat Rogers, 'Gulliver's Glasses', in *The Art of Jonathan Swift*, ed. Clive T. Probyn (London: Vision Press, 1978), 179–88 (184).

moral limits, placing the process of observation itself under satiric scrutiny, partly in order to interrogate the colonial project in which it was implicated. Observation is characterised as an empiricist reduction to the physical which struggles to produce useful or even objective knowledge. Indeed, physiological inspection normally results in Gulliver's revulsion – at, for instance, 'monstrous Breast[s]' in Brobdingnag (II, i, 130), or the realisation that he himself shares the Yahoo anatomy (IV, ii, 342). Whilst the entirety of the *Travels* is based in Gulliver's ostensibly neutral observations of phenomena, this further analysis is most apparent in those moments when Gulliver is himself observed by the species he meets, all the while gazing back, observing the observers. These vignettes of interspecies or intercultural viewing ironise the colonial contact zone. The identity of the 'other' in these meetings is never absolutely clear for the reader: it is at once Gulliver and the 'alien' species, complicated further by their potential to stand as defamiliarised mirrors of English and/or European society. Nevertheless, the relativity of viewing and of knowledge within these encounters serves to undermine Western knowledge at a time when its superiority was undoubted and used to justify imperial conquest. Moreover, the plain style of these observations can create a false sense of objectivity which itself becomes an assertion of authority over the 'other'.

Critics exploring the scientific gaze often recall Gulliver's inspection within the Brobdingnagian court, when the 'three great Scholars' can only determine him to be a '*Lusus Naturæ*' (II, iii, pp. 145, 146). However, the most significant (but overlooked) moment of meta-observation occurs when he is first discovered in that country:

> The Farmer [. . .] lifted up the Lappets of my Coat; which it seems he thought to be some kind of Covering that Nature had given me. He blew my Hairs aside to take a better View of my Face. He called his Hinds about him, and asked them [. . .] whether they had ever seen in the Fields any little Creature that resembled me. He then placed me softly on the Ground upon all four; but I got immediately up, and walked slowly backwards and forwards [. . .]. They all sate down in a Circle about me, the better to observe my Motions. I pulled off my Hat, and made a low Bow [. . .]: I fell on my Knees, and lifted up my Hands and Eyes, and spoke several Words as loud as I could: I took a Purse of Gold out of my Pocket, and [. . .] poured all the Gold into his Palm [. . .] He made me a Sign to put them again into my Purse, [. . .] which, after offering it to him several times, I thought it best to do.
>
> The Farmer by this time was convinced I must be a rational Creature. (II, i, 126–7)

Initially, the farmer assumes that a 'little Creature' of Gulliver's size would be a quadruped; in contrast, the King of Brobdingnag conceives of him as an automaton (II, iii, 145). Standing up, Gulliver distinguishes himself from the animals. Ancient philosophers believed that it was man's upright posture and the ability to look up which confirmed the existence of his rational faculty,[13] but the farmer needs further evidence (and the 'Hinds' – labourers – assist him by providing collective witness and, earlier, the authority of comparison). An empirical observer himself, Gulliver presents himself in a way which seeks to aid and speed up the process of observation for the farmer and his workers, making him the perfect object of science: yet this highlights that observation and classification are not neutral but conceptually pre-structured, and involve looking for specific characteristics and behaviours.

Furthermore, in Brobdingnag, Gulliver is subject to two kinds of scientific gaze, differentiated by educational status – and it is clear that Swift wishes the reader to compare them, given that the farmer is invited back into the court immediately following the scholars' observations (II, iii, 147). The scholars (called 'Virtuosi' in the first edition, a term often applied disparagingly to those engaged in natural philosophical and natural historical studies) are supposedly more credible, but Gulliver-as-specimen serves to test this view, in a social experiment in which the learned are found wanting, and common sense prevails via both farmer and king. However, the scholars' observations are not without some (satiric) value, since they identify the deficiencies of the human body in comparison to those of other species. Yet the scholars are judging Gulliver from the wrong premise, unaware of his natural environment, imposing their own 'regular Laws of Nature' and Brobdingnagian gaze upon this foreign body (II, iii, 146), revealing the relativity of scientific knowledge.

Colonial Transactions

Sprat believed that the existence of the Royal Society proved England to be uniquely blessed as a 'Land of *Experimental knowledge*', attributable to its climate, the 'composition of the English blood', and 'embraces of the Ocean'.[14] The minutes of the Society's first meeting in November 1660 record its main objective: to found a college for the 'promoting of

---

[13] C. A. Patrides, 'Renaissance Ideas on Man's Upright Form', *Journal of the History of Ideas*, 19 (1958), 256–8.

[14] Sprat, *History*, 114.

experimentall philosophy'. This emphasis upon experiment was wholly unique, as was the importance it placed upon the public witnessing of experimental results as the guarantor of authority.[15] Reports of experiments performed at Society meetings, or extracts of correspondence containing field observations, were published in its *Philosophical Transactions*, established in 1665. Although Swift makes no direct reference to having read the *Transactions*, it is generally assumed that the 'Voyage to Laputa' – particularly Gulliver's visit to the Academy of Lagado – burlesques and conflates various Royal Society experiments to produce hilarious and grotesque inventions and projects.[16] Reduced to a disinterested observer of a succession of harmful, unseemly, or worthless interventions in nature which yield impractical results or misinterpretations of data, Gulliver leaves each Lagadan experiment to 'speak for itself', placing readers in the position of (what Sprat calls) '*debating* on its consequences', as the *Transactions* did.[17]

Moreover, the *Travels* as a whole seems partially inspired by the *form* of many of the journal's papers.[18] A notable example is the third chapter of Part III, which describes in detail the magnetic mechanism of the flying island, and even incorporates a kind of force diagram. This section is arguably more pastiche than parody, revelling in the scientific treatise as a literary form. Yet this indulgence in form is combined with a deep suspicion of how scientific knowledge might be applied, and how the discourse of science is deployed to obscure or even justify the potential harm of such application. The flying island is 'under the Care of certain Astronomers, who from Time to Time give it such Positions as the Monarch directs' (III, iii, 244) and utilised as a weapon of state, the Laputans bending nature to their will to subordinate or at the very least cause distress to the people of Balnibarbi (depriving them of the sun and rain, or threatening to crush them), enshrining the use of science in the project of empire. This has been interpreted as alluding to Britain's political and economic grip over Ireland, and particularly the 'Wood's

---

[15] Quoted in Marie Boas Hall, *Promoting Experimental Learning: Experiment and the Royal Society, 1660–1727* (Cambridge: Cambridge University Press, 1991), 9.

[16] Marjorie Nicolson and Nora M. Mohler, 'The Scientific Background of Swift's *Voyage to Laputa*' and 'Swift's "Flying Island" in the *Voyage to Laputa*', *Annals of Science*, 2 (1937), 299–334, 405–30. The slightly dissenting voice on this is Pat Rogers, 'Gulliver and the Engineers', *MLR*, 70 (1975), 260–70, who argues that Swift mainly has practical projects in mind.

[17] Sprat, *History*, 102.

[18] Frederick N. Smith, 'Scientific Discourse: *Gulliver's Travels* and *The Philosophical Transactions*', in *The Genres of 'Gulliver's Travels'*, ed. Frederick N. Smith (Newark: University of Delaware Press, 1990), 139–62 (141).

Halfpence affair', which had provoked Swift into writing *The Drapier's Letters* (1724–5), thereby interrupting the composition of the *Travels*. Significantly, Newton, in his position of Master of the Mint, assessed the quality of the copper coinage being imposed upon Ireland, and it is likely that Swift drew upon these circumstances when composing the 'Voyage to Laputa', written last, making further connections between imperial rule and institutions of natural knowledge. In Swift's eyes, Newton's involvement continued a tradition of men of science interfering in Irish 'Matters of State' (III, ii, 235). Such figures included Sir William Petty (1623–87), anatomist, fellow of the Royal Society, and President of the Dublin Philosophical Society, who applied 'political arithmetic' in topographical and demographical studies (such as the Down Survey, which reallocated to English, usually Protestant, soldiers and investors the Irish property forfeited by Civil War rebels), and was parodied by Swift in *A Modest Proposal* (1729).[19]

The *Philosophical Transactions* was an eclectic periodical. A single issue might feature, for instance, the description of a water-store in France, responses to Newton's theory of light and colours, and observations on stones found in a dog's bladder and 'fastnd to the Back-Bone of a Horse'.[20] Early satirical responses, such as William King's *The Transactioneer* (1700), consequently suggested that the periodical placed more emphasis on the trivial, exotic, and prurient than valuable, ordered knowledge and matter of fact. Gulliver's accounts of exploration are similarly miscellaneous, with a single chapter encompassing such topics as a country's geography, the size of its marine life, a cancerous breast, and the king's kitchen (II, iv). In this respect, Gulliver was following the recommendations of the Royal Society, which had recognised that it should encourage those on foreign voyages to supply information 'highly conducive to the improvement of *True Philosophy*, and the well-fare of *Mankind*', and provided guidance to such inquisitive travellers on how best to make observations of natural environments.[21] The first volume of the *Philosophical Transactions* included 'Directions for Sea-men, Bound for Far Voyages' and Robert Boyle's 'General Heads for a Natural History of a Countrey', whilst in his *History*, Sprat hoped 'there will scarce a ship come up the Thames, that does not make return of experiments'.[22] It was in this context, therefore,

---

[19] Gregory Lynall, 'Swift's Caricatures of Newton: "Taylor," "Conjurer" and "Workman in the Mint"', *BJECS*, 28 (2005), 19–32; Lynall, *Swift and Science*, 107.

[20] *Philosophical Transactions*, 7: 84 (17 June 1672), 4094.

[21] Robert Boyle, 'General Heads for a Natural History of a Countrey Great or Small, Imparted Likewise by Mr. Boyle', *Philosophical Transactions*, 1: 11 (12 April 1666), 186–9 (189).

[22] *Philosophical Transactions*, 1: 8 (8 January 1665/6), 140–3; Boyle, 'General Heads'; Sprat, *History*, 86.

that the explorer William Dampier (1651–1715) dedicated his *A New Voyage Round the World* (1697) to Charles Montagu, President of the Royal Society, and asserted his 'hearty Zeal for the promoting of useful Knowledge, and of anything [...] to my Countries advantage' from his 'Gleanings here and there in Remote Regions'.[23] The natural-historical, ethnographical, meteorological, and nautical knowledge his book contained did not disappoint members of that illustrious society and, soon after it was published, Dampier received numerous appeals for his acquaintance from some of the most learned men in London. Later, Dampier was commissioned by the Admiralty for voyages which were explicitly 'scientific' in aim, mapping compass variation and conducting other kinds of experiments. Whilst Dampier was the first to report (at least in English) on a large number of natural specimens, the style of his 'plain piece' belied the excitement of these new discoveries.[24] Gulliver declared his writerly affinity with 'my Cousin *Dampier*' in his letter to Sympson (*GT*, 7), and there are numerous echoes between these real and fictional South Sea voyagers, including the simplicity and matter-of-factness of the observational prose, the compulsion to 'make what Discoveries I could' in each new land (II, i, 122), and the hopes that a philosopher would use the account's 'Particulars' for the 'Benefit of publick as well as private Life' (II, i, 133). Furthermore, Dampier's notorious description of Indigenous Australians is at least one inspiration for Gulliver's similarly horrified observations of the Yahoos (IV, i, 333–4). Such borrowings from Dampier emphasise how Gulliver's ostensibly objective narration both critiques and is deeply implicated in colonial, racialised discourse.

The colonial infrastructure of British knowledge-making is perhaps nowhere more obvious than in the life and career of Sir Hans Sloane (1660–1753), a natural historian and collector known to Swift (*Correspondence*, I, 243). Sloane became a Royal Society member in 1685 and was appointed secretary in 1695, thereafter responsible for editing the *Philosophical Transactions*. Newly established as a physician, in 1687 Sloane joined the entourage of the governor of Jamaica, and for fifteen months kept a journal logging his observations of Caribbean plants, animals, weather, and other phenomena, and also gathered over 800 botanical specimens. Returning to London in 1689, he married Elizabeth Langley, daughter of a London alderman and the widower of a plantation owner.

[23] William Dampier, *A New Voyage Round the World* (1697), 'To the Right Honourable Charles Montague'.
[24] Joseph C. Shipman, *William Dampier: Seaman Scientist* (Lawrence: University of Kansas Libraries, 1962), 51; Dampier, *New Voyage*, 'Preface'.

Enabled by his West Indian wealth, Sloane was a generous supporter of
other practitioners of natural history and natural philosophy, and an
acquirer of thousands of curious objects from across the globe (collections
which had no rival in Britain, and in 1759 became the foundation of the
British Museum).[25] Sloane first set about publishing accounts of his time in
Jamaica in the *Philosophical Transactions*, and in 1707 appeared the first
volume of *A Voyage to the Islands Madera, Barbados, Nieves, S. Christophers
and Jamaica*. Its title page epigraph was taken from the Book of Daniel –
'Many shall run to and fro, and Knowledge shall be increased' – a fitting
motto for the Royal Society's ambitions for international travel.[26] We do
not know if Swift read Sloane's account specifically, but its empirical
impulse and its immersion in the triangular slave trade illustrate the
colonial-scientific context in which the *Travels* emerged. In particular, in
its Preface, Sloane remarks upon the purpose of his book: 'the Knowlege of
Natural-History, being Observation of Matters of Fact, is more certain than
most Others, and [. . .] less subject to Mistakes than *Reasonings*, *Hypotheses*,
and *Deductions* are [. . .] so far as our Senses are not fallible'.[27] The *Travels*,
however, shows us the limitations of the human senses, and how a focus
merely upon sense impressions can significantly distort our view of the
world. Demonstrating the close alignment between the scientific mindset,
racism, and slavery, Sloane's empirical, dispassionate, and often dehumanising prose documents the shocking treatment of slaves on the plantations.
Like Gulliver when celebrating the 'Wisdom, Care, and Justice' of the
'*British* Nation' in 'planting Colonies' and granting 'liberal Endowments
for the Advancement of Religion and Learning' while others 'give a free
Licence to all Acts of Inhumanity' in their 'new Dominion' (IV, xii, 441–2),
Sloane excuses the actions of the imperial power with reference to the
severity of other countries: 'These Punishments [. . .] appear harsh, yet are
[. . .] inferior to what Punishments other *European* Nations inflict on their
slaves in the *East-Indies*'.[28]

Swift's friend Anthony Henley (c.1666–1711) had told him in July 1709
that 'Dr Sloan is of Opinion that modern Travels are very behovefull
towards forming the Mind and Inlarging the thoughts of the Curious
part of Mankind' (*Correspondence*, I, 261). *Gulliver's Travels* could be read
as a striking riposte to such an assertion, instead suggesting that published

[25] Arthur MacGregor, 'Sloane, Sir Hans, baronet', *ODNB*.
[26] Hans Sloane, *A Voyage to the Islands Madera, Barbados, Nieves, S. Christophers and Jamaica, with the
Natural History of the Herbs and Trees, Four-Footed Beasts, Fishes, Birds, Insects, Reptiles, &c. of the last
of those Islands*, 2 vols. (1707), I, titlepage.
[27] Sloane, *Voyage*, sig. A3^v.   [28] Sloane, *Voyage*, sig. A3^v.

voyages of discovery are not only frequently untrustworthy, but also detrimental to all concerned (author, readers, and described inhabitants), and demonstrating that curiosity and (self-)knowledge come at a severe price. This cost is made apparent during the *Travels'* meta-observational climax in Houyhnhnm-land, when the Master and Servant 'diligently compare' the 'Countenances' of Gulliver and one of the island's degenerate beasts. Prompted by the Houyhnhnms' repetition of 'the word *Yahoo*', Gulliver's stance as passive empiricist breaks down as he visits upon himself a terrifying taxonomy: 'My Horror and Astonishment are not to be described, when I observed, in this abominable Animal, a perfect human Figure; the Face of it indeed was flat and broad, the Nose depressed, the Lips large, and the Mouth wide: But these Differences are common to all savage Nations' (IV, ii, 342). This moment of comparative anatomy shatters Gulliver's sense of self, whilst for the Houyhnhnms it eventually becomes a means of control over him, as they do already the Yahoos. Gulliver's classification as Yahoo motivates the Houyhnhnm assembly to order his Master to 'employ [him] like the rest of [his] Species' or to banish him, for fear of him leading a slave rebellion (IV, x, 421). But Gulliver is not a Yahoo: he is himself dehumanised by the Houyhnhnms' observations, just as Gulliver dehumanises 'all savage Nations' using conventional racist tropes. Yet whilst the *Travels* interrogates the colonial gaze, and finds scientific observation to be anything but neutral, Part IV also uses this distortion for satiric purposes – some of the satire only works because the reader is invited to recognise similarities with the grotesque, defamiliarised other. Both science and satire create objects of us all.

PART II

Genres

CHAPTER 5

Popular Fiction

J. A. Downie

'I am now writing a History of my Travells, which will be a large Volume, and gives Account of Countryes hitherto unknown', Swift wrote to his friend, Charles Ford, on 15 April 1721, 'but they go on slowly for want of Health and Humor' (*Correspondence*, II, 372). This, Swift's first reference to *Gulliver's Travels*, suggests that he was consciously working within a popular narrative tradition – the travel book – while playing games with readers' expectations at the same time. That Swift was perfectly aware of what he was doing is implied by the anecdote, almost certainly apocryphal, he told about the reaction to the publication of *Gulliver's Travels* in Ireland: 'A Bishop here said, that book was full of improbable lies, and for his part, he hardly believed a word of it; and so much for Gulliver' (*Correspondence*, III, 56). It is not so much Swift's implicit comment on Irish credulity to which I wish to draw attention as his final throwaway remark. In dismissing 'Gulliver' in this way, is he referring to his central character or to his book – to the narrator or to the travels themselves? This is an important consideration. Claude Rawson rightly draws attention to 'that teasing fluctuation, or bewildering uncertainty, of *genre* which critics have noted in some of Swift's works, and which gives a curious precariousness to the reader's grasp of what is going on'.[1] For modern readers of *Gulliver's Travels*, familiar with realistic narratives as well as a wide range of science fiction and fantasy fiction, the dominant literary genre is the novel. But this was not the case as far as early eighteenth-century readers were concerned. In relating his anecdote about the Irish bishop who 'said, that book was full of improbable lies', Swift was tacitly drawing attention to two markedly different popular fictional traditions: one ancient; the other brand new.

[1] Claude Rawson, *Gulliver and the Gentle Reader: Studies in Swift and Our Time* (London: Routledge & Kegan Paul, 1973), 5.

Gulliver's Travels and Lucian's True History

'The general idea of the work is unquestionably borrowed from the *True History* of Lucian, a fictitious journey through imaginary countries', Walter Scott observed about *Gulliver's Travels*, 'prefaced by an introduction, in an exquisite vein of irony, upon the art of writing history'.[2] Scott, writing in the 1820s, was not the first to a discern a connection between the two works. Almost a century earlier, in the Preface to the second edition of his translation of *Gulliver's Travels*, L'Abbé Desfontaines observed that, although 'this work of Mr. Swift is new and original in its kind', it had a number of predecessors, even if the principal feature in common was merely 'the idea of an imaginary voyage and an imaginary country'.[3] Desfontaines listed Lucian's *True History* in this category, along with Plato's *Republic*, More's *Utopia*, Bacon's *New Atlantis*, the *History of the Sevarambes*, and the voyages of Sadeur, Jacques Macé, and Cyrano de Bergerac. Scott also identified de Bergerac's *A Journey to the Moon* along with Rabelais' 'more famous *Voyage of Pantagruel*' as Swift's most important sources. 'Swift has consulted both, as well as their common original', he argued, 'but is more particularly indebted to the work of Rabelais, which satirised severely the various orders of the law and clergy of his period'.[4]

Whether Swift was hinting at this aspect of the *True History* in his anecdote about the Irish bishop who said that 'that book was full of improbable lies', it is perhaps significant that Lucian freely acknowledged that 'the only true Word in the following History is, that 'tis wholly made up of Lyes'. 'I honestly declare', he explained,

> that what I here write I neither saw my self, nor suffer'd in my own Person, nor yet heard from other People, that never were, and what is more, never will be in the World, let it last never so long: Wherefore the Reader is advised beforehand not to believe one Syllable of this Story, for if he does, he must e'en take it for his pains.[5]

---

[2] Walter Scott, *The Works of Jonathan Swift, D.D., Dean of St. Patrick's Dublin*, 2nd ed. (1824), in *Jonathan Swift: The Critical Heritage*, ed. Kathleen Williams (London: Routledge & Kegan Paul, 1970), 306.

[3] Abbé Desfontaines, 'Preface du Traducteur', *Voyages de Gulliver* (1727), in *Jonathan Swift: The Critical Heritage*, ed. Williams, 80.

[4] Desfontaines, 'Preface', in *Jonathan Swift: The Critical Heritage*, ed. Williams, 80.

[5] *The Third Volume of the Works of Lucian: Translated from the Greek by Several Eminent Hands* (1711), 125. I quote from this, the so-called 'Dryden Lucian', as it is the one with which Swift's first readers are likely to have been familiar. The most thorough treatment of the relationship between the two remains J. T. Parnell, 'Swift and Lucian', in *Münster* 3, 295–308.

By having 'Richard Sympson' insist that 'There is an Air of Truth apparent through the whole; and indeed the Author was so distinguished for his Veracity, that it became a Sort of Proverb among his Neighbours at *Redriff*, when any one affirmed a Thing, to say, it was as true as if Mr. *Gulliver* had spoke it' (*GT*, 15–16), Swift adopted a very different satirical strategy. However, several points of resemblance between the *True History* and *Gulliver's Travels* can be readily identified. At the outset, Lucian announced his intention to follow the example of 'the ancient Writers, Poets and Philosophers, who have left abundance of fabulous and absurd things in their Writings', specifically those who

> have left behind them strange Narrations of their Travels, and wandring up and down, of strange Beasts, of savage People, and odd fantastical Customs, which liberty they copied from that Father of Legends *Homer's Ulysses*, who at *Alcinous's* Table banter'd the poor *Phæacians* with Stories of the Wind's being imprison'd in Leather Bottles; of an one-ey'd Generation of People that never regal'd in oil'd or roasted but eat their Victual raw; of strange Animals, with the Lord knows how many Sets of Heads; of his Companions being changed into Swine by the Enchantments of a confounded Harlot, with the Devil and all of such unaccountable *Otisms* of the same stamp.[6]

After visiting lands inhabited by little men and big men, respectively, Gulliver encounters the Yahoos and the Houyhnhnms (assuming at first that they 'must needs be Magicians' (IV, i, 337)). Perhaps of more significance, he repeatedly comes across examples of 'odd fantastical customs'.

This is of course the principal satirical strategy of *Gulliver's Travels*: Swift invites his readers to compare the ways they construct reality with those of the fictitious Lilliputians, the Brobdingnagians, the Laputans and, above all, the Houyhnhnms. 'There are some Laws and Customs in this Empire very peculiar', he makes Gulliver explain about Lilliput, 'and if they were not so directly contrary to those of my own dear Country, I should be tempted to say a little in their Justification' (I, vi, 84). Swift's satirical challenge to the mindset of those in positions of power in early eighteenth-century Europe is given greater prominence in his account of the reaction of the wise King of Brobdingnag's horror-struck reaction to Gulliver's proposal to share with him the secret of gunpowder:

> A strange Effect of *narrow Principles* and *short Views!* that a Prince possessed of every Quality which procures Veneration, Love and Esteem; of strong Parts, great Wisdom and profound Learning; endued with admirable

---

[6] *The Third Volume of the Works of Lucian*, 124.

Talents for Government, and almost adored by his Subjects; should from
a *nice unnecessary Scruple*, whereof in *Europe* we can have no Conception, let
slip an Opportunity put into his Hands, that would have made him absolute
Master of the Lives, the Liberties, and the Fortunes of his People. (II,
vii, 193)

In this way, the reader is prepared for Part IV of *Gulliver's Travels* in which
Gulliver encounters creatures outwardly resembling human beings that do
not appear to be rational, and creatures outwardly resembling horses that
profess to be entirely guided in their conduct by the dictates of reason and
which, despite patently not being created in the image of the Christian
conception of God, regard themselves as '*the Perfection of Nature*' (IV,
iii, 350).

   In addition to these rhetorical similarities, there are also clear plot
resemblances between the *True History* and *Gulliver's Travels*. Soon after
setting out on his travels, Lucian's ship is blown 'about some three
thousand furlongs into the Air'. 'We thus continu'd our Course through
the Sky for the space of seven Days and as many Nights', he explains. 'At
last, on the eighth Day, we discover'd a great Land in the Sky, like a shining
island, round and bright, where we arriv'd, and coming into a convenient
Harbour, went ashore, and soon found it to be inhabited'. Here, after
meeting Endymion, the King of the Moon, he becomes involved in his
unsuccessful war with Phaeton, King of the Sun. On being defeated,
Endymion resolves 'to enter into a League Offensive and Defensive, and
to make War no more'. Before departing the celestial zones, Lucian relates
'what remarkable things fell under my Observation, during my stay in the
Moon [...] tho' some of them may seem to exceed belief.[7] While
Gulliver's encounter with the flying island of Laputa bears at least
a passing resemblance to Lucian's adventures in space, what happens on
the latter's return to earth calls to mind other episodes from Part III of his
travels. Whether Swift simply reversed Lucian's observation that 'No one
grows old in this Country, but in that Age he came so he continues'[8] for his
account of the immortal Struldbruggs, the questions Gulliver asks of the
spirits he meets during his visit to 'the Island of *Sorcerers* or *Magicians*' (III,
vii, 286) recall Lucian's conversations with ancient Greek authors. Ordered
by the governor of Glubbdubdrib 'to call up whatever Persons I would
chuse to name, and in whatever Numbers among all the Dead from the
Beginning of the World to the present Time' (III, vii, 288), Gulliver

[7] *The Third Volume of the Works of Lucian*, 128–9, 136, 137.
[8] *The Third Volume of the Works of Lucian*, 161.

understandably seeks 'to gratify that insatiable Desire I had to see the World in every Period of Antiquity placed before me' (III, vii, 292). He therefore views not only Homer and Aristotle but Alexander, Hannibal, Caesar, Pompey and Brutus (at the sight of whom he 'was struck with a profound Veneration'), as well as moderns such as Descartes and Gassendi. Swift's treatment of notable figures from the past perhaps takes its cue from Lucian, who explains how Socrates 'swore until he looked black in the Face, that he was never naughty with [boys], but innocently toy'd and sported with them, but all the Company knew him to be perjur'd', before going on to observe about Homer that 'the report of his being blind was without any Foundation'.[9] Gulliver proposes 'that *Homer* and *Aristotle* might appear at the Head of all their Commentators'. Able to 'distinguish those two Heroes at first Sight', he 'soon discovered, that both of them were perfect Strangers to the rest of the Company [of commentators], and had never seen or heard of them before' (III, viii, 294).

Gulliver's Travels and Contemporary Prose Fiction

In addition to identifying a connection between *Gulliver's Travels* and Lucian's *True History*, Scott also suggested a way in which Swift might have been consciously engaging with contemporary literature. There had been a significant upturn in the publication of volumes of prose fiction following the appearance in 1719 of Defoe's *The Life and Strange Surprizing Adventures of Robinson Crusoe, of York, Mariner*, 'Written by Himself'. The Preface maintained that 'The Editor believes the thing to be a just History of Fact; neither is there any Appearance of Fiction in it', but Defoe's protestations were given short shrift in Charles Gildon's lampoon, *The Life And Strange Surprizing Adventures of Mr. D– De F– of London, Hosier* (1719), and other works of fiction, such as the Preface to Penelope Aubin's *The Strange Adventures of the Count de Vinevil And his Family* (1721): 'As for the truth of what this Narrative contains, since *Robinson Cruso* has been so well receiv'd, which is more improbable, I know no reason why this should be thought a Fiction'.[10]

Travellers' tales were in vogue at the turn of the eighteenth century, especially if they were about countries hitherto unknown, hence the flurry of publications with similar titles taking their cue from William Dampier's *A New Voyage Round the World* (1697). In 'A Letter from Capt. Gulliver, to

[9] *The Third Volume of the Works of Lucian*, 165, 167.
[10] Penelope Aubin, *The Strange Adventures of the Count de Vinevil and His Family* (1721), 6.

his Cousin Sympson', first published in 1735 in Faulkner's edition of his *Works*, Swift made Gulliver claim that he had advised his 'Cousin *Dampier*' to 'correct the Style [...] in his Book call'd, *A Voyage Round the World*' (*GT*, 7), and Dampier had indeed drawn attention to his 'Stile' to explain that while he had 'frequently [...] divested my self of Sea Phrases, to gratify the Land Reader', he 'still retain[ed] the use of so many Sea-terms'.[11] Patently, Swift was playing games with passages such as this when, in 'The Publisher to the Reader' section of the first edition, 'Richard Sympson' explained that:

> This Volume would have been at least twice as large, if I had not made bold to strike out innumerable Passages relating to the Winds and Tides, as well as to the Variations and Bearings in the several Voyages; together with the minute Descriptions of the Management of the Ship in Storms, in the Style of Sailors: Likewise the Account of the Longitudes and Latitudes; wherein I have Reason to apprehend that Mr. *Gulliver* may be a little dissatisfied. But I was resolved to fit the Work as much as possible to the general Capacity of Readers. (*GT*, 16)

Whether 'The Publisher to the Reader' section of *Gulliver's Travels* succeeds in establishing Gulliver's credentials as a reliable narrator, it prepares the ground for the two occasions in 'A Voyage to Lilliput' where Gulliver feels called upon to defend his character or reputation 'to the World' (I, ii, 44; I, vi, 95). 'This art of introducing trifling and minute anecdotes, upon which nothing depends, or is made to turn', Scott perceptively observed, 'was perhaps imitated by Swift from the romances of De Foe, who carried the air of authenticity to the highest pitch of perfection in his *Robinson Crusoe*, and *Memoirs of a Cavalier*'.[12]

   In turning from questions of genre to issues of narrative technique, Scott was joining the list of eighteenth-century critics, including William Congreve and Clara Reeve, who pre-empted Ian Watt in identifying 'formal realism' as the new novel's distinguishing characteristic: 'the premise, or primary convention' that it comprises 'a full and authentic report of human experience, and is therefore under an obligation to satisfy the reader with such details of the story as the individuality of the actors concerned, the particulars of the times and places of their actions'.[13] As virtually the very first thing Gulliver does on arriving in Lilliput is to supply the unsuspecting

---

[11] William Dampier, *A New Voyage Round the World* (1697), sig. A3^v.

[12] Scott, *The Works of Jonathan Swift*, in *Jonathan Swift: The Critical Heritage*, ed. Williams, 307.

[13] Ian Watt, *The Rise of the Novel: Studies in Defoe, Richardson and Fielding* (London: Chatto and Windus, 1957), 32.

reader with the time and place of his bowel movements, it would be difficult to deny that *Gulliver's Travels* provides readers with 'particulars of the times and places of their actions'. In this respect, it could be argued that Swift was offering a clear instance of 'formal realism' *avant la lettre*. 'Even Robinson Crusoe (though detailing events so much more probable)', Scott contends, 'hardly excels Gulliver in gravity and verisimilitude of narrative'.[14]

Whether this makes *Gulliver's Travels*, in Shklovsky's famous phrase, a 'parodying novel',[15] is an interesting question which largely depends upon the extent to which Swift might be said to be intentionally drawing attention to the pseudo-autobiographical narratives made popular by *Robinson Crusoe* in order to ridicule the sort of circumstantial detail they presented to the reader. Defoe introduced, if not a new style of novel, at any rate a new form of popular fiction which, in striving for an air of authenticity, claimed to be 'not a Story, but a History'.[16] Gulliver begins his account of his travels by offering autobiographical details in a similar vein to Crusoe. 'My Father had a small Estate in *Nottinghamshire*; I was the Third of five Sons', he explains. 'He sent me to *Emanuel-College* in *Cambridge* at Fourteen Years old, where I resided three Years, and applied my self close to my Studies' (I, i, 29–30). Critics have remarked on the correspondence between this circumstantial detail and Swift's own experience in matriculating at Trinity College, Dublin, at the age of fourteen. When he goes on to explain that after a four-year apprenticeship with 'Mr. *James Bates*, an eminent Surgeon in London', he 'married Mrs. *Mary Burton*, second Daughter to Mr. *Edmund Burton*, Hosier, in *Newgate-street*, with whom [he] received four Hundred Pounds for a Portion' (I, i, 30–1), however, Gulliver provides information which seems to associate him with the author of *Robinson Crusoe*. Defoe started out as a hosier, his wife was called Mary, and he had done time in Newgate prison after being charged with seditious libel. One contemporary method of demeaning Defoe, exemplified by Gildon's *The Life And Strange Surprizing Adventures of Mr. D– De F– of London, Hosier*, drew attention to his humble origins. The connection between Swift and Defoe, Gulliver and Crusoe, was made by at least one early reader who pretended 'to vindicate the Reverend D–, on whom it is maliciously father'd', as well as offering 'probable Conjectures concerning the real Author'. 'The Account which the Author is said to give of himself and Family, his Travels, &c. are manifest Forgeries, not one Word of them being

---

[14] Scott, *The Works of Jonathan Swift*, in *Jonathan Swift: The Critical Heritage*, ed. Williams, 293.
[15] See Viktor Shklovsky, 'A Parodying Novel: Sterne's *Tristram Shandy*', in *Laurence Sterne: A Collection of Critical Essays*, ed. John Traugott (Mornington Heights: Prentice Hall, 1968), 66–89.
[16] Daniel Defoe, *The Fortunate Mistress*, ed. P. N. Furbank (London: Pickering & Chatto, 2009), 21.

in the Original', the author of *Gulliver Decypher'd* maintained, 'so that they seem to have been added to the *English* Version by the Author of *Robinson Crusoe*, to inhance the Price, and other Reasons very obvious'.[17]

That contemporaries associated *Gulliver's Travels* with what we now know to have been other spurious examples of autobiography is indicated by an advertisement in the *Daily Post* for 20 October 1727:

> Printed for Thomas Worrall at the Judge's Head over against St. Dunstan's Church in Fleetstreet.
> Where may be had the following entertaining Books.
>
> 1. Captain Gulliver's Travels in three volumes, 8vo.
> 2. The Fortunes and Misfortunes of the famous Moll Flanders.
> 3. The remarkable Life of Colonel Jack.
> 4. The Fortunate Mistress, or the Life, &c. of the Lady Roxana
> 5. The Life, Adventures and Pyracies, of Captain Singleton.
> 6. The Voyages, Adventures, &c. of Capt. Richard Falconer.

It is interesting that this advertisement links two of the most popular forms of fiction of the 1720s – travel literature and criminal biography – because it again draws attention to that 'bewildering uncertainty, of *genre*' identified by Claude Rawson in connection with some of Swift's works, including *Gulliver's Travels*. In 1725, in the Preface to a subscription edition of her *Works*, Mary Davys explained that 'those Sort of Writings call'd Novels have been a great deal out of Use and Fashion' because 'the Ladies (for whose Service they were chiefly design'd) have been taken up with Amusements of more Use and Improvement; I mean History and Travels'.[18] I have previously drawn attention to Davys's statement as an indication of the generic confusion – the generic instability at any rate – current in the 1720s,[19] possibly as a consequence of Defoe's insistence in the Preface to *The Fortunate Mistress* (1724)

> That this *Story* differs from most of the Modern Performances of this Kind, tho' some of them have met with a very good Reception in the World: *I say*, It differs from them in this Great and Essential Article, *Namely*, That the Foundation of This is laid in Truth of *Fact*; and so the Work is not a Story, but a History.[20]

---

[17] *Gulliver Decypher'd: Or Remarks on a Late Book, Intitled, Travels Into Several Remote Nations of the World. By Capt. Lemuel Gulliver. Vindicating the Reverend Dean on Whom it is Maliciously Father'd. With Some Probable Conjectures Concerning the Real Author* [1727], 16–17.

[18] *The Works of Mrs. Davys: Consisting of, Plays, Novels, Poems, and Familiar Letters*, 2 vols. (1725), I, iii.

[19] J. A. Downie, 'Mary Davys's "Probable Feign'd Stories" and Critical Shibboleths about "The Rise of the Novel"', *Eighteenth-Century Fiction*, 12 (2000), 309–26.

[20] Defoe, *The Fortunate Mistress*, 21.

When Davys referred to 'those Sort of Writings call'd Novels', she was evidently using the term as it was defined in Johnson's *Dictionary* (1755): 'A small tale, generally of love'. Davys was herself an 'amatory' novelist, and her *Works* included four examples of them.

Whether contemporaries knew that when they were reading *The Voyages, Dangerous Adventures, And Miraculous Escapes of Capt. Richard Falconer* (1720) and *The Strange Adventures of the Count de Vinevil And his Family* (1721) they were actually reading, not authentic 'History and Travels', but fiction, the commercial success of *Robinson Crusoe* seems to have acted as a stimulus to the market for various kinds of 'novels'. David Oakleaf's contention that '*Travels into Several Remote Nations of the World*, "By Lemuel Gulliver, First a Surgeon, and then a Captain of several Ships," places itself subversively among Crusoe's heirs while parodying 1720s fiction'[21] appears to be borne out by Swift's informing Ford that 'I am now writing a History of my Travells'. And if Swift was implicitly acknowledging the existence of, and playing off, the new type of realistic fiction masquerading as authentic autobiography introduced by Defoe a few years earlier, it would appear to raise questions about recent critical assumptions that the 1720s was the decade in which a process of 'novelization' was taking place.

According to Mikhail Bakhtin's hugely influential dialogic theory of the novel, novelistic discourse constitutes a 'parodic stylization of canonized genres and styles'. 'In the era of the novel's creative ascendancy – and even more in the periods of preparation preceding this era', he insists, 'literature was flooded with parodies and travesties of all the high genres (parodies precisely of genres, and not of individual authors) – parodies that are the precursors, "companions" to the novel in their own ways studies for it'.[22] On this view, the emerging novel is in dynamic dialogue with other, established genres and therefore 'novelizes' existing literary forms. But the novel was scarcely a 'high genre' in the 1720s, and the comments from Defoe, Davys, and Johnson I have just quoted suggest that references to 'novels' in this period do not necessarily mean the type of long prose fiction we now associate with the term. On the contrary, as the repeated use by contemporaries of the phrase, 'novels and romances', insinuates, early eighteenth-century readers do not appear to have been sufficiently aware of the generic issues involved in the classification of prose fiction for the terms

---

[21] David Oakleaf, 'Testing the Market: *Robinson Crusoe* and After', in *The Oxford Handbook of the Eighteenth-Century Novel*, ed. J. A. Downie (Oxford: Oxford University Press, 2016), 172–86 (183).

[22] M. M. Bakhtin, *The Dialogic Imagination: Four Essays*, ed. Michael Holquist, trans. Caryl Emerson and Michael Holquist (Austin: University of Texas Press, 1981), 6.

they used to describe them to have been at all stable. However, were we to view *Gulliver's Travels* as a parody not only of the verisimilitude of Defoe and his imitators, but also of the various voyages round the world published in the previous decade, it would chime in with critical insights about its generic ambivalence.

David Oakleaf has recently taken the proposition that *Gulliver's Travels* is a 'parodying novel' one stage further by referring to another hugely popular form of prose fiction. 'The scene in which a female Yahoo sexually assaults Gulliver after watching him strip to bathe in a stream', he suggests, 'reverses genders to parody amatory fiction's voyeurism'.[23] A little over three months before *Robinson Crusoe* appeared in April 1719, Eliza Haywood published *Love in Excess; or the Fatal Enquiry*. It led to a brief boom in the market for amatory fiction, hitherto associated primarily with Aphra Behn and Delarivier Manley, and Haywood sought to exploit this new-found popularity by publishing numerous individual titles as well as collections such as *The Works of Mrs. Eliza Haywood* (1724) and *Secret Histories, Novels and Poems. In Four Volumes. By Mrs. Eliza Haywood* (1725). In the middle of the decade, however, she turned to political satire in the two volumes of *Memoirs Of a Certain Island Adjacent to the Kingdom of Utopia* (1725–6). It is unlikely that Swift was responding to this specific text, given that he told Charles Ford on 14 August 1725 that he had 'finished my Travells, and I am now transcribing them'. But there has been a tendency, particularly since the publication of Watt's seminal study in 1957, to underplay the extent to which *Gulliver's Travels* was intertextually aware of the various forms of prose fiction that were being published in the early eighteenth century. If this is suggestive of the marked reluctance, despite its evident influence on subsequent prose fiction, to consider *Gulliver's Travels* in relation to the emergence and development of the novel, it seems distinctly odd that the concept of novelization allegedly taking place in the 1720s can apparently accommodate dramatic entertainments such as *The Beggar's Opera* (1728) but not a fictional work in prose which had appeared a little over a year earlier.

The Afterlife of *Gulliver's Travels*

'Is *Gulliver's Travels* a novel?', Northrop Frye memorably enquired in the same year that *The Rise of the Novel* was published. 'Here most would demur', he continued. 'But surely everyone would call it fiction, and if it

[23] Oakleaf, 'Testing the Market', 183.

is fiction, a distinction appears between fiction as a genus and the novel as a species of that genus'.[24] Although Watt failed to mention Swift's bestseller, *Gulliver's Travels* was routinely included in lists of novels in the century following its initial publication. It was reprinted in 1782 in volume IX of James Harrison's *The Novelists' Magazine* along with *A Sentimental Journey, David Simple, Sir Lancelot Greaves, Letters Written by a Peruvian Princess*, and *Jonathan Wild*. The following year James Beattie described *Gulliver's Travels* as 'a sort of allegory; but rather Satirical and Political than Moral',[25] though Clara Reeve did not hesitate to include it alongside *The Pilgrim's Progress, Don Quixote* and *Robinson Crusoe* at the beginning of the 'list of Novels and Stories Original and uncommon' offered in *The Progress of Romance* (1785).[26] 'Cook's Cheap and Elegant Pocket Library Containing the most esteemed and popular Works in the English Language', extensively advertised in a range of newspapers at the turn of the nineteenth century, listed *Gulliver's Travels* among its 'Select Novels' at the price of 2s. 'Fictitious adventures, in one form or other, have made a part of the polite literature of every age and nation', Anna Laetitia Barbauld observed in her prefatory essay to the fifty-volume collection of *British Novelists* (1810). 'They are often made the vehicles of satire, as in Swift's *Gulliver's Travels*, and the *Candide* and *Babouc* of Voltaire'.[27] She chose not to include it in her collection of the best British novels, however, and this was perhaps a factor in Scott's decision to reprint *Gulliver's Travels* in Volume IX of *Ballantyne's Novelists Library* which was devoted to 'The Novels of Swift, Bage, and Cumberland'.

The Author of the Waverley Novels was not in the business of propounding a teleological theory of the rise of the novel. Given that by 1820 the novel's generic identity had still to be firmly established it would have been anachronistic to do so. Yet, as both a practising novelist and a biographer and critic, Scott was perfectly aware of the existence of earlier fictional forms, hence his contention in his famous review of *Emma* that a new 'style of novel' had emerged at the turn of the nineteenth century which was different from both 'the original style of romantic fiction' and the kind of novels that had previously been derived from it.[28] In this essay,

---

[24] Northrop Frye, *Anatomy of Criticism: Four Essays* (Princeton: Princeton University Press, 1957), 303.
[25] James Beattie, 'On Fable and Romance', in *Dissertations Moral and Critical* (1783), 51.
[26] C[lara] R[eeve], *The Progress of Romance*, 2 vols. (Colchester, 1785), II, 52.
[27] Anna Barbauld, 'On the Origin and Progress of Novel-Writing', in *The British Novelists; with an Essay and Prefaces, Biographical and Critical*, 50 vols. (1810), I, 5–6.
[28] [Walter Scott], 'ART. IX. *Emma, a Novel*', *The Quarterly Review* (October 1815), 188–201 (192–3).

I have made extensive use of Scott's remarks on Swift's bestseller with the purpose of indicating that, regardless of any generic uncertainty they might have experienced, eighteenth-century readers of *Gulliver's Travels* had no difficulty appreciating that, if it was not a novel, it was unquestionably working within a recognisable popular literary tradition.

CHAPTER 6

Satire

Pat Rogers

To put the question, 'What is satiric about *Gulliver's Travels?*', has an absurd ring. It is like asking whether there is any romance in the novels of Jane Austen. Satire is present everywhere in the book, in its mode, its generic roots, its form, its plot, its narrative manner, its dialogue, its rhetoric, its language, its descriptive techniques, its allusions, and its humour. The work draws on several forms of earlier writing in the genre, and although it is not itself a novel it has influenced much later fiction. These aspects are illustrated elsewhere in the present volume, and this chapter will outline the way that some become visible in the course of the *Travels*. More perhaps than any other work, *Gulliver* illustrates the truth of Matthew Hodgart's comment, 'The perennial topic of satire is the human condition itself. Man, part ape and part essence, is born for trouble as the sparks fly upwards'.[1] However, it is impossible to specify every single example of satiric detail within the text. To attempt that would be to risk incurring the fate of the critic described in a story by Jorge Luis Borges, Pierre Menard, whose 'reading' of *Don Quixote* ultimately takes the form of a line-for-line reproduction of the Spanish masterpiece.

Here we shall look at the place of *Gulliver* in the satiric tradition and in contemporary practice. This will involve touching at times on Swift's own output besides the *Travels*. Certain genres he parodied (travel writing, scientific discourse, and treatises on philosophy and logic) form the subject of other chapters in this volume. We could add to the list of these submerged genres that the author embedded in his text: for example, complacent political moralising, excitable accounts of 'wonders' and providential rescues from disaster, flat journalistic recitals, and so on. A good example is supplied by the contemptuous description of 'the Roguery and Ignorance of those who pretend to write *Anecdotes,* or secret History', mentioned in the visit to Glubbdubdrib (III, viii, 299). Swift found an

[1] Matthew Hodgart, *Satire* (London: Weidenfeld & Nicolson, 1969), 10.

abundance of bad writing to expose in every branch of literature, as he had continued to do throughout his career. In the *Travels* he does not deal with some issues in such a frontal way as he did elsewhere, for instance matters such as religion, Irish politics, or the literary feuds of London and Dublin. None the less, he brings a number of topical subjects to the fore in the course of Gulliver's adventures. In the final reckoning, the *Travels* is as distinctively a product of the age of George I as other satiric masterpieces are of their own time. We might think of the manner in which Byron's *Don Juan* (1819–24) portrays the Regency era, or that Orwell's *Animal Farm* (1945) constructs a beast fable for the era of Stalin in the mid-twentieth century. It follows that the book needs to be set in a precise historical context if its satire is to be properly understood.

Satiric Traditions

In a broad sense, Swift draws on a corpus of ancient and modern literature that formed a loosely defined 'tradition of satire'. This does not mean that he borrows directly from every writer who helped to establish this line of writing. He was certainly well aware of the fifth-century Greek author Democritus, popularly associated with the 'laughing philosophy' that underlay later comic aspects of satire; but he did not quote this salient figure as an inspiration for any of his own work. Homer and Aristotle are the first representatives of classical literature whose ghosts Gulliver chooses to call up in Glubbdubdrib, while the major satirists hardly enter the text at all – even if the portrait of Swift used as a frontispiece in early editions did carry with it at various times some apt quotations. First came a couplet from the second satire of Persius and later a striking phrase from Horace, *Spendide mendax* (gloriously false) – though this actually derives from an ode, III.xi, not a satire. In brief, Swift may have inherited tone and approach from the great writers of antiquity, including also Juvenal and Martial, but he did not allude explicitly to their works in *Gulliver* in the fashion that he did in *A Tale of a Tub* and many of his poems.

Portions of the *Travels* suggest that he recalled certain moments in Greek and Latin fiction, such as the metamorphosis of the hero in *The Golden Ass* by Lucius Apuleius (*c.* AD 150), which is distantly related to comments on the Houyhnhnms (IV, i, 337). There may be a glancing allusion to the fragmentary *Satyricon* of Petronius Arbiter. However, the only extensive debt is that to the Greek author Lucian (*c.* AD 115–80), Swiftian in his wit and parodic skills, whose miscellaneous works almost all contain some satiric admixture, with a constant urge to demythologise the tales that prop up a culture. The influence is seen at its clearest in the third part of the *Travels*, where several overt reminiscences can be traced in Gulliver's adventures as he progresses from Laputa and Balnibarbi to Luggnagg and Glubbdubdrib, as part of an imaginary voyage whose episodes are in places directly reminiscent of Lucian's *Verae historiae* ('True histories'). Like Swift, Lucian constantly raises issues of truth and falsehood (*Splendide mendax* once more). Unlike Lucian's hero, who is formally identical with the author, Gulliver never ventures into space, or finds himself in the belly of an enormous whale, but he does encounter equally unsettling environments and equally fantastic creatures. The conversations with departed souls in the *Travels* (III, viii, 294–304) draw on a section on the Isles of the Blessed in the second part of Lucian's work, and they could hardly have been written without the example of the lastingly popular 'Dialogues of the Dead' that he pioneered. In his own set, Lucian describes exchanges between characters such as Socrates and Diogenes as they are transported to the underworld. The form was revived in the Renaissance, for example by Trajano Boccalini, whose *Ragguagli di Parnasso* ('Information from Parnassus', 1612) lies behind both *A Tale of a Tub* and *The Battle of the Books*. It had been translated into English in the seventeenth century and a revised version by Pope's friend John Hughes went through several editions in Swift's lifetime. The most important legatee of this tradition in the circle of Swift was Matthew Prior (1664–1721), who owned editions of Lucian in four languages, as well as a copy of *Nouveaux Dialogues des Morts* (1683) by Bernard le Bovier de Fontenelle. Towards the end of his career Prior produced four accomplished exercises in this form. They were not published until 1907, but it is possible that Swift knew of their existence.

If we leap forward to the early modern period, bypassing the bulk of medieval literature (as the reading of Swift and his contemporaries largely did), we encounter a number of available models. These include Thomas More's *Utopia* (1516), to which 'Capt. Gulliver' refers in his prefatory letter (*GT*, 13), and which could be seen to provide an ironic contrast to some of the institutions and practices in Houyhnhnm-land. The imaginary traveller here is a Portuguese named Hythloday, and some of his reactions to the idealised commonwealth are only a little less naive than those of Gulliver in the countries that he visits. Comparison is also possible with Francis Bacon's fragment, *The New Atlantis* (1626), although this is not a satire, but rather a blueprint for a future science-based society on the mythical island of Bensalem. The classic demonstration of an unreliable satiric narrator occurs in *The Praise of Folly* (1513) by More's friend Desiderius

Erasmus. In a general sense Gulliver resembles the narrator of the *Praise* by reason of his overweening confidence in his own rectitude, as well as his perverse recommendation of stupid behaviour, but he is blind and without self-knowledge, whereas the goddess Folly is completely aware of what she is doing when she adopts the fool's motley.

Among early works of space fiction, the most relevant is the moon voyage in Cyrano de Bergerac's *Les États and Empires de la Lune* (1657), where the traveller finds himself reduced to the role of a freak show exhibit, much like Gulliver in Brobdingnag. In addition, Swift could well have encountered other allegorical voyages into the unknown such as *The Consolidator: or Memoirs of Sundry Transactions from the World in the Moon* (1705). This was said to be 'Translated from the Lunar Language' by its supposed editor, that is Daniel Defoe. The *Consolidator* is very different from the *Travels*, but there are occasional convergences, as in this passage early on, which offers a hint of Gulliver's complacent way of displaying his mastery in all matters Lilliputian:

> If these Labours of mine shall prove successful, I may in my next Journey that way, take an Abstract of their most admirable Tracts in Navigation, and the Mysteries of *Chinese* Mathematicks; which out-do all Modern Invention at that Rate, that 'tis Inconceivable: In this Elaborate Work I must run thro' the 365 Volumes of *Augro-machi-lanquaro-zi*, the most ancient Mathematician in all *China*: From thence I shall give a Description of a Fleet of Ships of 100000 Sail, built at the Expence of the Emperor *Tangro* the 15th; who having Notice of the General Deluge, prepar'd these Vessels, to every City and Town in his Dominions One, and in Bulk proportion'd to the number of its Inhabitants.[2]

Two major figures in world literature played a large part in forming Swift's notion of satire. Pope, who knew him as well as anyone in England, referred to these masters when he wrote a quasi-dedicatory tribute to his friend in *The Dunciad*, which appeared two years after the *Travels*. The lines begin by running over some of the great achievements of Swift, especially as polemicist and satirist:

> O thou! Whatever Title please thine ear,
> Dean, Drapier, Bickerstaff, or Gulliver!
> Whether thou chuse Cervantes' serious air,
> Or laugh and shake in Rab'lais' easy Chair.[3]

---

[2] Daniel Defoe, *The Consolidator: Or Memoirs of Sundry Transactions from the World in the Moon* (1705), 7.
[3] Alexander Pope, *The Dunciad*, I, 17–20, *The Twickenham Edition of the Poems of Alexander Pope*, 11 vols. (New Haven: Yale University Press, 1961–9), V, 68.

There are signs that people in those days read *Don Quixote* more narrowly than we do today, judging by a passage that Pope wrote into his copy of the novel. It came from René Rapin, one of the most influential critical theorists of the age. Pope's marginalium cites the translation by Basil Kennett (1716), which commends the 'Romance' as 'a most fine and ingenious Satire on his own Country; because the Nobility of Spain, whom he renders ridiculous by this work, were all bit in the head & intoxicated with Knight Errantry'.[4] Rapin supplies a testimony to the effect that Cervantes wrote his novel in a spirit of revenge against a powerful nobleman. The same view of *Quixote* was expressed by Defoe, in the preface to his *Serious Reflections during the Life and Surprising Adventures of Robinson Crusoe* (1720), in the course of an argument justifying Crusoe's story as a 'true' account of the hero's life. This parallel suggests that Swift, too, may have seen his book as Cervantic, because it allowed him to get his own back surreptitiously on former patrons who had dashed his hopes of preferment. The petty manoeuvres of the leaders of Lilliput bear an uncomfortable resemblance to the stratagems of the quarrelsome politicians who had triumphed over Swift and his allies.

Nevertheless, the most pervasive influence visible throughout the *Travels* is that of François Rabelais, with his *Gargantua and Pantagruel* (1532–64). Famously, Voltaire declared that 'Dean *Swift* is *Rabelais* in his Senses, and frequenting the politest Company', meaning that unlike his fellow countryman, a drunken 'Prince of Buffoons', Swift always had a sane and civilised outlook – some may demur.[5] The debt can be observed in particular episodes, such as the moment early on when Gulliver urinates on the blazing palace of the Emperor of Lilliput (I, v, 79–80). This recalls a scene in Rabelais (Book I, Chapter xvii) where the giant Gargantua confronts the residents of Paris as he leans on the tower of Notre Dame and 'so bitterly all-to-bepissed them, that he drowned two hundred and sixty Thousand, four hundred and eighteen, besides the Women and little Children'. A more extended parallel can be found between the experiments conducted in the Academy of Lagado (III, v–vi) and the activities witnessed by Pantagruel at the court of La Dame Quinte Essance, whose name was translated by Swift's contemporary Peter Motteux as Queen Whim (Book V, Chapter xxii). This crotchety lady presides over a strange collection of hangers on, one of the ways in which she resembles Pope's Queen

---

[4] Cited by Maynard Mack, *Collected in Himself* (Newark: University of Delaware Press, 1982), 400–1. Like Voltaire, Rapin offered a more qualified admiration of Rabelais, whose wit he considered to be tainted by crude ribaldry.
[5] Voltaire, *Letters Concerning the English Nation* (1733), 182.

Dulness. The exploits of these deluded courtiers include such futile Lagadan feats as making chalk from cheese, and honey from a dog's turd. Throughout the *Travels* we are reminded of the learning, gusto, verbal invention and sheer smut that have given rise to the term 'Rabelaisian humour'. According to Pope, Swift was a great reader and admirer of the French author. Just as much to the point, another of the Scriblerian group, Dr John Arbuthnot, cherished the same fondness and often drew on Rabelais in his own comic pamphlets (see below).

Contemporary Satire

Neither in the ancient world nor in the Renaissance did satire occupy an exalted place among the literary kinds. Aristotle spent little time on comedy in the *Poetics* (he may have written a lost treatise on the subject), and it is astounding for us to realise that commentators on literary theory seldom paid any attention to the dramatic art of Aristophanes, whose portrait of fifth-century Athens now looks to us like one of the greatest satiric achievements of all time. Equally, Britain produced some brilliant examples of complaint and invective during the medieval period, with writers such as Chaucer and Dunbar. In the Elizabethan age compelling use was made of varied satiric motifs by Shakespeare, John Marston, and Ben Jonson in drama, by John Donne and Joseph Hall in verse, and by Thomas Nashe in prose – all this despite the ever-present threat of legal reprisals.

Nevertheless, it was not until the seventeenth century that a body of criticism grew up recognising the distinctive attributes of this form of writing. Greater clarity emerged with discussions by the French scholar Isaac Casaubon and then by John Dryden (who was incidentally Swift's second cousin once removed). Significantly, the most influential treatises on the art of poetry, as they followed the ancient example of Horace, would come from Boileau and Pope, each a satirist who wrote in an acid vein about the work of others. For the first time, a full defence of satire could be elaborated by commentators on literature. When *A Tale of a Tub* and *The Battle of the Books* appeared in 1704, the form was widely practised and debated, even if it remained open to dismissal by moralists and vulnerable to prosecution. Through a range of devices, Swift managed to stay out of prison, which is where his opponents regularly wished him to be consigned (and his cloth would not have saved him), but he often rode a very fine line.

The most helpful conspectus of activity in the field has been given by Ashley Marshall, in her comprehensive survey of *The Practice of Satire in*

England 1658–1770 (2013), which leaves out hardly anything that would have mattered to Swift.[6] It covers contemporary views of satire as well as the canon of major writing, from Dryden, Marvell, Rochester, Butler, and Oldham onwards. Swift's own era is described with close analysis of work by Defoe, Pope, and Gay among others, before the story moves on to Fielding, Churchill, Smollett, Sterne, and still uncanonical writers such as Charlotte Lennox and Samuel Foote. Marshall also brings out the penetration of satire into drama and the novel, as formal satire in the mode of Horace and Juvenal became less dominant. From this source we can assemble a good picture of the nature of satire almost up to the time of Byron. Most of the earlier writers mentioned had some importance in moulding Swift's approach to his art. However, the example of Rochester and Samuel Butler in particular was more applicable to his work in verse, where it can be felt both in major poems such as *Verses on the Death of Dr. Swift* and in the informal items he addressed to his friends like Thomas Sheridan or Lady Acheson. The direct impact of earlier poets on *Gulliver* is negligible, but we do find occasional passages in the text where the narrator takes up issues that had already surfaced in Swift's own verse, for example, the bitter attack on informers and lying witnesses used in 'Tribnia' (Walpole's Britain) that emerges in the hero's visit to the Grand Academy (III, vi, 281–4). This section had been heralded in a work entitled 'Upon the Horrid Plot' (1722), dealing with the trial of Bishop Francis Atterbury in connection with a planned Jacobite rising.

The situation is different with respect to more immediately contemporary writing. Swift undoubtedly knew the *Amusements Serious and Comical* (1700) by Thomas Brown, better known as 'Tom Brown of Facetious Memory'. The title of this book would fit almost all the multifarious productions of Brown (1662–1704), a man of some learning who wrote a life of Erasmus as well as translations of Petronius, the French comic author Paul Scarron, and (oddly perhaps) Cicero. Most relevantly, he supplied his own 'letters from the dead to the living' in a volume with that title in 1702, and contributed to a version of Lucian published in 1710. Though soon relegated to the lower status of a 'popular author', Brown's books show considerable verve and energy. Swift possibly had some of these items in his head when drafting the *Travels*. The most obvious instances come from the ninth of the *Amusements*, styled 'The City Circle', where we meet a Rabelaisian Lady Wimsey, President of the

[6] Ashley Marshall, *The Practice of Satire in England 1658–1770* (Baltimore: Johns Hopkins University Press, 2013).

Board of scandalmongers (here, too, a hint of Swift's *Verses*); the tenth, on 'The Philosophical, or *Virtuosi* Country', where we find such Laputan projects as buildings designed on a geometrical principle with their foundations in the air, leading to the inevitable collapse of the structure while 'the Architects tumble down to the Earth'; and the eleventh, describing the college set up in the land of Physick 'for the improvement of the Mystery of *Manslaughter*'.[7] Some of Brown's absurd pseudo-scientific experiments rival those of Lagado in comic invention.

Another possible model from the world of Grub Street is Edward 'Ned' Ward (1667–1731), long cited by social historians, especially on the morals and manners of London. His works, while often lively, embody more gusto than subtlety in their descriptions, and the intention seems to be less to provoke outrage and consequent reformatory zeal than to supply entertainment from known scandalous subjects. It has been suggested that Swift may have raided Ward at least once: in the latter's most famous production, *The London Spy* (1698–1700), the narrator tells of a visit to '*Wise-Acres-Hall*, more commonly call'd *Gresham-College*', the home in the capital of investigations of natural science.[8] The ensuing passage gives a sketch of an unworldly philosopher (that is, scientist) with a 'mathematical countenance', a phrase recalling features of the inhabitants of Swift's academy. In this portion of the third voyage, the debts accrue more heavily than in any other phase of the *Travels*. There is a simple reason: the episode contains more precise and concrete parallels with defined targets than we find in the generalised sections on the human condition that predominate elsewhere, while the topics had been more frequently approached in the same style by earlier satirists.

Among writers outside the Scriblerian set who were personally known to Swift, the most interesting connection is with William King (1662–1712), whose role among the wits of Christ Church, Oxford, placed him on the same side as Swift in the great battle of the books. Some even thought he might be the author of *A Tale of a Tub*. In his *Dialogues of the Dead* (1699) he ridiculed Richard Bentley, a major target of Pope's *Dunciad*, as a footling dabbler – unfairly but amusingly. He satirised the trivial contents of travel books in *A Journey to London* (1698), with which we might compare the absurdly over-documented details of Gulliver's storm on the way to Brobdingnag (II, i, 119–21). In his *Useful Transactions in Philosophy* (1709), too, King had mocked Royal Society transactions in a manner that anticipates the proceedings in the Grand Academy.

---

[7] *The Third Volume of the Works of Mr. Tho. Brown*, 3rd ed. (1715), 94, 98.
[8] Edward Ward, *The London Spy: Part III* (1699), 8–9. See *GT*, 226 n 2.

Scriblerian Connections

An especially fruitful context in which to view Swift's debt to his contemporaries will emerge if we look at the work of his fellows within the Scriblerian group. Ashley Marshall argues that scholars have assumed more commonality among their number than actually exists.[9] Some evidence lends support to that view. The Club as a human entity met only for a short spell in the later years of Queen Anne, with a few slight efforts at resuscitation of their meetings. One of the team, Swift, soon left for permanent exile in Ireland. He was followed by the poet Thomas Parnell, who died not very long afterwards. This left Pope, Arbuthnot and Gay as the only founding members still around. Their major collective production did not come out until there was just one left – Pope, who published *The Memoirs of Martinus Scriblerus* in 1741. It is also true that the individual writers had some specialisms of their own, and that some of their works have little relation to the overall satiric project (Gay's *Fables*, to take a single example). But even *The Beggar's Opera* (1728), which belongs to an alternative tradition of mock musicals, had its roots in a suggestion from Swift concerning the opportunity for a 'Newgate pastoral'.

These circumstances, indicating divergence, are overridden by a greater weight of evidence which serves to augment the cohesiveness of the satirists' output. First, they did not need to be in one another's company to get their Scriblerian act together. Pope, Gay, and Arbuthnot all corresponded extensively with Swift during his absence in Ireland, and as soon as he was able to visit England in 1726 and 1727 immediately resumed their intimate relations. The letters contain plans for forthcoming works. Long after Swift left for Dublin, his colleagues kept exhorting him to carry on with his Scriblerian activity. It is here, along with messages to a close associate, Charles Ford, that we can trace the origins of the *Travels* and the progress Swift made on them in the early 1720s. In the immediate aftermath of publication, it would be Arbuthnot who gave the author his first account of the ways in which the book had been received.

Second, the friends went on collaborating for many years after the breakup of their meetings. Pope and Arbuthnot seem to have shared responsibility for a number of pamphlets from around 1716, and it has never been doubted that they are the joint authors of the *Memoirs*, the key text in assessing how the project evolved over time. The three London Scriblerians were identified by hostile critics as a 'triumvirate' who put

---

[9] Ashley Marshall, 'The Myth of Scriblerus', *JECS*, 31 (2008), 77–99.

together the farce *Three Hours after Marriage* (1717). It is often impossible to tell where one writer breaks off and the other takes over. Pope wrote a parody of his friend in the form of a Horatian epistle 'Imitated in the Manner of Dr. Swift', which never strays far at all from the Dean's language and versification. A poem called 'Bounce to Fop', published in 1736, is full of innuendo concerning political figures. Swift may have started this item, and Pope completed it. But if so (a large concession), at what point did he seize the pen, and did he revise Swift's supposed portion extensively? We do not know. Despite periodic differences, the two men remained extraordinarily close to one another in outlook and in literary mannerisms.

A clinching point is that the group maintained their identity by producing a series of jointly written *Miscellanies* from 1727. *The Dunciad* was originally scheduled to appear in this setting. Items that did make their debut include *Peri Bathous*, another Pope-Arbuthnot collaboration. A host of smaller items were included in the set, originally running to four volumes. Pope included numerous well-known works by Swift, who had a very good idea of what was going on and did not raise any objections until much later. By the time he brought the *Travels* before the public, the author had an inkling of his friend's intentions. Thus, the masterpiece emerged from a larger matrix of satiric practice in which all four survivors among the group took part.

What is the relation of *Gulliver* to the original project of the Scriblerian group? The fullest answer has been given by a careful student, Charles Kerby-Miller, who concludes that 'though Swift never publicly said so, it seems likely that he actually began writing the travels as a direct contribution to the club scheme'. In the event, Swift went his own way, and so the penultimate chapter in *The Memoirs of Martinus Scriblerus*, as published in 1741, gives only 'some Hint of his Travels'. The four voyages are briskly summarised, starting with the Lilliputian adventures, where the hero makes 'a Discovery of the Remains of the ancient *Pygmæan* Empire' – this sounds like pure Arbuthnot, as the doctor had a particular fascination with this subject. For that matter, the Yahoos bear an uncomfortable resemblance to the simian creatures anatomised by Arbuthnot's Royal Society colleague Edward Tyson and mentioned in *An Essay Concerning the Origin of Sciences*.[10] Kerby-Miller details a number of passages where the supposed travels outlined in the *Memoirs* closely mesh with episodes in *Gulliver*.[11]

---

[10] Published in the *Miscellanies* in 1732, but written earlier, mostly if not completely by Arbuthnot.
[11] *The Memoirs of the Extraordinary Life, Works, and Discoveries of Martinus Scriblerus*, ed. Charles Kerby-Miller (New York: Oxford University Press, 1988), 164–5, 315–23.

We can detect a broader congruence. The central goal in the Scriblerus movement had been to produce items of learned wit, in which attacks were launched on pomposity, pretentiousness, bogus scholarship, fatuous intellectual schemes, and preposterous innovations. Some of these targets are most evident in the third book of the *Travels*, but the ridicule of figures at the court of Lilliput who institute impeachment (I, ii, 96–104) and the Houyhnhnm senators sitting in judgment on Gulliver (IV, x, 421–3) partake of the same quality. Beyond this, the plot of the book enacts a movement common in satires by members of the group, whereby an apparently rational narrator turns out to be thoroughly demented, like Gulliver skulking in the stable at the end of his story. Among Swift's other works, this process of gradual revelation is found most obviously in *A Modest Proposal* (1729), where it takes a little time before we realise just how crazed the proposer is. The parallel effect of a shifting narrative voice occurs in the writings of the highly unreliable narrator 'Isaac Bickerstaff', as well as the tricksy persona to be found in the *Drapier's Letters* (1724–5) and the *Verses on the Death of Dr. Swift*. But we must keep in mind that the reader has to negotiate similar hermeneutic twists in Pope's *Key to the Lock* (1715), with its absurd Jacobite interpretation of *The Rape of the Lock*, and in Arbuthnot's pamphlets casting scorn on quacks and pedants. Thus, techniques as well as topics are shared.

The different writers often choose identical targets. A frenzied ideologue or system-maker commonly appears at the centre of the story, as with the critic John Dennis in Pope's *Narrative of Dr. Robert Norris* (1713), told by a quack. It is only a single step to the once competent medical man Lemuel Gulliver, now become a deluded misanthrope as a result of his voyages. Three pamphlets concern the descent into madness of the publisher Edmund Curll, who also figures in Swift's *Verses*: two of these are by Pope, the third may have been written partly or wholly by Arbuthnot. Other short pieces by the group attack the self-important geologist John Woodward, along with astrologers and astronomers like William Whiston, in terms similar to those used in the third voyage. 'Jeremy Thacker', a mathematician created by Arbuthnot to make fun of wild proposals to find the longitude, would have little difficulty fitting into Laputan society, so long as he had the aid of a flapper to bring his attention back to the real world.

Conclusion

None of the works mentioned in this chapter would provide Swift with a prescriptive model. Rather, they were part of his mental furniture – Lucian and Rabelais perhaps most of all, along with the works of his

Scriblerian colleagues – and they stimulated his powers of invention. He brought to the composition of the *Travels* a range of literary skills, honed in different departments of writing. The book does not operate in an inter-textual mode, that is to say the reader is never asked to remember the precise context of any passage by an earlier writer to which glancing allusion is made. Moreover, Gulliver is a more unremarkable man than most of his progenitors among the heroes of the satiric canon. Despite that, his story carries with it a more intense level of feeling, and it provokes in us a greater release of potentially disruptive emotions (outrage, scorn, antagonism, incomprehension, wild hilarity, plain disbelief). All with the help, naturally, of that prime weapon in the satirist's armoury – a gift for comedy. The *Travels* do not contain such obvious examples of learned wit as we find in the coruscating wordplay of the digressions in the *Tale*, or in the barbed allusions that permeate *The Dunciad*, but they assuredly carry with them in places the weight of Swift's learning and the almost unbearable lightness of his wit.

CHAPTER 7

Travel Writing

Dirk F. Passmann

Swift's interest in travel literature dates back to 1696/97, when he was employed as secretary to Sir William Temple at Moor Park, and when, as he stated in the 'Apology' to the fifth edition of *A Tale of a Tub*, '*his Invention [was] at the Height, and his Reading fresh in his Head*' (*Tale*, 5). On the reading list Swift drew up from this period occur titles like 'Voyage de *Syam*', 'Voyage de *Maroc* &c' or '*Bernier's* Grand Mogol 2 Vol:' (*Tale*, 273–4), the latter referring to the highly influential travel accounts of the French physician François Bernier about the realm of the Indian Great Mogul, whose works are referred to in the mock notes of the *Tale* and *The Mechanical Operations of the Spirit*.[1]

Surely a number of the books Swift enumerates in his list must have been from Temple's Library. As a tentative catalogue shows, Temple's library held a substantial number of voyages and travels, works the retired diplomat drew on at large in the composition of, among other works, *Of Heroick Virtue* and *Upon the Gardens of Epicurus*.[2] Since Swift was entrusted with the editing of Temple's works, he would have reverted to his patron's library and surely would have consulted and verified the sources of his mentor's essays. Temple had continued to acquire the most recent travel books well into the late 1690s, as becomes evident from a list of books Temple bought from the bookseller Ralph Sympson in 1698, which contained, among others, *A New Voyage and Description of the Isthmus of America* (1698) by the surgeon Lionel Wafer, a work that was also later to be found in Swift's own library.[3]

---

[1] *Tale*, 175, 387, 485, 516. For details of Swift's reading in 1697/98, see Dirk F. Passmann and Hermann J. Real, 'Annotating J. S. Swift's Reading at Moor Park in 1697/8', in *Münster 7*, 101–24.

[2] Dirk F. Passmann and Heinz J. Vienken, *The Library and Reading of Jonathan Swift: A Bio-Bibliographical Handbook. Part I: Swift's Library*, 4 vols. (Frankfurt am Main: Peter Lang, 2003), IV, 185–215; Dirk F. Passmann, *'Full of Improbable Lies': Gulliver's Travels und die Reiseliteratur vor 1726* (Frankfurt am Main: Peter Lang, 1987), 475–7.

[3] Ehrenpreis, I, 286–7; Passmann and Vienken, *Library*, III, 1948–9.

Many of Temple's contemporaries shared his interest in travel books. The libraries of Robert Hooke and Edward Millington, for instance, contained more than 140 titles of travel literature. Whether Isaac Newton, John Ray, Thomas Browne, John Woodward, Edward Waller, Elias Ashmole, John Arbuthnot, Edward Stillingfleet, Charles Boyle, 4th Earl of Orrery, Elijah Fenton, Anthony Collins, or John Locke, on whose shelves there were about 195 works of travel literature, the learned of the age were well read in this popular genre.[4] Shaftesbury viewed that development, however, with dismay: 'Our Relish or *Taste* must of necessity grow barbarous, whilst *Barbarian* Customs, *Savage* Manners, *Indian* Wars, and Wonders of the *Terra Incognita*, employ our leisure Hours, and are the chief Materials to furnish out a Library. These are in our present Days, what Books of Chivalry were, in those of our Forefathers'.[5]

Despite this scepticism, travel books had become an established genre that had come a long way from the pilgrims' itineraries of the Middle Ages or the sober ship's logs of the early discoverers. The discovery and colonisation of the New World in America and the establishment of trade in Africa, Asia, and the East and West Indies had brought news from even some of the remotest parts of the world, and the reports of the voyagers were eagerly read. The expansion of the colonial powers produced a massive flow of information composed by discoverers, explorers, merchants, missionaries, ambassadors, scientists, naturalists, or buccaneers and adventurers alike. Accounts of voyages and descriptive geographies were among the most popular literary genres in Restoration and Augustan England.

With the emergence of the new science in the later seventeenth century, a new type of voyager emerged, that of the scientific explorer, whose expeditions amassed the facts on which the age of reason thrived. They collected specimens of plants, fruits, and animals that fed the virtuoso's cabinets; they recorded nautical and geographical details and data on minerals, ore, timber, grain and other raw materials important for overseas trade; and they reported on newly discovered civilisations and religions which nourished the emerging theories of empirical philosophers like Locke or deists and freethinkers like Blount, Toland and Collins. 'Useful knowledge' was the universal formula applied now, and *The Philosophical Transactions of the Royal Society of London* praised the scientific traveller, whose writings 'must needs contain many uncommon and useful Things

[4] Passmann, *'Full of Improbable Lies'*, 125–32.
[5] *Characteristics of Men, Manners, Opinions, Times*, ed. Philip Ayres, 2 vols. (Oxford: Oxford University Press, 1999), II, 177.

upon most of the Heads of Natural and Mathematical Sciences, as well as Trade and other Profitable Knowledge, which contribute to the enlarging of the Mind and Empire of Man'.[6]

At the same time, the voyagers' narrations dealt with the unknown, dangerous adventures, savage nations, hardships and tempests, and the exotic, and even the driest style could not diminish readers' fascination. Thus, William Dampier's *A New Voyage Round the World* (1697) and *A Voyage to New Holland* (1703) went into several editions in the early eighteenth century.

Pigmies, Giants and Savages

When on 28 October 1726, the travels of a certain Lemuel Gulliver came out, Benjamin Motte, the publisher, could be sure of a commercial success and the author could not have made a better choice to attract a large audience when he gave his most famous satire the framework of a travel account. Swift's keen interest in the genre had continued, and the inventories as well as the sale catalogue of his library list a considerable stock of travel literature. The individual works and the various anthologies of, among others, Grynaeus, Hakluyt, and Purchas numbered roughly 520 authors and their reports, among them some of the most popular exponents of the genre like Bernier, Linschoten, Dampier, Wafer, Herbert, Leo Africanus, Niehof, Rycaut, Busbecq and others.[7] His attitude towards the genre was, however, ambivalent. In a letter to Esther Vanhomrigh on 13 July 1722, he writes: 'The use I have made of [the bad weather] was to read I know not how many diverting Books of History and Travells' (*Correspondence*, II, 424). At the same time, however, he informs his friend Charles Ford that he had been reading an 'abundance of Trash' (*Correspondence*, II, 428).

Gulliver emerges as a competent scientific observer, a surgeon like Wafer or Bernier, interested in navigation and languages, who is established as a trustworthy reporter even before his first voyage begins. Like many of his 'colleagues', Gulliver is driven by an insatiable curiosity, and like almost all travel writers of the age he repeatedly affirms the authenticity and truthfulness of his relation. Although we would not today seriously expect a contemporary reader to accept the account of Lilliput at face value,

[6] *Philosophical Transactions*, 18 (June 1694), 167. For the Royal Society's impact on travel writing, see Michael McKeon, *The Origins of the English Novel, 1600–1740* (Baltimore: Johns Hopkins University Press, 1987), 101–5.
[7] Passmann and Vienken, *Library*, IV, 418–21.

reports of pygmy tribes were common stock in contemporaneous travelogues. Paolo Giovio or Johannes Scheffer asserted their existence in Lapland, and Olaus Magnus and Dithmar Blefkens (both authors in Swift's library) located them in Greenland, a fact asserted as late as 1698 in Jodocus Crull's *Antient and Present State of Muscovy*, one of the books Temple bought in 1698.[8] Even the famous geographer Herman Moll, whom Gulliver names as a 'friend' (IV, xi, 428), confirmed the existence of pygmies on the *Nowaja Semlja* peninsula in his *Compleat Geographer*,[9] and Jodocus Hondius's map of the Northern Regions in Samuel Purchas's *Pilgrimes* (1625) showed an area near the pole to which the legend reads 'Pygmaei hic habitant'. Further reliable accounts of pygmies could be found in Andrew Battel's report on his sojourn in Angola, contained in Purchas.[10] Although there were sceptical voices the existence of that race was thought at least probable.

The same applies to the possible existence of giants like the Brobdingnagians. There was the conviction in many cultures that, from paleontological and historical evidence, a race of giants existed in former times, as Linschoten reported of Peru, Acosta of the Aztecs, or Ovington of Hindu idols in India.[11] Therefore, it is amusing to note that both Acosta and Linschoten mention as a proof of the discovery of a giant's tooth, as Gulliver does when taking home a footman's tooth as a souvenir from Brobdingnag (II, viii, 211). Moreover, ever since Antonio Pigafetta's account of the Patagonian giants near the Strait of Magellan, travellers were quick to enlarge the actual size of natives treated in eye-witness accounts, so much so that even North American tribes like that of the Sasquehannocs were described as 'gyant-like people' in the report of John Smith.[12] The existence of a race of giants could not be ruled out altogether, especially since there were too many white spots on the landscape. Thus, even in 1724, the Jesuit missionary Joseph-François Lafitau asserted that giants will surely be discovered in *Terrae Australes*.[13]

Another almost classical topos in travel reports was the description of savage tribes, and if Swift wanted to model the Yahoos in Part IV on similar accounts in travel books, the genre offered a generous choice. Prominent in

---

[8] Ehrenpreis, I, 286.   [9] Herman Moll, *The Compleat Geographer* (1723), Pt. I, 326.
[10] Samuel Purchas, *Hakluytus Posthumous, or, Purchas His Pilgrimes* (Glasgow: J. MacLehose, 1905–7), VI, 401; Passmann, 'Full of Improbable Lies', 145–66.
[11] Dirk F. Passmann, 'Degeneration in *Gulliver's Travels*: Excavations from Brobdingnag', *SStud*, 1 (1986), 46–50; *GT*, II, vii, 198 nn 31–3.
[12] Purchas, *Purchas His Pilgrimes*, XVIII, 540.
[13] Joseph-François Lafitau, *Customs of the American Indians*, ed. W. N. Fenton and E. L. Moore, 2 vols. (Toronto: Champlain Society, 1974–7), I, 61.

that class were the 'Hottentots' (a historical term used for the Khoekhoe people, which is now offensive), whose habit of eating guts was common stock in accounts of the Cape of Good Hope. In Thomas Herbert's *A Relation of Some Yeares Travaile . . . into Afrique and the Greater Asia* (1634), another book from Swift's shelves, 'Hottentot' women were illustrated with their long breasts thrown over their shoulders and suckling babies on their backs, holding at the same time a dish of guts. Like the Yahoos, the 'Hottentot' women were described as lustful.[14] From his reading of travel books, Swift acquired a wealth of rather unpleasant details of various 'barbarian' tribes, which he used in his treatment of the Yahoos.[15] Their insatiable avarice, manifest in their love of 'certain shining Stones of several Colours' (IV, vii, 392), may have been indebted to Linschoten's account of a tribe on an island near Florida, where the Amerindians have the same love for jewels they gather from the sand,[16] or may have been influenced by the description of the tribe of the 'Tracoides' in the spurious relation of 'John Mandeville' (available to Swift in Hakluyt's anthology), who live like beasts, have no language and cherish 'preciosos lapides' that shine in 60 different colours.[17] However, whereas the travellers' descriptions of savage tribes served to underline the superior status of the 'civilised' traveller, the same vocabulary was used to prepare the cultural shock of Gulliver, who finds himself on the same footing with the abominable Yahoos.

Moreover, the Yahoos are a biological and cultural cross-breed, who not only bear a resemblance to barbarous 'natives' but also to the apes and monkeys described in travel reports. Travellers rarely failed to notice the physiological similarities between man and ape, whether in the description of the 'Pongo' in Angola or the Orang-Utang of Borneo and Java. Some illustrations of apes, as in John Ogilby's *Atlas Japannensis* (1670) or Daniel Beeckman's *A Voyage to . . . Borneo* (1718), reveal a striking similarity between humans and anthropoid *simiae*.[18] Moreover, aggressiveness was a typical characteristic of apes, and travellers like Charles Dellon (*A Voyage to the East Indies*, 1698) or William Bosman (*A New and Accurate Description of the Coast of Guinea*, 1705) recount members of their crew being attacked by monkeys. Gulliver is likewise

---

[14] Passmann, *'Full of Improbable Lies'*, 190–3; Passmann and Vienken, *Library*, II, 831–3.
[15] John Robert Moore, 'The Yahoos of the African Travellers', *N&Q*, 195 (1950), 182–5; Ray Frantz, 'Swift's Yahoos and the Voyagers', *MP*, 29 (1931/32), 49–57. See also *GT*, 329 n 3.
[16] Ian Higgins, 'Possible "Hints" for *Gulliver's Travels* in the *Voyages* of Jan Hughen van Linschoten', *N&Q*, 231 (1986), 47–50.
[17] Passmann, *'Full of Improbable Lies'*, 195; Dirk F. Passmann, 'An Allusion to Mandeville in *Gulliver's Travels*: The "Air of Truth" Polluted', *N&Q*, 230 (1985), 205–7.
[18] Passmann, *'Full of Improbable Lies'*, 197–211.

threatened by the Yahoos and they even discharge their excrements on his head, an incident which Swift is almost certain to have 'drawn' from similar scenes in the works of William Dampier and Lionel Wafer.

The geographical data provided in the *Travels* are often contradictory if not highly misleading. In order to increase his reliability, Gulliver invokes his friendship with the cartographer Herman Moll, and he forestalls criticism of the geographical detail by blaming any faults on his 'editor' Richard Sympson, who had supposedly purged from his original account 'innumerable Passages relating to the Winds and Tides, as well as to the Variations and Bearings' in order to 'fit the Work as much as possible to the general Capacity of Readers' (*GT*, 16). However, Swift was highly critical of the geography and cartography of his time, evidenced in these lines in 'On Poetry: A Rapsody':

> So Geographers in *Afric*-Maps
> With Savage-Picture fill their Gaps;
> And o'er unhabitable Downs
> Place Elephants for want of Towns.   (*Poems*, II, 645–6)

Swift apparently imbibed this scepticism from Temple, who in his *Essay upon the Ancient and Modern Learning* had voiced serious criticism as to the state of geographical knowledge:

> How little has been performed, of what has been so often and so confidently promised, of a *North-West* Passage to the *East* of *Tartary*, and *North* of *China*? How little do we know of the Lands on that side of the *Magellan Straits*, that lie towards the *South Pole*, which may be vast Islands or Continents, for [aught] any can yet aver, though that Passage was so long since found out? Whether *Japan* be Island or Continent, with some Parts of *Tartary*, on the *North* side, is not certainly agreed. The Lands of *Yedso* upon the *North-East* Continent, have been no more than Coasted, and whether they may not join to the *Northern* Continent of *America* is by some doubted.[19]

It seems to be more than coincidence that Swift locates all his imaginary countries in these regions.

The only country Gulliver visits that could be found on a map was Japan.[20] The description was influenced by the letters of Will Adams, who resided in Japan during the days of the Shogun Jeyasu and whose works were printed in *Purchas his Pilgrimes*. Certainly, the most memorable part is that dealing with the ceremony of Jefumi (trampling on the crucifix), a test required by

---

[19] William Temple, *Miscellanea. In Two Parts. The Fifth Edition* (1697), Pt. II, 48.
[20] Takau Shimada, 'Xamoschi Where Gulliver Landed', *N&Q*, 228 (1983), 33; Maurice O. Johnson, Muneharu Kitagaki, and Philip E. Williams, *'Gulliver's Travels' and Japan: A New Reading* (Kyoto: Amherst House, Doshisha University, 1977); Passmann, *'Full of Improbable Lies'*, 448–51.

the Japanese from all visitors who wanted to enter the country, and with which the Dutch had purportedly no problem complying. The source Swift most probably relied on here was the spurious travel account of 'George Psalmanazar', *An Historical and Geographical Description of Formosa* (1704), an author Swift invoked in *A Modest Proposal* several years later. Another allusion to the infamous Dutch doings in the Far East is the name of the ship *Amboyna*, on which Gulliver leaves Japan. The name alludes to the massacre committed by the Dutch on that spice island when they killed ten English residents, which had been treated at length in Purchas and was repeated even in the works of William Funnell and Herman Moll in the early eighteenth century.

Finally, there are several particular incidents and customs in *Gulliver's Travels* that contemporary readers could also find in travel books. To name but a few, we learn that the peculiar habit of the Lilliputians to bury their dead upright and upside down (I, vi, 83) is similar to the burial rites of the 'Vartias' in India as described by Jean de Thevenot.[21] Whatever Swift may have had in mind when he chose the horse as a vehicle for the theriophilic paradox in the fourth voyage, the noble Houyhnhnms were not the only horses with the capacity of speech. In the account of Hernando Cortez's conquest of Mexico contained in *Purchas his Pilgrimes*, the reader learns that the Indians thought horse and rider to be 'but one creature . . . When they heard the Horses ney, they had thought the Horses could speake, and demanded what they said: . . . the simple Indians presented Roses and Hens to the beasts, desiring them to eate, and to pardon them'.[22] And Gulliver was apparently not the only human to be carried away by a giant eagle. The same incident had happened in Joseph de Acosta's account of Mexico to a man who had been taken up in the talons of a huge bird. Only recently the striking similarities between the mutiny aboard the *Adventure* at the beginning of Gulliver's fourth voyage and the authentic mutiny aboard a ship of the same name, commanded by a captain named 'Gullock' have been revealed. The mutineers were tried at the Old Bailey in 1700 and a popular broadsheet published in the same year described the whole incident.[23]

Another detail drawn from a travel book comes when Gulliver recounts his box being dropped by the giant eagle in Part II, stating that his 'Fall was stopped by a terrible Squash, that sounded louder to mine Ears than the

[21] Dirk F. Passmann, 'Jean de Thevenot and Burials in Lilliput', *N&Q*, 231 (1986), 50–1.
[22] Purchas, *Purchas His Pilgrimes*, XV, 506–7; Dirk F. Passmann, 'Purchas and Swift: Where Horses Talk and Eagles Carry Men', *N&Q*, 229 (1984), 390–1.
[23] Alain Bony, 'Mutiny on the Adventure: A Possible Source of *Gulliver's Travels*', *SStud*, 19 (2004), 72–85.

Cataract of *Niagara* (II, viii, 205). Swift apparently recalled this detail from his reading of Louis Hennepin's *A New Discovery of a Vast Country in America* (1698), of which he made notes on a leaf originally designed as a letter to his mother, dated 5 August 1699: 'The prodigious fall of Niagara in the lake Erie, R. of St. Laurence'.[24] Hennepin's book contained a plate depicting the Falls that shows a group of spectators, of which one holds his ears because of the noise. Even Gulliver's account of the rope-dancing contests at the court of Lilliput is reminiscent of similar descriptions in travel books of the time, notably that of the 'sports and pastimes' of the Laplanders, described by Jocodus Crull (I, iii, 56 n 1, 477–81).

The best-known example of Swift's use of voyages and travels to authenticate Gulliver's account is the famous description of the storm at the beginning of the second voyage (II, i, 119–21), which was copied verbatim from Samuel Sturmy's *Mariner's Magazine* (1669). The literary joke was, however, not discovered until the nineteenth century. Whether all these parallels and similarities were actually sources in the sense that Swift's imagination fed on them is not really important. What matters is the fact that the reader met with authentic elements he was accustomed to when he expected to read a travel book.

Playing Hide and Seek

Another question, however, is whether the contemporary reader of travel books was able to assess the authenticity of a travel account. If even John Locke in his *Essay Concerning Human Understanding* (1689) accepted travellers' reports on the existence of mermaids, less sceptical minds would surely have been even more credulous. Addison and Steele pointed out the weak spot in *Tatler* 254: 'There are no books, which I more delight in than in travels, especially those that describe remote countries, and give the writer an opportunity of showing his parts without incurring any danger of being examined or contradicted'.[25] In other words, there was no way the contemporary reader could verify the information given in the travel books. And surely there were many authors who dished out purportedly authentic adventures that had never occurred. Some travellers 'augmented' their reports by blatant plagiarisms from earlier travel books, such as *The World Surveyed: Or, The Famous Voyages and Travailes of Vincent Le*

---

[24] Irvin Ehrenpreis and James L. Clifford, 'Swiftiana in Rylands English MS. 659 and Related Documents', *Bulletin of the John Rylands Library*, 37 (1954–5), 368–92; Frederick N. Smith and Karen K. Dudra, 'Gulliver and Niagara', *The Scriblerian*, 13 (1981), 116–18.

[25] *The Tatler*, ed. George A. Aitken, 4 vols. (London: Duckworth, 1899), IV, 287–8.

Blanc (1660) – also in Swift's library – or Louis Hennepin's voyages, which Swift had read in 1698/99. The boisterous Recollect friar had freely borrowed from earlier writers and the inaccuracy of his report had been noted in the *Philosophical Transactions of the Royal Society.*

But there was a considerable number of purported travel narratives, the so-called 'travel lies', that went much further than just a loose handling of the truth. Travel liars wrote with a clearly deceptive purpose and owed their success to the growing popularity of the genre. Ever since the notorious 'John Mandeville', whose travels had been concocted from the writings of Marco Polo, William of Rubrucq, and John Plano Carpini, the travel-liars tried to fool readers with seemingly authentic accounts. And they succeeded extremely well with their fabrications: Mandeville's book was trusted even in the late seventeenth century.

Similarly successful was Maximilian Misson's *New Voyage to the East Indies* (1708), allegedly written by the purely fictitious traveller 'Francois Leguat', which was taken for granted even by its nineteenth-century editor Pasfield Oliver, who published the narrative in the prestigious *Publications of the Hakluyt Society.* As Percy Adams puts it: 'Because the eighteenth century was so avid in its search for data about man and his physical surroundings, it was inclined to be gullible and fall victim to facts that were not facts and travel books that were partly, even completely, false'.[26] Even imaginary voyages like Henry Neville's *Isle of Pines* (1668), Denis Vairasse's *Histoire des Sévarambes* (1677–9), and Simon Tyssot de Patot's *Voyages of Jacques Massé* (1710) were regarded as authentic for some time.[27] A rather peculiar case in point was 'George Psalmanazar's' *Formosa*, the book Swift had relied on in the passage dealing with the trampling on the crucifix. Psalmanazar's ludicrous hoax managed to deceive the London public for some time. He soon becomes a public celebrity because of his fanciful exotic appearance, his made-up 'Formosan' pronunciation and his appetite for raw meat. By 1711, however, the authenticity of his report had been called into question and its author became an object of ridicule.[28]

---

[26] Percy G. Adams, *Travelers and Travel Liars, 1660–1800* (Berkeley: University of California Press, 1962), viii.

[27] Passmann, *'Full of Improbable Lies'*, 99–101; Kate Loveman, *Reading Fictions, 1660–1740: Deception in English Literary and Political Culture* (Aldershot: Ashgate, 2008), 69–81.

[28] Passmann, *'Full of Improbable Lies'*, 267–9; Dirk F. Passmann, '"Many Diverting Books of History and Travels" and *A Modest Proposal*', *Eighteenth-Century Ireland*, 2 (1987), 167–76 (173); Daniel Eilon, 'Gulliver's Fellow-Traveller Psalmanaazaar', *BJECS*, 8 (1985), 173–8.

Of singular significance for the context of *Gulliver's Travels* was the travel
lie of a certain William Symson entitled *A New Voyage to the East Indies*, first
published by Edmund Curll in 1715. We remember that a 'Richard
Sympson' acted as the fictitious 'publisher' of *Gulliver's Travels* and introduced Gulliver as an authentic sailor and reliable narrator (*Correspondence*,
III, 9–14). There was in fact a travel account by a member of John Strong's
South Sea expedition of 1689–91 written by a Richard Simson, and his report
has recently been considered in the context of the *Travels*. The report,
however, was never published and is still in the Sloane Collection of
Manuscripts.[29] Naming Sympson as a publisher was a particular feat for
another reason, since he was soon, in Curll's *Key* to *Gulliver's Travels* (1726),
which appeared shortly after the publication, identified as a 'near Relation' of
'Capt. William Sympson'. Curll, one of the most enterprising publishers of
the day, capitalised on this lucky coincidence. He could advertise
a production of his press as closely related to the mammoth success of
Gulliver's Travels. In fact, Swift may have anticipated this development,
because he was familiar with Simson's book and it provided the source for
the peculiar handwriting of the Lilliputians (I, vi, 83 nn 5–6).

The problem for the contemporary reader was that he had no means to
verify the information of the travellers. Whereas today we consider the travel
report a clearly non-fictional or rather a hetero-referential text that relates to
a verifiable reality as opposed to a fictional, that is, decidedly auto-referential
text creating its own universe, this distinction was blurred for the reader of
Swift's time. Unless he set sail for the unknown himself, he had no chance to
put the authenticity of the travel authors to the test. Important here is what
Hans Robert Jauß called the 'generic expectation' of the reader.[30] When he
read a travel book he expected to find authentic, realistic accounts of actual
events and places. Moreover, readers were tolerant towards travel fabrications because they *wanted* the text to be factual, as much as today's TV
audiences toy with the thought of even the wildest Science Fiction proving
true in some part of the universe. Pierre Bayle was right when he pointed out
that the reader has more pleasure in reading a text that informs him about
real people and events.

Swift reverted to this strategy of authentification in the *Travels* in order to
increase the impact of the satiric shock of his attack on the political and
human corruptions of his time. For his major work he could have chosen

---

[29] Clement Hawes, 'Cousins Sympson and Simson: Gulliverian Intertextuality', *SStud*, 19 (2004),
49–71.
[30] Hans Robert Jauß, 'Literaturgeschichte als Provokation der Literaturwissenschaft', in
Rezeptionsästhetik, ed. Rainer Warning (Munich: Wilhelm Fink, 1979), 126–62.

other literary genres over the travel book. He could have moulded it into the shape of a philosophical verse essay, as Pope did in *An Essay on Man* (1733–4). He could have settled Lilliput or Brobdingnag on the moon, as authors of imaginary or extraordinary voyages like Francis Godwin or Cyrano de Bergerac had done with their imaginary civilisations. But then he would have run the risk of his readers being left in 'amused distance' from his story. Instead, he chose the factual travelogue to convey his satiric attack.

Gulliver's Travels is not only a satire on corrupt politics, on a hypocritical anthropology, or degenerate morals of institutions and individuals. It is also a witty game of hide and seek with his reader, a clever sham, a wild goose chase with deceptive impetus. Swift had always liked playing jokes on friends and foes alike, as in his April fool's joke on Sir Andrew Fountaine, his successful hoax on the astrologer John Partrige, or the one he played with *The Last Speech and Dying Words of Ebenezor Elliston* (1722).[31] It may be true that the *Travels* were not designed to deceive readers and that the hoax was over after a few pages. Swift, however, might well have noted with satisfaction that his sham was recognised and appreciated by some of his Scriblerian friends, as demonstrated in John Arbuthnot's letter to Swift of 5 November 1726, which reported that some readers took the *Travels* at face value (*Correspondence*, III, 45).

Whatever we think *Gulliver's Travels* is – a satire, an allegory, a novel – generically the work is a travel book, obeying the structural rules the narration of a journey demanded and containing many of the standard topics the genre provided. Further than that, Swift's major satire was not only a travel lie but also a parody of the travel book inasmuch as he created a satiric inversion of the genre. The purpose of the traveller, as defined by the Royal Society, was to gain useful knowledge, and Swift makes Gulliver declare this noble end in the last chapter of the fourth voyage: 'Whereas, a Traveller's chief Aim should be to make Men wiser and better, and to improve their Minds by the bad, as well as good Example of what they deliver concerning foreign Places' (IV, xii, 436).

---

[31] Irvin Ehrenpreis, 'Swift's April Fool for a Bibliophile', *The Book Collector*, 2 (1953), 205–8; Loveman, *Reading Fictions*, 159–66; Passmann, *'Full of Improbable Lies'*, 342–3.

CHAPTER 8

Philosophical Tale

Paddy Bullard

Why should we read *Gulliver's Travels* as a philosophical tale? Jonathan Swift wrote the book as a satire, and expected his readers to laugh at some very silly jokes. But there is plenty of internal evidence that he wanted them to read like philosophers too, at least from time to time. 'The main concern of philosophy', writes the American philosopher Thomas Nagel, 'is to question and understand very common ideas that all of us use every day without thinking about them [. . .] The aim is to push our understanding of the world and ourselves a bit deeper'.[1] These are Swift's aims in *Gulliver's Travels* as well. The reversals of physical scale that Gulliver experiences in Lilliput and Brobdingnag raise some classic philosophical questions about how we perceive the world. They also trouble our everyday assumptions about what is hugely significant or minutely trivial within it. In Part III the ridiculous mathematicians of Laputa bring Gulliver to doubt that abstract science can ever be the basis for a sound understanding of the universe, as many philosophers of his day argued it should. And in Part IV Gulliver has some deeply held ideas about his species-identity as a rational being put to the test by a race of philosopher-horses. In each fantastic episode the world that Gulliver experiences remains solid and recognisable, and the style in which he describes it plain and matter-of-fact. Gulliver speaks to us, that is, 'rather in a Philosophical than a Rhetorical strain', as the scientist Robert Boyle characterised his own method of writing, 'rather clear and signifi-cant, than curiously adorn'd'.[2] Swift gives us journeys in which our common, everyday ideas are fully operational, but in which many of them cannot be taken for granted.

Swift's contemporaries would have been less surprised than we are to find such philosophical provocations in a book of travel stories.

[1] Thomas Nagel, *What Does it All Mean?* (Oxford: Oxford University Press, 1987), 5.
[2] Robert Boyle, 'Proemial Essay', *Certain Physiological Essays* (1661), 1–36 (11); cf. *GT*, IV, xii, 436: 'I have not been so studious of Ornament as of Truth'.

The association of philosophy with travelling was well established in the early modern period. Michel de Montaigne praised travel as the great improver of the human soul, 'and I do not know, as I have often said, a better School wherein to model Life, than by incessantly exposing to it the diversity of so many other lives, fancies, and usances'.[3] René Descartes provided a famous example of such plural modelling in his *Discourse on Method*, tracing the freedom of his thinking back to his experiences as a young traveller:

> For having learnt from the very School, That one can imagin nothing so strange or incredible, which had not been said by some one of the Philosophers; And having since observ'd in my travails [i.e. travels], That all those whose opinions are contrary to ours, are not therefore barbarous or savage, but that many use as much or more reason then we, [. . .] I found my self even constrain'd to undertake the conduct of my self.[4]

Gulliver echoes Descartes's observation about the extravagance of philosophers (III, vi, 275), and he discovers the use of reason in some far-flung places.[5] But it is in the overall shape of his *Travels*, in their structure as four interrelated thought experiments, that the philosophical character of the writing is most apparent. Swift's friend and colleague George Berkeley described returning to 'the simple Dictates of Nature' after losing himself in philosophical problems. It was 'like coming home from a long Voyage: a Man reflects with Pleasure on the many Difficulties and Perplexities he has passed thorow'.[6] Gulliver makes a journey into the realm of ideas as well, and it is a sign of the restlessness of Swift's thinking that the satirist grants his hero no such peace of mind when finally he does return home.

Montaigne, Descartes, and Berkeley help us to identify a philosophical component in *Gulliver's Travels*, but they offer no straightforward encouragement to philosophical reading. Our first attempts to find contemporary contexts for this component have led us to passages that reject earlier philosophical writing. They remind us that hostility to philosophers is not incompatible with philosophical engagement. *Gulliver's Travels* is full of anti-philosophical reflections. In Part II Gulliver tries to give lessons in scholastic philosophy to the sensible giants of Brobdingnag, but 'as to Ideas, Entities, Abstractions and Transcendentals, I could never drive the

---

[3] Michel de Montaigne, *Essays*, trans. Charles Cotton, 3 vols. (1685), III, 320 ('Of Vanitie', III, 9).

[4] René Descartes, *A Discourse of a Method for the Well-Guiding of Reason* (1649), 26–7.

[5] Swift may have been echoing Descartes, or he may have been referring to Cicero's *De divinitatione*, in *De senectute, De amicitial, De divination*, ed. W. A. Falconer (Cambridge, MA: Harvard University Press, 2015), 505 [2.58.119]: 'Somehow or other no statement is too absurd for some philosophers to make'.

[6] George Berkeley, *Three Dialogues between Hylas and Philonous* (1713), sig. A4ᵛ.

least Conception into their Heads' (II, vii, 195). Swift had his fill of these topics while studying at Trinity College, Dublin: 'to enter upon causes of Philosophy', he complained at the time, 'is what I protest I will rather dy in a ditch than go about'.[7] When Gulliver explains contemporary Natural Philosophy to the Houyhnhnms, his master, a horse not given to humour, cannot help but laugh 'that a Creature pretending to *Reason*, should value itself upon the Knowledge of other Peoples Conjectures' (IV, viii, 402). When Gulliver visits Glubbdubdrib, an island of sorcerers, the governor conjures the ghosts of Descartes and Pierre Gassendi to explain their ideas to the ghost of Aristotle, who reports that their systems are already 'exploded' (III, viii, 295–6). Metaphysics were a particular bugbear. When Swift's friend Lord Bolingbroke wrote in 1734 with news of his own metaphysical projects, he expected trouble: 'I know how little regard you pay to Writings of this kind', Bolingbroke apologised, 'but I imagine that if you can like any such, it must be those that strip Metaphysics of all their bombast [. . .] and never bewilder themselves whilst they pretend to guide the reason of others'.[8] Swift replied with stiff compliments. One of his earliest biographers reported that he 'held logic and metaphysics in the utmost contempt'.[9] Any reading of *Gulliver's Travels* as a philosophical tale must adjust to this negative frame of reference.

One way of accommodating a philosophical reading of *Gulliver's Travels* to its author's anti-philosophical attitudes is to focus readings on the themes of writers with whom we know Swift aligned himself intellectually. Swift recognised George Berkeley as 'a very ingenious man, & great Philosoph' (*Journal to Stella*, 528). They were both Tory in their political outlook, both senior officeholders in the Church of Ireland, and both took critical positions on mainstream philosophical opinion within that church.[10] Berkeley's books were in Swift's library, although there is no evidence of how Swift read them, if he read them at all.[11] But their presence there shows some of the affordances that contemporary philosophical debate allowed Swift, in terms of the problems that were most pressing in 1726. Berkeley's writings on the relationship between sight and touch indicate the issues at stake when Swift swapped Gulliver between two

[7] Swift to Thomas Swift, 3 May 1692, *Correspondence*, I, 111.

[8] Pope and Bolingbroke to Swift, 15 September 1734, *Correspondence*, III, 759.

[9] John Boyle, Earl of Orrery, *Remarks on the Life and Writings of Dr Jonathan Swift* (1752), 7.

[10] On their shared rejection of Irish representational theories of ideas see David Berman, *Berkeley and Irish Philosophy* (London: Continuum, 2005), 39, 97–102, 125–6.

[11] Dirk F. Passmann and Heinz J. Vienken, *The Library and Reading of Jonathan Swift: A Bio-Bibliographical Handbook. Part 1: Swift's Library*, 4 vols. (Frankfurt am Main: Peter Lang, 2003), I, 180–8.

radically distorted and imaginary subject positions, those of very large and very diminutive persons.

These indications also highlight the perspectivism of *Gulliver's Travels*. Perspectivism, the idea that objectivity is impossible because knowledge is circumscribed by subject position, is implicit in the structure of Swift's satire.[12] The differences between the four Parts of *Gulliver's Travels* suggest that there is no stable relationship between truth 'in itself' and what individuals believe about the world, but only comparisons in quality or scope between different perspectives. The first section of this chapter will look further into these questions. A second writer of philosophy with whom Swift had a close (though often antagonistic) friendship was the poet Alexander Pope. Pope's correspondence with Swift during the 1720s and the later systematic statement of Pope's optimistic and harmonising philosophy in *An Essay on Man* (1733–4) set up contrasts with *Gulliver's Travels* that bring the philosophical character of Swift's satire into relief. They allow us to see the outlines of its broadly anti-Stoic positions: its scepticism about the beneficence of God and nature; its pessimism about the narrow limits of human wisdom and reason; its horror at the prospect of inciting human pride. The second section of this chapter focuses on these darker tendencies.

Gulliver, Perception and Perspectivism

One peculiarity of *Gulliver's Travels* is the heightened and intimate character of the physical perceptions reported by its narrator, especially in the first two Parts. In Brobdingnag Gulliver is lacerated by ears of corn, deafened by a cat's purr, nipped and be-slimed in a marrow bone, and knocked out by perfumes (I, i, 123; i, 129, iii, 152, v, 167). In Lilliput it is the visible world that makes deepest impressions. On first waking in Lilliputian bondage Gulliver is half-blinded by the sun while trying to glimpse his six-inch captors. Later, in a puzzlingly intense episode, Gulliver displays his sword for the king. Three thousand bowmen are poised to discharge their arrows, 'but I did not observe it, for mine Eyes were wholly fixed upon his Majesty'. As Gulliver draws his blade the sun shines 'and the Reflexion dazzled their Eyes' (I, ii, 53). These exchanges of bedazzlement and display, of curiosity and surprise, make odd and asymmetrical tableaux within the narrative. But their awkwardness conveys a basic naturalism of

---

[12] Perspectivism is associated especially with Nietzsche: see Alexander Nehemas, *Nietzsche: Life as Literature* (Cambridge, MA: Harvard University Press, 1985), 42–73.

style and perceptive psychology, even within the fiction's fantastic setting. Soon Gulliver realises that his eyes are his great vulnerability. He saves them from arrows while raiding the Blefuscudian fleet by the lucky expedient of spectacles – tools for sharpening perception repurposed as eye-armour (I, v, 74). On falling from royal favour Gulliver learns that he is to be blinded: he preserves 'mine Eyes, and consequently my Liberty', only by flight (I, vii, 100, 105). It may also be significant, much later, that 'Sight' is the final word of *Gulliver's Travels* (IV, xii, 444; cf. 4). But what relevance does this have to the book's arguments about perception?

Swift took a position on contemporary debates about perception, and their significance becomes evident when we look more closely at the character of his descriptive naturalism. An important aspect of Gulliver's reports on his experiences is that in neither Lilliput nor Brobdingnag does the possibility of misapprehension or visual illusion arise. In Houyhnhnm-land, by contrast, where bodily scale is undistorted, he fears his 'Brain was disturbed by Sufferings and Misfortunes [. . .] I rubbed mine Eyes often, but the same Objects still occurred' (IV, ii, 341; cf. 13; IV, xi, 431). Why is Gulliver sure of his perceptions among the visual surprises of Parts I and II, but not in physically straightforward Part IV? After all, seventeenth-century philosophers warned their readers continually that the senses, and particularly sight, cannot tell us the truth about the world. Their function is to help us preserve our bodies, not to let us know what things are in themselves: 'our eyes generally deceive us in everything they represent to us', warned Nicolas Malebranche; 'we are very uncertain about the true size of the bodies we see and all we can know of it by sight is the relation between their size and our own'.[13] Gulliver pays lip service to this sort of argument: 'undoubtedly Philosophers are in the Right, when they tell us, that nothing is great or little otherwise than by Comparison', he pronounces. 'It might have pleased Fortune to let the *Lilliputians* find some Nation, where the People were as diminutive with respect to them, as they were to me' (II, i, 124). But the unreflective naturalism of Gulliver's descriptions, which seldom involve comparative calculation of scale, does not align with Malebranche's position. Although Gulliver may be a splendid liar, he gives us no reason to doubt his senses, or to think that the reports he gives of everyday experiences in Lilliput and Brobdingnag are prone to error. The naturalism of *Gulliver's Travels* directs us towards a position similar to the one George Berkeley took against Malebranche: that if no visual scale of size or diminution is right intrinsically,

---

[13] Nicolas Malebranche, *The Search after Truth*, trans. Thomas M. Lennon and Paul J. Olscamp (Cambridge: Cambridge University Press, 1997), 32, 25, 30.

it is illogical to describe any given measure as illusive. Even when we understand Gulliver's reports as fictions, they are neither non-veridical nor veridical: 'by *Sensible Things* I mean those only which are perceived by Sense', Berkeley writes; 'in truth the Senses perceive nothing which they do not perceive immediately: for they make no Inferences'.[14] Gulliver tries to reason like Malebranche, but it is to Berkeley's universe of sensible things that he belongs.

Berkeley argues that sight gives us no immediate information about the magnitude of objects, for example, or their distance from us. Our senses make no direct inferences, although meaning is created, when one sense operates along with another, by the inferences we make between them.[15] The ideas we derive from sight and touch are 'twisted, blended, and incorporated together' especially closely, Berkeley emphasises, having 'a far more strict and near Connexion, than *Ideas* have with Words'.[16] The connection between seeing and touching in our efforts to make sense of '*sensible Things*' was also important to Swift in *Gulliver's Travels*. This becomes clear in Part IV of the satire.

The earliest indication of intelligence in the first two Houyhnhnms Gulliver meets is that their earnest survey of his person involves both looking and touching: 'The grey Steed rubbed my Hat all round with his Right Fore-hoof, and discomposed it so much, that I was forced to adjust it better'; the other, a brown bay, 'stroked my Right Hand, seeming to admire the Softness, and Colour; but he squeezed it so hard between his Hoof and his Pastern, that I was forced to roar; after which he touched me with all possible Tenderness' (IV, i, 337). In Brobdingnag a giant examined Gulliver's clothes, lifting the lappet of his jacket with a straw; now a Houyhnhnm 'felt the lappet of my coat', surprised to find it hang loose (II, i, 126; IV, i, 337). Swift is drawing attention to these gestures. The idea that a horse's hoof could be prehensile gives the scene a satirical spin, but it also appeals to our ideas about what intelligent persons look like when working out problems. Here and elsewhere the Houyhnhnms make gestures 'not unlike those of a Philosopher, when he would attempt to solve some new and difficult Phænomenon' (IV, i, 337; cf. II, iv, 157 and III, i, 223). There is a strong current of psychological naturalism flowing beneath the satire and absurdity of Gulliver's encounter with the dapple-grey and brown-bay Houyhnhnms, and it makes its own argument. It shows Swift's

[14] Berkeley, *Three Dialogues*, 7.
[15] George Berkeley, *An Essay towards a New Theory of Vision* (1709), 172–3 [CXLVII].
[16] Berkeley, *New Theory of Vision*, 56 [LI].

position on the modes of intelligent perception – that they are plural – and his understanding that they are distinct from rational problem-solving. Swift's writing is not philosophical as such, but we can see how his friend Berkeley might have recognised it as congenial to his philosophical thinking, and especially to his preference for explanations of human cognition that focus on habitual, immediate, and associative processes, rather than cogitative or inferential ones.

The flatness of Swift's style in *Gulliver's Travels* has been remarked upon often.[17] The prose is polished to a dull burnish, as though to deflect our conjectures about what authorial intention or affect might lurk beneath its surface. And the book has a correspondingly flat ontology. Gulliver makes his reports on midget armadas and giant moralists, on flying islands, ghosts, and immortal Struldbrugs, with the same undistinguishing attentiveness. The kindling of Gulliver's level curiosity into a sort of devotion among the philosopher-horses is the norm-defining exception. At the other extreme of recognisability, there are several incidents in *Gulliver's Travels* in which differences in scale make very familiar objects unidentifiable. In Part IV, the Sorrel Nag is unable to see the small island that Gulliver spots five leagues off the Houyhnhnm-land coast: 'For, as he had no Conception of any Country beside his own, so he could not be as expert in distinguishing remote Objects at Sea, as we who so much converse in that Element' (IV, x, 423). In Part I two Lilliputian functionaries, charged with making an inventory, have mixed success at identifying the everyday contents of Gulliver's pockets (I, ii, 50–5). When Gulliver shows the ship's captain who rescues him from Brobdingnag some souvenirs, including a comb made of beard shavings set in a thumbnail, we understand the complacency with which the captain accepts the report of their origin to be absurd (II, viii, 210). The more general point that Swift makes in each of these cases – that perception is itself governed by local experience and habit – is implicit throughout *Gulliver's Travels*.

The implication has parallels with a famous remark of the philosopher J. L. Austin, who disparaged both the attempts of other thinkers to define what they mean by the classification 'material things', and the objects they gave as examples: chairs, tables, books, pens, cigarettes, and so on. 'But does the ordinary man believe that what he perceived is always something like furniture', Austin wondered, 'or like these other "familiar

[17] For example Adam Smith, *Lectures on Rhetoric and Belles Lettres*, ed. J. C. Bryce (Oxford: Oxford University Press, 1983), 38–9; Barbara Everett, 'The Sense of Nothing', in *The Spirit of Wit: Reconsiderations of Rochester*, ed. Jeremy Treglown (Oxford: Blackwell, 1982), 1–14 (7).

objects" – moderately-sized specimens of dry goods?"[18] Swift, who was quick to find humour in bundles of moderately sized dry goods, would have enjoyed this, and also Austin's refusal to enter into ontological classifications of the things (including 'material things') that ordinary people ordinarily perceive. Berkeley took a similar line: 'The Word *Matter* shou'd never be missed in common Talk. And, in Philosophical Discourses, it seems the best way to leave it quite out'.[19] Swift, like Berkeley and Austin, is carrying out an exercise in philosophical hygiene. The fictitious surprises that Gulliver reports to us are not in themselves lies or misrepresentations. Swift insists we read them as direct accounts of the visible and tangible qualities of sensible things, without groping irritably after the truth of their being.

Gulliver, Reason and Moral Perception

Islands five leagues distant are not the only things that the Houyhnhnms have difficulty seeing. As Gulliver learns their language and begins to tell them about his home, it becomes clear that they have neither the verbal materials nor the cognitive scaffolding with which to build an understanding of everyday human life. Clothes, lawyers, 'Stargazing', and 'Free-Thinking' are all incomprehensible (IV, iii, 351; vi, 373; vi, 375). It is not only for human practices that Houyhnhnms have blind spots. Gulliver finds that his moral vocabulary is untranslatable, particularly the terms '*Lying*' (which they fumble for as '*the Thing which was not*'), '*Opinion*', and, in the final paragraphs of his travels, 'Pride': regarding the last, 'the wise and virtuous *Houyhnhnms* [...] have no Name for this Vice in their Language' (IV, iv, 354; viii, 402, xii, 444). The quick and natural rationality of the philosopher-horses is no help to them in their efforts to understand Gulliver's account of his moral life. Gulliver's Master suspects that usage might accustom him in time 'to such abominable Words'. Indeed,

> although he hated the *Yahoos* of this Country, yet he no more blamed them for their odious Qualities, then he did a *Gnnayh* (a Bird of Prey) for its Cruelty, or a sharp Stone for cutting his Hoof. But, when a Creature pretending to Reason, could be capable of such Enormities, he dreaded lest the Corruption of that Faculty might be worse than Brutality itself. He seemed therefore confident, that instead of Reason, we were only possessed of some Quality fitted to increase our natural Vices; as the Reflection from

---

[18] J. L. Austin, *Sense and Sensibilia* (Oxford: Clarendon Press, 1962), 7–8.
[19] Berkeley, *New Theory of Vision*, 163.

a troubled Stream returns to the image of an ill-shapen Body, not only *larger*, but more *distorted*. (IV, v, 367)

Gulliver internalises this idea, turning away 'in Horror and detestation of my self' when later he glimpses his reflection in a fountain (IV, x, 420; cf. xii, 443). Once again, the visual register of the reflection metaphor is vivid, even though the object of the Master-Houyhnhnm's moral insight in this case is 'some Quality' discerned in Gulliver but not known. What he can work out about this quality is that it has to do with self-relation: the ill-shapen body in the troubled stream is that of the European Yahoo subject, looking at itself. Otherwise, Houyhnhnms lack the conceptual resources to understand human reason. The poverty of the Houyhnhnms' intellectual system is one with the apparent perfection of their reasoning.

While he was writing *Gulliver's Travels* Swift adopted the Master-Houyhnhnm's pose of indifference to the cruelty of the *Gnnayh* in a famous sequence of letters to Alexander Pope. Swift begins with a paradox. Reflecting on the source of his energy as a writer, Swift decides that his animating indignation is triggered by the human being in abstract, or by any general categorisation of human being (nation, profession, community), but not by individuals: 'Upon this great foundation of Misanthropy (though not in Timons manner) the whole building of my Travells is erected'.[20] In his reply Pope makes an awkward joke about Swift's determination to 'be employ'd as an Avenging Angel of wrath'.[21] Swift replies with a demurral, and an allusion:

> I tell you after all that I do not hate Mankind, it is vous autr[e]s who hate them because you would have them reasonable Animals, and are Angry for being disappointed. I have always rejected that Definition and made another of my own. I am no more angry with — th[a]n I was with the Kite that last week flew away with one of my Chickins and yet I was pleas'd when one of my Servants shot him two days after[.] This I say, because you are so hardy to tell me of your Intentions to write Maxims in Opposition to Rochfoucault who is my Favorite because I found my whole character in him.[22]

Swift shares with the Master-Houyhnhnm his indifference to the bird of prey. But the satirist, writing *in propria persona*, does not avow any deeper resentment towards creatures who 'pretend' to reason (as Gulliver and his fellow non-Yahoo hominids do), and this distinguishes the author's

[20] Swift to Pope, 29 September 1725, *Correspondence*, II, 607.
[21] Pope to Swift, 15 October 1725, *Correspondence*, II, 612.
[22] Swift to Pope, 26 November 1725, *Correspondence*, II, 623.

position from that of his fictional creation. Swift attributes a truly misanthropic disappointment to Pope and his philosophical mentor Lord Bolingbroke ('vous autr[e]s') but denies it for himself. Swift's allusion here to the French moralist the Duc de La Rochefoucauld suggests that he and Pope both saw their quarrel in a particular philosophical context, and that Swift recognised that context as the foundation of his satire.

What do we know about this philosophical context? For Pope's part, the project of writing 'Maxims in Opposition to Rochfoucault' is on the side of moral optimism, and opposed to Swift's moral anger. 'As L'Esprit, Rochefoucauld, and that sort of people prove that all virtues are disguised vices', Pope explained later to Joseph Spence, 'I would engage to prove all vices to be disguised virtues'.[23] The allusion is to one of La Rochefoucauld's best-known maxims, which claims that 'what we take for virtues are really only vices which resemble them, and which self-love has disguised from us'.[24] The plan Pope makes to turn it upside down is fulfilled in 'Epistle II' of his philosophical poem *An Essay on Man*. Self-love in La Rochefoucauld is an obscure, restless, corrupting principle of the unconscious mind. In the *Essay* Pope gives it a positive role, as energy source for our moral passions ('Active its task, it prompts, impels, inspires'), and as counterbalance to slow, comparing reason.[25] The virtues are like grafts upon the 'savage stocks' of those passions: 'What crops of wit and honesty appear', Pope exclaims (perhaps with Swift in mind), 'From spleen, from obstinacy, hate, or fear!'[26]

Pope is positioning himself within a tradition of British moral thought that might be described as Christianised Stoicism. It saw human beings as benign in their deepest moral impulses, and it sought to explain their place in what is ultimately a rational universe.[27] Despite their closeness as friends and writers, as Tories and Scriblerians, Pope recognises Swift's allegiance to an opposing philosophical tradition, that of the seventeenth-century

---

[23] Joseph Spence, *Observations, Anecdotes, and Characters of Books and Men*, ed. James M. Osborn, 2 vols. (Oxford: Clarendon Press, 1966), I, 210 (no. 517).

[24] François de La Rochefoucauld, *Collected Maxims and Other Reflections*, trans. E. H. and A. M. Blackmore and Francine Giguère (Oxford: Oxford University Press, 2007), 173 (IV:172); from the fifth edition of 1678 it became the epigram for the collection.

[25] Alexander Pope, *An Essay on Man*, ed. Tom Jones (Princeton: Princeton University Press, 2016), 35 [II, 68].

[26] Pope, *Essay on Man*, 42 [II.185–6]; the suggestion that Pope has Swift in mind here is from Dustin Griffin, *Swift and Pope: Satirists in Dialogue* (Cambridge: Cambridge University Press, 2010), 166.

[27] See John Spurr, '"Latitudinarianism" and the Restoration Church', *Historical Journal*, 31 (1988), 61–82; Christopher Brooke, *Philosophic Pride: Stoicism and Political Thought from Lipsius to Rousseau* (Princeton: Princeton University Press, 2012), 101–26.

French *moralistes*. This tradition included thinkers like La Rochefoucauld, Montaigne, Jacques Esprit, and Blaise Pascal, who (following St Augustine) saw the human will as radically depraved by the Fall, and continually complicated by *amour-propre*, the self-love that 'gives man this inclination to disguise himself', as Esprit put it, 'because if he appeared as he really is, a self-idolator without concern or affection for any of his fellow creatures [. . .] he would cause them to rise up against him'.[28] The party lines between Stoic optimism and Augustinian pessimism are less distinct than Pope's scheme implies, but they help to organise the field of ideas in which he and Swift were working.

We need Pope to explain that context because Swift does not do so. A failure to make direct reference to the French seventeenth-century thinkers whom Pope, his closest literary friend and antagonist, understood to be Swift's immediate intellectual peers, is not inconsistent with the play on self-disguise, pride, and hypocrisy evident throughout *Gulliver's Travels*. However, Swift's approach to these topics does not quite match that of his favourite La Rochefoucauld. The *Maximes* focus on the internal experience of *amour-propre*, and on the intricacy of the operations by which pride blinds the subject to its own faults: 'nature', La Rochefoucauld observes, 'which has so wisely arranged the organs of our body for happiness, has also given us pride to spare us the pain of knowing our deficiencies'.[29] Swift is preoccupied more with the external spectacle that this process of delusive self-reflection presents to a virtuous and ideally rational observer. Such is the distorted image refracted by 'some Quality' unknown, like 'the Reflection from a troubled Stream' (IV, v, 367); such is the 'Lump of Deformity, and Diseases both in Body and Mind, smitten with *Pride*', that breaks the measures of Gulliver's patience in Part IV's climactic paragraphs (IV, xii, 442). Although Gulliver is as full of distorting *amour-propre* as the rest of us, he has a crucial role in that tableau of external observation, because the Houyhnhnms cannot even see the moral character of semi-rational Yahoos without his explications. 'Certain good qualities are like physical senses', writes La Rochefoucault: 'people who lack them altogether can neither perceive nor understand them'.[30] Houyhnhnm-land is Swift's conjecture that the reverse would also be true for bad qualities, if beings who lacked them could be imagined.

[28] Jacques Esprit, *De la fausseté des virtus humaines*, 2 vols. (1709), II, 233, cited by Michael Moriarty, *Fallen Natures, Fallen Selves: Early Modern French Thought II* (Oxford: Oxford University Press, 2004), 241.
[29] La Rochefoucauld, *Collected Maxims*, 12–13 [V:36]; cf. 132–3 [V:494].
[30] La Rochefoucauld, *Collected Maxims*, 94–5 [V:337].

At the beginning of this chapter, we saw how the motif of travel was used by early modern philosophers as a figure for their different journeys through the realm of ideas. Gulliver's own stolid rationale for his voyage-writing refuses philosophical subtlety: 'a Traveller's chief Aim should be to make Men wiser and better', he pronounces, 'and to improve their Minds by the bad, as well as good Example of what they deliver concerning foreign Places' (IV, xii, 436). But the inconsistency of this sentiment with Gulliver's statements on his irregular and compulsive motivations for travel, as someone 'condemned by Nature and Fortune to an active and restless Life', is evident enough (II, i, 117; cf. I, viii, 112; III, i, 218). If we take the perspective of the French Augustinians, Gulliver's restlessness looks less like a metaphor for the curiosity proper to a modern philosopher and more like a primary symptom of his fallenness. Suspended between two states, Houyhnhnm *'Perfection of Nature'* and Yahoo baseness, Gulliver's exile from Houyhnhnm-land plunges him into the dilemma that Pascal rehearsed in his *Pensées*: 'Man does not know on which level to put himself. He is obviously fallen from his true place without being able to find it again. He looks for it everywhere restlessly and unsuccessfully in impenetrable darkness'.[31] La Rochefoucauld had a similar sense of human restlessness, although he expressed its consequences more mildly: 'Whatever discoveries have been made in the realm of self-love', he predicted, 'many unknown lands remain there still'.[32] Retired finally to his smallholding near Newark, Gulliver may finally have completed his travels to those unknown lands, but Swift has no reason to grant him a philosopher's peace.

[31] Blaise Pascal, *Pensées*, ed. Anthony Levi, trans. Honor Levi (Oxford: Oxford University Press, 1995), 8 (no. 19).
[32] La Rochefoucauld, *Collected Maxims*, 5 (V:3); cf. 147 (I.i) and 55 (V:191) on restlessness.

PART III

Reading Gulliver's Travels

CHAPTER 9

Advertisements and Authorship

Brean Hammond

This chapter is concerned initially with the material that precedes the chapter summaries and the main narrative of *Gulliver's Travels*. Later sections discuss the words that readers find on their page and how they come to be there.[1] Put succinctly, the purpose of the prefatory material to the main narrative of *Gulliver's Travels* is to make the reader uncertain whether or not they are reading a true story. The purpose of *that* is to tease and vex the reader, with the broader satirical intention of calling into question the very concept of truth. At this cultural juncture – England in 1726 – Swift is putting a case that English human beings, Yahoo-like physically but superior to them in linguistic capability, are systematically perverting language so as to express intentionally untrue statements. They are worse than Yahoos because they are endowed with reason but choose to pervert it. Human beings, whatever they once were, are now a corrupt species, one of the worst aspects of that corruption being their chronic mendacity.

The problem with lying, as Gulliver's Houyhnhnm 'Master' seems to apprehend, was (and is) that if it becomes a stable practice in a community, it threatens to destroy the integrity of the linguistic system. Long-term commitments between people(s) cannot be undertaken if lying for manipulative purposes becomes the norm. If there is indeed 'a Society of Men among us, bred up from their Youth in the Art of proving by Words multiplied for the Purpose, that *White* is *Black,* and *Black* is *White*', as Gulliver tells his Houyhnhnm Master exists in human society, what trust can possibly survive between a people, its legal representatives and its political office-bearers (IV, v, 368–9)? If human beings are a sociable species whose continued existence depends upon the formation of lasting bonds, then the systematic abuse of sincere language must sabotage their very

---

[1] This article extends and refines a previously published piece: Brean Hammond and Gregory Currie, 'Lying, Language and Intention: Reflections on Swift', *European Journal of English Studies*, 19 (2015), 220–33.

survival. When it is sometimes said that we are currently in a 'post-truth' era, in which populist politicians knowingly fabricate untruths as a means of securing short-term political gain, this is the critique that is implied.

Mendacity

Populist politicians of our own generation have not newly discovered how potent a political weapon it is to 'say the thing that is not'. They have *re*discovered it. Machiavelli advised Lorenzo de Medici that 'contemporary experience shows that princes who have achieved great things have been those who have given their word lightly [...] and who, in the end, have overcome those abiding by honest principles'.[2] The politicians and political pamphleteers of Swift's period seemed to him to have absorbed Machiavelli's doctrine. He was close to those in power at a point when the structure of politics denied legitimacy to opposition. As late as 1715, Robert Harley was arraigned and sent to the Tower when his administration fell: falling from power was its own punishment and ipso facto evidence of corruption in office. To oppose the government of the day was to be part of a narrow 'faction', not operating in the interests of the nation.[3] Such an understanding of political life imposes a binarism upon the conceptual apparatus with which politics was – and sometimes still is – thought. Controversialists and polemical pamphleteers of the period with whom Swift had to contend were not normally seeking complexity or nuance. They did not routinely emphasise that truth might be aspectual and might depend upon the position from which you were viewing the facts. Filter this rhetorical polarisation through Swift's individual psychology – his frequently extreme, intolerant, and vehement mode of expression, bristling with the certainty of being right – and we begin to understand the cognitive crisis that follows from routinely 'saying the thing that is not'.

At one level, Swift knew the impossibility of eliminating opinion and making everyone think alike. He expressed that memorably in *A Tale of a Tub*:

> For, what Man in the natural State, or Course of Thinking, did ever conceive it in his Power, to reduce the Notions of all Mankind, exactly to the same Length, and Breadth, and Heighth of his own? (*Tale*, 108)

---

[2] Niccolo Machiavelli, *The Prince* (*Il principe*, 1532), intro. and trans. George Bull (Harmondsworth: Penguin, 1961, repr. 1968), 99.

[3] See Pat Rogers, 'Swift and Bolingbroke on Faction', *Journal of British Studies*, 9 (1970), 71–101; Tom Jones, 'Pope and the Ends of History: Faction, Atterbury, and Clarendon's *History of the Rebellion*', *SP*, 110 (2013), 880–902.

Nevertheless, this was the task he undertook as a political writer; and in his *Examiner* campaign (1710–11) pursued against the conduct of the War of the Spanish Succession, he repeatedly sought to expose what he set about persuading his readers was the mendacity of Whig politicians:

> Considering that natural Disposition in many Men to Lie, and in Multitudes to Believe, I have been perplex'd what to do with that Maxim, so frequent in every Bodies Mouth, That *Truth will at last prevail* [...] Truth, who is said to *lie in a Well*, seem[s] now to be buried there under a heap of Stones.[4]

What Swift considered to be the biggest political lie in his later experience was the continuing claim that Ireland was an English dependency rather than a separate realm. This example of political mendacity preoccupied Swift in the years of *Gulliver's Travels*'s composition. The most egregious instance of this in practice was the deception deployed to require the Irish to accept copper coins struck in England by the Wolverhampton ironmonger William Wood. To accept Wood's halfpence as good coin suitable for Irish use and circulation was, by implication, to accept England's right to impose them. In *The Drapier's Letters* of 1724–5, we observe Swift's continuing concern for truth and his consuming anxiety that those in highest authority, even the King himself, have fallen victim to a deception on a grand scale. Swift's powerful but thwarted desire to gain the position of Historiographer Royal, a vocation partly fulfilled in his posthumously published *History of the Four Last Years of the Queen* (1758), was a near-obsessive commitment to the belief that he could tell the objective, non-partisan truth about the years 1710–14, the period when he was close to the centre of political events. We could say that he aspired to write Houyhnhnm history, history as written by a perfectly rational being, who is not expressing mere *opinion*, not merely telling it as he sees it, but telling it as it actually was.

Faction and Fiction

The term 'faction', applied in Swift's period to opponents of the party in power, can provide a bridge between the historical and the literary challenges facing Swift in his time, even if only by means of an elision punning on its modern generic meaning: 'A literary and cinematic genre in which fictional narrative is developed from a basis of real events or characters'

---

[4] Jonathan Swift, *The Examiner*, 15 (9 November 1710), *Swift vs Mainwaring: The Examiner and The Medley*, ed. Frank H. Ellis (Oxford: Clarendon Press, 1985), 24–5.

(*OED*). If, as suggested above, the separation between truth and lies in contemporary political commentary resulted from a conceptual matrix creating all opposition as 'faction', fiction too was, at the point of development reached in Swift's time, in a condition of 'faction'. Writers of imaginative fiction in the early eighteenth century were not certain how far they could emancipate themselves from the factual. Was pure invention legitimate? Could you, with a clear conscience, just make stories up? If you did, were you lying? Lying in print could, after all, have very serious real-world consequences, in the form of prosecution for seditious libel.

The most influential of the period's prose fiction writers, Daniel Defoe, did not think that stories could retain respectability as entire fictions. He deployed the Horatian justification that his stories were morally useful as well as pleasurable. One means of justifying their morality was to claim that they were based on the life experiences of real people. His characters can serve as role models or aversion therapy because they existed. Characteristic of Defoe's fiction is its claim to documentary status: it claims to be more faction than fiction. Typical in this respect is the uneasy Preface to *Robinson Crusoe* (1719), where a story that the title page claims is 'Written by Himself' now turns out to have an editor:

> The Editor believes the thing to be a just History of Fact; neither is there any Appearance of Fiction in it: And however thinks . . . that the Improvement of it, as well to the Diversion, as to the Instruction of the Reader, will be the same.[5]

Well-known accounts of the story of the Scottish sailor Alexander Selkirk's isolation on Juan Fernandez, available in print shortly before *Robinson Crusoe* was published, further occluded the boundary between fiction and documentary fact.[6] Defoe appears to have thought fiction defensible only if it had a factual basis. The duty of imaginative writing to instruct its reader could only be fulfilled if it was insulated from being a whole-cloth fabrication.

Defoe is important here because in my opinion the success of *Robinson Crusoe*, which went into four editions between its date of publication, 25 April 1719, and 7 August 1719, was a major catalyst for Swift to begin writing his fictional travelogue. This is a difficult case to prove because, as the authoritative Cambridge edition says, 'Swift disdained to mention Defoe'; and the edition does not redress that balance.[7] Nevertheless one can make

[5] Daniel Defoe, *The Life and Strange Surprizing Adventures of Robinson Crusoe*, ed. Evan R. Davis (Peterborough: Broadview Press, 2010), 45.
[6] Maximillian E. Novak, *Daniel Defoe: Master of Fictions* (Oxford: Oxford University Press, 2001), 538–9.
[7] See *GT*, I, i, 29 n 2.

a strong case that *Gulliver's Travels* is in a structurally parodic dialogue with *Robinson Crusoe*. Swift's first mention of the *Travels* occurs in April 1721; there is some evidence that he was thinking about it and even writing it before that.[8] One of his targets is Defoe's slippery tactic of positioning his fictional writing between fact and fiction. If Defoe's fictions are 'factual fictions', then Swift's will be, as the legend inscribed on the 'author' portrait of Lemuel Gulliver in the frontispiece to the 1735 Faulkner edition puts it (quoting from one of Horace's *Odes*) 'gloriously false' ('Splendide Mendax')

Figure 9.1 Frontispiece portrait of Lemuel Gulliver, from *The Works of J. S, D.D, D. S.P.D.*, 4 vols. (Dublin: George Faulkner, 1735), volume 3, Bodleian Library, University of Oxford (Bodl. Radcl. e.233)

8 See *GT*, 627 nn 1–2.

(Figure 9.1).[9] If, in his prefatory material, Defoe indirectly claims the respectable Horatian virtues for his text, Swift will take his title-page motto, 'Vulgus abhorret ab his', from Lucretius's materialist and atheist *De rerum natura* IV, 19–20. Rather than being educated and instructed by the *Travels*, 'the people' will 'shrink away from it', because the truths it contains will be unpalatable, so they may prefer to think it tells lies.

The progressive emancipation from 'faction' in *Gulliver's Travels*, its glorying in a fictionality that, simultaneously, it challenges the reader to disbelieve, its poking fun at realistic conventions (such as the mariners' jargon to which the prefatory material in the *Travels* calls attention) that define the very nature of Defoe's achievement, is one of its hallmark originalities. *Gulliver's Travels* is deliberately positioned between fact and fiction, its individual sentences frequently poised between truth and falsehood, intentionally mystifying the grounds upon which such distinctions are made. In spirit, therefore, despite being a collection of good stories, the *Gulliver* project is a critique of reader-credulity and 'absorptive' reading that might have stopped fiction in its tracks – but, despite itself, contributed to such self-consciously metafictional developments as Sterne's *Tristram Shandy*. The protagonist's name, Lemuel Gulliver, appears to have been a very late addition to the text, gleaned by Swift on his 1726 visit to England when he stayed at an inn kept by one Samuel Gulliver. There is a further irony in that Gulliver could have been modelled upon one Richard Coleire, whom Swift befriended in 1708.[10] *Gulliver's Travels* too may be a 'faction'.

Authorship and Advertisements

Who did the earliest readers of the *Travels* believe was its author? Nowadays we might think of authorship as on a spectrum with a 'strong' conception at one end – authorship as agency, original creativity, realisation of specific intentions and intellectual ownership – and at the opposite end, a 'weak' conception of it as a product of various cultural networks. The entire book trade, with all the intermediary stages necessary to the conversion of a manuscript into a printed book and its distribution to a reading public, would be seen as vital aspects of

---

[9] *Factual Fictions: The Origins of the English Novel* (New York: Columbia University Press, 1983) is the title of Lennard Davis's influential book arguing that prose fiction destined to evolve into the novel derived from history and journalism, was middle-class, was concerned with present-day actuality, and usually adopted the first person or epistolary form. 'Splendide mendax' derives from Horace's *Odes* 3.xi.35.

[10] Leo Damrosch, *Jonathan Swift: His Life and His World* (New Haven: Yale University Press, 2013), 176; Michael Treadwell, 'Swift, Richard Coleire, and the Origins of *Gulliver's Travels*', *RES*, 34: 135 (1983), 304–11.

authorship on the 'weak' view. Swift vacillated between, and played fast and loose with, those conceptions of authorship. He rarely acknowledged authorship of his writings on title pages, but as his series of letters written to Esther Johnson and Rebecca Dingley, familiarly entitled the *Journal to Stella*, make clear, he had a very strong sense of proprietorship of them. He wanted to be known, and yet not known, as the author of such controversial works as the *Tale* and *The Conduct of the Allies*. *Gulliver's Travels* was exceptional in that, mainly through his friend Alexander Pope's negotiating skills, Swift received a payment of £200 for the copyright. As a rule, he did not profit from his own writings, neither did he seek to do so. In part, this was a protection against prosecution, offering Swift an opportunity to disown his most subversive writing. As he reportedly told Lord Somers, it was also to avoid having authorship of works he did not write foisted upon him: altogether better if readers remained unsure. As significantly, it was an expression of an authorial personality addicted to hoaxes, practical jokes and 'bites'. Nowhere in his oeuvre does Swift more successfully dissolve the function of authorship into the processes of book production than in the lead-up to, the publication and the subsequent print history of *Gulliver's Travels*.

One of the paratextual features of the *Travels* is its 'Advertisement'. Advertisements in the modern sense of the promotion of goods and services was a well-established aspect of newspapers in Swift's era. Readers picking up the *Daily Journal* for Friday 28 October 1726 would find in the advertisements section a 'what's on' notice about the play being performed at the Theatre Royal in Lincoln's Inn Fields, news of auctions, publishers' information, promotions for remedies and dire warnings against bogus panaceas. They would also learn that:

> *This Day is Published,*
> Travels into several remote Nations of the World. By LEMUEL GULLIVER, first a Surgeon, afterwards Captain of Several Ships. In Two Volumes.
> Compositum jus, fasque animi, sanctosque recessus
> Mentis, & incoctum generoso pectus honesto.
> Printed for BENJ. MOTTE, at the Middle Temple Gate, Fleet-street.
> N, B. There are a few Printed on a Royal Paper.

The motto, taken from the second satire of Persius, celebrates human virtues that money cannot buy: 'In spirit, to be reconciled to what is holy and to what is just; to be thoroughly pure in mind; and to have a heart infused with nobleness and honour'. Those persuaded to buy the *Travels*

Figure 9.2 Frontispiece portrait of Lemuel Gulliver (second state), from *Travels into Several Remote Nations of the World. By Lemuel Gulliver*, 2 vols. (London: Benj. Motte, 1726), vol. 1, Bodleian Library, University of Oxford (Bodl. Vet. A4 e.2217 v.1)

a little later than its very first edition would find this motto inscribed on the frontispiece, on a tablet beneath what claims to be a portrait of Lemuel Gulliver, the 'author' at age 58 – a portrait executed by John Sturt, that some have thought resembles the 1725 portrait of Sir Isaac Newton by Vanderbank (Figure 9.2).[11] The frontispiece to the second state of the 1726 Motte edition sets up purity, nobility, and honour as the by-words to describe Lemuel Gulliver, author of this authentic travelogue.

Advertising and authorship are closely associated in Swift's writings. Catalogues serving the book trade, listing works available for sale, have

---

[11] Newton became a target for Swift in the third of the *Drapier's Letters*, because as Master of the Mint he weighed Wood's coin and found it to be good. But as Swift pointed out, only the samples brought to Newton might have been good.

existed since the late fifteenth century. Auction catalogues were first used in England in 1676, and between 1668 and 1709, Term Catalogues listing books for sale in each Law Term were obtainable. In *A Tale of a Tub*, Swift produced a parodic list of mock books containing such titles as 'A General History of Ears' and 'A Description of the Kingdom of Absurdities' referred to as 'Treatises wrote by the same Author' (*Tale*, 4). Advertisements were parodied by Swift as a joke in themselves and also to occlude and confound discovery of his own authorship: for example, the mock-advertisement for a non-existent auction that he set up as an April Fool in 1709, placing a notice in *The Post-Boy* for 29 March. He used them as a strategy in the cat-and-mouse game he played with authorship throughout his writing career.

The Text and its Preliminaries: 1726[12]

As we have seen, Swift is known to have been writing the *Travels* in 1721, though its inspiration goes back further. References to its progress surface in his correspondence, showing that the order of composition of the parts was not the order of publication. By September 1725 he speaks directly to Pope of 'finishing correcting, amending, and Transcribing my Travells in four parts Compleat newly Augmented' (*GT*, 628–9). In March 1726, Swift travelled from Dublin with a copy in someone else's hand of the manuscript of the *Travels*. His friend Charles Ford brought Swift's own handwritten copy to London a little later. London friends, in particular Alexander Pope and John Gay, became involved in the project. A persona was invented, 'Richard Sympson', who would play a significant part in the ensuing print history. 'Sympson' (actually John Gay) sent a letter enclosing a portion of the text to the London publisher Benjamin Motte, who was now sole partner in the established bookselling firm of Tooke, a rising firm gaining a reputation for sermons, instructional manuals, historical studies, scientific treatises and classical editions as well as literature. Pope's account of how Motte received the remainder of the text captures the hugger-mugger spirit of the enterprise, positioned somewhere between practical joke and conspiracy:

> Motte receiv'd the copy (he tells me) he knew not from whence, nor from whom, dropp'd at his house in the dark, from a Hackney-coach. (*GT*, 633)

---

[12] The story of the *Travels*'s textual transmission is best told by David Womersley in *GT*, 627–52. Although I do not concur with all his critical stances, I am indebted for my textual sections to his authoritative edition.

Benjamin Motte was anxious about this clandestinely conveyed manuscript from the outset. It appeared to be a much more satirical and subversive text than he was used to handling, offering clear opportunities to those who would read it as a *pièce à clef*: that is, a narrative with veiled allusions to real people. Equally disconcerting was its radical critique of a range of English institutions and its apparently misanthropic and negative appraisal of the human condition itself. While claiming to be an authentic account of actual travels – in dialogue, as we have seen, with a developing fictional form that draws its strength from the claims it makes to being 'true history', to being real – its real or imaginary communities suspended the laws of human physiology and physics. His business associate Andrew Tooke became involved in a bowdlerisation process, slashing and burning without any consultation with Swift and his 'team'. Thus the text published on 28 October 1726 as *Travels into Several Remote Regions of the World* (*not* as *Gulliver's Travels*) gave its author a nasty surprise, despite its becoming the talk of the town and its three 1726 editions, comprising in total some 10,000 copies, selling out.

For the next few years, the recurring theme in Swift's correspondence in respect of the *Travels* was the carelessness of the printing, the non-authorial exclusions and inclusions that murdered the text especially in its later sections. Swift's friend Charles Ford took up the cudgels with Motte in January 1727, presenting him with a list of over a hundred passages that required alteration. An edition incorporating some corrections was produced by the Dublin publisher John Hyde in 1726, many of those corrections corresponding to corrections marked in a copy of the *Travels* now in Armagh Public Library, possibly a copy belonging to Swift himself. A second edition published by Motte in May 1727 restored some minor alterations to the original text but did not restore longer and more major passages that had been excised by Tooke.

Readers who bought the first (1726) Motte edition would immediately encounter the portrait discussed above, though the tablet beneath it does not yet have the motto from Persius, reading simply: '*Captain Lemuel Gulliver, of* Redriff Aetat. suae 58'. Those early readers, encouraged by the cursive font in which the name is written, as though it were in Gulliver's own hand, are to think that this is a likeness of the author himself. After the contents, there is an 'advertisement' in the older sense of that word: 'a (written) statement calling attention to anything; a notification; *esp.* a notice to readers in a book (typically, a preface)' (*OED*). 'The Publisher to the Reader' is signed by Richard Sympson, the persona invented, as we saw, for the initial conveying of the manuscript to Motte. Confusingly, though,

Sympson is not actually the publisher. Sympson tells us that Gulliver is his 'antient and intimate Friend', in fact a distant relation. Local celebrity has forced him to move from Redriff (Rotherhithe) to Newark where he was born, though his family derives from the Banbury area where Gulliver tombs are to be found – as they still are in our own time. Although there is a little too much circumstantial detail for Sympson's liking, and too much sea-jargon, he judges that 'there is an Air of Truth apparent through the Whole' and indeed, Gulliver's name is proverbial in Redriff for truth-telling. Heading off at the pass an obvious objection that we do not know where the lands are of which the travelogue speaks, Sympson tells us that he has struck out 'the Account of Longitudes and Latitudes' so as not to bore the reader. Sympson curiously anticipates the real publisher Motte in his cavalier attitude to his author's text. Everything has been done, however, to establish that Lemuel Gulliver is a real person, whose reliability and honesty are beyond question and it is under this aspect that the first purchasers must have commenced their reading.

The Text and Its Preliminaries: 1735

Swift's continuing dissatisfaction with the published text of *Gulliver* was one factor in the accumulating case for a revised complete edition of his works, a proposition with which the Dublin publisher George Faulkner approached Swift in 1733. James McLaverty sums up the commercial thinking behind the 1735 Dublin edition of *The Works of Jonathan Swift DSPD* thus:

> The advantages proposed for the edition were four: disentanglement of Swift's writings from those of his friends; inclusion of new works (especially two new Drapier's letters and many original poems); amalgamation of pieces independently published and those collected in the Miscellanies; and restoration of the text of *Gulliver's Travels*.[13]

McLaverty makes clear that Swift was an active contributor to the creation of this text, and it has been thought that Faulkner had the benefit of an interleaved large-paper copy of the *Travels* with very many annotations and insertions in the handwriting of Charles Ford, probably compiled by Ford shortly after the Motte edition was published. This copy still exists in the Victoria and Albert Museum (*GT*, 644). McLaverty argues that a set of

---

[13] James McLaverty, 'George Faulkner and Swift's Collected Works', in *Jonathan Swift and the Eighteenth-Century Book*, ed. Paddy Bullard and James McLaverty (Cambridge: Cambridge University Press, 2013), 154–75 (163).

corrections was given to Faulkner *not* via this copy, but through the agency of Matthew Pilkington, another of Swift's Irish-domiciled friends. It is now thought that this printing, as Volume III of a collected edition, did not merely restore original readings, but also incorporated fresh thinking – revisions, that is to say. One important passage present in Ford's interleaved copy (the V&A copy), remains mysterious, a passage describing a rebellion taking place in Lindalino, the 'second City in the Kingdom'. This section containing five paragraphs appears consonant with the material in the *Travels* III, iii, where the state of mutually assured destruction existing between the flying island of Laputa and its dependent territory Balnibarbi is described. The Lindalino material is an allegory of the Dubliners' resolute opposition to Wood's halfpence. James McLaverty, again, has shed most light on this matter, concluding that the Lindalino episode was never intended for insertion in the Faulkner *Gulliver*. Bibliographical analysis of the V&A interleaved copy gets close to proof that Lindalino was not in the holograph copy that Swift provided to Motte in 1726.[14] One conjecture is that this material was left over from the *Drapier's Letters* writings and that Swift decided against it for inclusion in *Gulliver* (*GT*, 722–4).

Readers of *Travels into Several Remote Nations of the World* located in Faulkner's third volume of Swift's *Works* would have a different, and more complex, reading experience than those of the Motte edition in 1726. It made the question of the narrative's truth-to-fact a larger and even more vexed one than had the 1726 Motte edition. If they had a Motte edition in the library, they would be surprised by a different pictorial representation of the supposed author/teller, 'Capt. Lemuel Gulliver'. In Faulkner's edition, the depicted features, orientation of the head and costume details bear an uncanny resemblance to George Vertue's engraving of the real-life Jonathan Swift, after the well-known Charles Jervas portrait. Confusion persists in the reader's mind about who the 'real' author of this travel book is, and about whether it is a real travel book. Such obfuscations continue to problematise the distinction between fact and fiction, truth and falsehood. As discussed above, the caption on the portrait of Gulliver, 'Splendide Mendax. Hor.', might suggest that Gulliver is a fake, or that the story he tells is a fabrication, but it is in some sense a virtuous, or 'glorious' deception.

The 1735 edition comes equipped with prefatory material from which 1726 readers did not benefit. In early 1727, when, as recorded earlier, Motte

[14] James McLaverty, 'The Revision of the First Edition of *Gulliver's Travels*: Book-Trade Context, Interleaving, Two Cancels, and a Failure to Catch', *The Papers of the Bibliographical Society of America*, 106 (2012), 5–35.

was preparing an edition corrected by Charles Ford's errata list, Swift was busy on another bewildering preface, cast in the form of 'A LETTER FROM Capt. *GULLIVER* TO HIS Cousin SYMPSON'. Not published in any earlier edition, this first saw the light in 1735; but before it, there is an 'Advertisement' which is again new. It speaks of 'Mr. Sympson's Letter to Captain Gulliver' but actually it is a letter from Captain Gulliver to Mr Sympson that the text contains. What is this – a slip, or a deliberate error? The 'Advertisement' is very difficult to make out, anticipating as it does the complaints in Gulliver's letter about interpolated passages and referring to '*a Person since deceased*' who was responsible for the unhappy state of the first edition (Andrew Tooke?). One non-authorial passage is singled out as particularly heinous: where it is said that '*her late Majesty* [Queen Anne] [. . .] governed without a Chief Minister' (5). The bemused reader, though, will not find such a passage in the book s/he currently has open, because Faulkner does not print it. It occurs in IV, vi of the Motte edition. Picking that from the library shelf, the reader will find that actually Queen Anne is *complimented* upon her benign, if autocratic style of leadership. She 'never puts any such Confidence in any of her Subjects as to entrust them with the whole and entire Administration of her Affairs'. Powerful ministers of state have been known in England but only 'in some former Reigns' (*GT*, 711). The Advertisement concludes by promising that this edition incorporates all the corrections sent forward by '*a most intimate Friend of the Authors*' (*GT*, 5), presumably Charles Ford – though actually it does not.

The following 'Letter from Capt. Gulliver, to his Cousin Sympson' appears to reinforce the title page's claim that there is a real Lemuel Gulliver, who has a real cousin called Sympson (though the name is oddly spelt). Gulliver claims in this letter that William Dampier, a famous buccaneer and explorer who really had published a highly influential account of his travels called *A New Voyage Round the World* in 1697, is his cousin. And there follows a series of references that anticipate the story in a wholly mysterious way. We hear about 'my Master Houyhnhnm' and about 'Yahoos' before we can have any idea what these exotic names can signify. Very uncomfortably, we come to discern that Gulliver somehow does not consider himself to be a member of the human race, because he speaks of it as though he were not included in it. We need to remember that this edition of the *Travels* is published as volume three of a collected edition of Swift's entire *oeuvre*. Captain Gulliver's letter has to be based on the assumption that there will be very few first-time readers – that most people reading his letter already know who the Houyhnhnms and the Yahoos are, and their interest resides as much in what the corrections amount to (as we have seen, an important strand of the commercial prospectus for a new collected Swift) as in the fiction itself. What are they getting for their money?

Capt. Gulliver's first major concern in the letter is that the first edition of the text is a mingle-mangle. One example deserves special notice because it is particularly unsettling: the name BrobdingNag should actually have been BrobdingRag, unsettling because the name is itself difficult enough to pronounce without also having a misprint to reckon with. As David Womersley astutely points out, Charles Ford's interleaved, annotated copy of the text (the V&A copy) does not list this as an error, so it is likely to be a 'bite', 'satirising the very notion of literary correctness' (*GT*, lxxxiii). But the significance of this correction of a single character is missed. In the King James Bible, the name of NebuchadNezzar, King of Babylon, is in some books spelt thus, and in others spelt NebuchadRezzar, so Swift is likely to be alluding to that relatively well-known crux concerning n and r – resulting from the fact that the Hebrew text used by the translators of the King James Version has both spellings, deploying the Hebrew letter nun in most cases but the letter resh in some.[15] A reader who notices this is alerted, therefore, to the disconcerting fact that there are even textual cruces in the Scriptures themselves.

Gulliver's other major concern in his letter is that the wholesale reform of the human race that he expected his book to effect has not transpired. What is the reader to make of this absurd expectation that Gulliver's book would reform the human race? How can we regard such a naive, utopian expectation as this, except perhaps as the raving of a lunatic? Having made their way through this preliminary material, original readers of *Gulliver's Travels* must have been very uncertain indeed about what they were about to read. The letter is dated 'April 2, 1727', suspiciously close, that is, to being an April Fool (*GT*, 14). At the letter's close, veracity is again what is at issue in Gulliver's arrogant, exasperated and world-weary tone. 'The Publisher to the Reader' is the same as in the 1726 text. If you were beginning to suspect that the whole thing is a fiction, or even some kind of hoax, you have to confront a very aggressively expressed opinion that Lemuel Gulliver is the most truthful man who ever lived!

We are ready to begin reading.

---

[15] It became clear, when the original language was cracked in the middle of the nineteenth century, that resh is closer to providing a correct pronunciation of the Akkadian.

CHAPTER 10

A Voyage to Lilliput

Melinda Alliker Rabb

Wading In

A reader embarking for the first time on Gulliver's voyages to 'Several Remote Nations of the World' would be unlikely to anticipate the depths or dangers of the journeys that lie ahead. No obvious warnings signal that neither the protagonist nor the thoughtful reader who accompanies him will reach the end of the narrative unscathed and unchanged. This satiric strategy – disarming the reader – is one of several crucial Swiftian techniques that will be the focus of this chapter. These strategies explain the effectiveness of the miniature world of Lilliput and also prepare the way for the journeys that follow: selective use of detail; topical allusions to real people and events; a questionable narrator; competing claims of the abstract (language and human ideals) and the concrete (the human body and the physical world); reversals; and, of course, manipulation of size and perspective. Lilliput, where everything shrinks by a scale of twelve to one, has proven to be the most beguiling fantasy among the satiric fictions in *Gulliver's Travels* that ultimately entrap Swift's readers in painful truths.[1] The charm of the miniature, its aesthetic appeal, its toy-like associations, its intimation of sentimentality and nostalgia, and its promise of easy control prove deceptive. In small-scale, all of the worst human tendencies are merely concentrated, not diminished. Swift's narrative tactics in Lilliput both entertain and vex readers. These tactics, sometimes overlapping although analysed separately here, carry out his satiric attack on a broken world he knows he cannot mend.

In the first four paragraphs of Book One, thirty-eight years of the protagonist's life pass by with disarming vagueness (I, i, 29–32). Gulliver's

---

[1] See Susan Stewart, *On Longing: Narratives of the Miniature, the Gigantic, the Souvenir, the Collection* (Baltimore: Johns Hopkins University Press, 1984); Melinda Alliker Rabb, *Miniature and the English Imagination: Literature, Cognition, and Small-Scale Culture, 1650–1765* (Cambridge: Cambridge University Press, 2019).

birth, education, apprenticeship, professional accomplishments, family, and career seem unremarkable. His autobiography is measured in modest units of property ('a small Estate', 'a very scanty Allowance', 'small Sums of Money', 'narrow Fortune', 'Part of a small House in the Old Jury', business 'not proving very fortunate'), and short spans of time (three years at college, four as apprentice, two years and seven months in Leyden, three moving about London, and so on). Little information about his relationships or his prior work as a ship's surgeon can be gleaned from Gulliver's perfunctory mention of marrying Mary Burton or 'making a Voyage or two in the Levant, and some other Parts'. We learn in general of his facility with foreign languages, his reading of 'the Best Authors', his interest in observing foreigners, and his good memory, but despite this good memory, actual details are few. What books did he study? Which 'manners and Dispositions' of which 'People' did he notice? Did he encounter the slave trade in the West Indies? Did he make one or two trips to the Levant? What exactly was his on-shore 'business' and why does he claim that it failed repeatedly because his 'conscience would not suffer [him] to imitate the bad Practice of too many of [his] Brethren'? A reader easily might overlook the possible implications in the first four paragraphs in which Gulliver travels widely from Nottinghamshire to Cambridge, London, Leyden, the Middle East, the West and East Indies, and the South Seas. The information gap between the explicit and the implicit will continue to widen, making room for a great deal of irony. We know essentially everything and essentially nothing about him.

Gulliver's curious mixture of precision (staying in Leyden for exactly two years and seven months) and imprecision (not explaining why his businesses fail) continues as he sets sail on the voyage that will bring him to Lilliput. He simply glosses over the suffering of nameless sailors because '[i]t would not be proper for some Reasons' and summarily reports the eventual death of the entire ship's crew:

> It would not be proper for some Reasons, to trouble the Reader with the Particulars of our Adventures in those Seas. Let it suffice to inform him, that in our Passage from thence to the *East-Indies*, we were driven by a violent Storm [. . .] Twelve of our Crew were dead by immoderate Labour, and ill Food; the rest were in a very weak Condition [. . .] We trusted ourselves to the Mercy of the Waves [. . .] [the remaining men] were all lost. (I, i, 32–3)

Attention focuses on his own survival as he swims into shallow water, reaches shore, falls into an exhausted sleep, and awakens into a nightmarish state. He is flat on his back, pinioned under the sun's glare, and unable even to lift his head in order to see the living thing that is crawling on his leg. The discovery of a 'Human Creature not six Inches high' – just the right size for a doll – initially seems something of a relief. But Swift is just beginning to construct the complex satire of Lilliput.

Politics

An oft-noted distinction of the first voyage is its political topicality. Although Gulliver will give accounts of England in Brobdingnag and Houyhnhnm-land in Parts II and IV, and Laputa will represent colonial oppression of Ireland in Part III, the most specific correspondence between fictional characters and actual public figures occurs in Lilliput. Explanatory 'keys' (such as those used in then-popular secret history and roman à clef) were published to confirm these parallels.[2] The tiny nation stands for England, a reduced-scale version of home, with counterparts to recognisable ministers, royalty, courtiers, circumstances, and events in early eighteenth-century Britain. Blefuscu represents France; High Heels and Low Heels are Tories and Whigs; Big-Endians and Little-Endians are Catholics and Anglicans; imperial troops signify the English standing army; the rope-dancing contest ridicules court preferment. Parallels are drawn between Flimnap and Robert Walpole, Reldresal and Lord Townshend, the Emperor and William III, Skyresh Bolgolam and Daniel Finch, Earl of Nottingham. These and other topical references have been well documented and extensively discussed by scholars.[3] Allusions to contemporary politics situate *Gulliver's Travels* in its own historical moment of party-faction, compromised monarchy, ambitious ministers, and governmental corruption. Even a miniature version of inter-necine squabbling harkens back to the sweeping trauma of England's disastrous civil wars. Swift's first readers, accustomed to reading thinly disguised political attacks in pamphlets and broadsides, would have recognised many specific identities that we must learn from helpful footnotes and commentary.

But for readers then and now, such references, however interesting, do not adequately explain the full satiric purpose of 'A Voyage to Lilliput' which, like the later journeys, reaches beyond local history in order to complicate the moral purpose of the satire. Larger questions arise from the play on perspective: specific issues that matter enough to send one group to the barricades appear trivial to another. Lilliput's standing army is ready for battle, but based on what justification or what distinction between warring

---

[2] For example, [Edmund Curll], *A Key, Being Observations and Explanatory Notes, upon the Travels of Lemuel Gulliver. By Signor Coroloni*, 4 Parts (1726).

[3] In addition to David Womersley's comprehensive notes in *GT*, see Ehrenpreis, *Swift*, and Ian Higgins, *Swift's Politics: A Study in Disaffection* (Cambridge: Cambridge University Press, 1994).

parties? During the second voyage, the King of Brobdingnag, disgusted by the petty viciousness of political faction will laugh dismissively at whether Gulliver identifies as Whig or Tory and be appalled by the disproportionate bloodletting that instigated those labels. By the fourth voyage, the Houyhnhnm Master will efface all local differences among Yahoos.

In certain ways, Lilliput seems to differ from England. Although ambitious claims are made about the six-inch Emperor whose 'Dominions extend [...] to the extremities of the Globe' and whose nod makes 'the Princes of the Earth shake their Knees' (I, iii, 63), Lilliput's interests appear relatively isolated and circumscribed; its international ambitions extend only to Blefuscu. We do not witness large-scale global exploration, commercial expansion, or the foreign slave trade. Its economy, when strained by the expense of supporting Gulliver, seems dependent on its own national resources. Lilliputians prefer to believe that Gulliver dropped from the moon rather than embrace the notion that whole nations of his same proportion exist and engage in larger-scale partisan struggles. Their narrow-mindedness allows Part I to shift away from specific ridicule of Walpole, Marlborough, or Nottingham, to the general danger of ideological myopia.

Further, Swift's ironic use of inverted perspective in the Lilliputian world also allows him to look beyond local politics and introduce a pattern of anti-colonialist ideas that will intensify in each voyage. The seeming confinement of Lilliput's territorial ambitions does not negate their pursuit of dominion. They have not conquered vast foreign populations or territories in a conventional sense. But when they secure with ropes and chains, and walk upon the sleeping Gulliver, they literally occupy his body. They conquer and colonise a mountain, or rather a Man-Mountain with (ironically) an enormous population of one. Like true colonial powers, they assume Gulliver's willingness to do their bidding until their extreme cruelty instigates his rebellion and escape. This presumptive abuse of power initiates an escalating anxiety about the relationship between local and remote, an anxiety even more explicitly expressed in the later voyages.

Size and Small Details

The small-scale world of Lilliput immediately captured the popular imagination in 1726, and it has continued to do so. Fascination with miniature objects owes much to the fineness of their detail which must be wrought with convincing accuracy in order to replicate the full-scale world. Accordingly, Gulliver's narration of Lilliput is full of descriptive particulars. When hungry, he is brought 'Baskets full of Meat', containing the 'Flesh of several Animals

[...] Shoulders, Legs, and Loins shaped like those of Mutton, and very well dressed, but smaller than the Wings of a Lark [which he eats] by two or three at a Mouthful' (I, i, 36). Living sheep can be carried in his pockets. Little seamstresses sew with dainty needles and silken thread too fine for Gulliver's sight. He scrutinises the Emperor's physical features – '*Austrian* Lip, and arched Nose, his Complexion Olive, his Countenance erect, his Body and Limbs well proportioned' – and inspects the royal attire – 'His Dress was very plain and simple [...] but he had on his Head a light Helmet of Gold, adorned with Jewels, and a Plume on the Crest' and held a sword 'almost three Inches long, the Hilt and Scabbard were Gold enriched with Diamonds' (I, ii, 45–6). The ratio of twelve to one is maintained to the smallest fraction. When explaining the political differences between High Heels and Low Heels, Gulliver notes that 'his Majesty's Imperial Heels are lower at least by a *Drurr* [...] a Measure about the fourteenth Part of an Inch' (I, iv, 69).

Reduction in scale usually makes things appear more attractive. The heaviest Lilliputian prison-chains are 'like those that hang to a Lady's Watch in Europe' (I, i, 41). The dollhouse-sized palace has 'the most splendid Apartments that can be imagined' (I, iv, 67). The fields 'resembled Beds of Flowers' (I, ii, 43); the town 'looked like the painted Scene of a City in a Theatre' (I, ii, 43), the gathering of 'Ladies and Courtiers [...] resemble[s] a Petticoat spread on the Ground, embroidered with Figures of Gold and Silver' (I, ii, 46). However, Swift also uses descriptive detail ironically, in order to disrupt the illusion of the miniature's beauty and to distance the reader from Gulliver's perspective. Hyper-focus on the attractions of the small can distract an observer from larger concerns and truths. Consider the odd effect of irrelevant information included in Gulliver's critical act of extinguishing the palace fire with his urine: 'I had the Evening before drank plentifully of a most delicious Wine, called *Glimigrim*, (the *Blefuscudians* call it *Flunec*, but ours is esteemed the better Sort) which is very diuretick' (I, v, 79). In the midst of a raging conflagration, literally in the heat of a moment that will materially and figuratively pollute Gulliver's fate, what possible significance can be gleaned from specifying the precise name of the variety of wine he drank, or that of a comparable foreign vintage, or of a connoisseur-like assessment of the taste? When accused of adultery with Lord Chancellor Flimnap's wife, Gulliver takes pains to 'vindicate the Reputation of an excellent Lady' (I, vi, 94) with a lengthy description of her chaperoned visits, the respectability of her companions, his careful practice of lifting her coach and horses onto a table of his contrivance, including the table's exact measurements around which he 'had fixed a moveable Rim quite round, of five Inches high, to prevent

Accidents' (I, vi, 95). The obvious impossibility of the sexual transgression of which he is accused, which in keeping with the book's mathematical calculations is beyond ludicrous, receives no mention. Yet we know the exact height of the table's rim. These comical instances of misplaced attention to detail are related to another means of challenging the efficacy of human perspective: for Gulliver, the world of minutiae is also a world of vast quantities.

Disproportion is fundamental to the account of Lilliput. Small objects accrue in excessively huge numbers as Gulliver counts 'above an Hundred Arrows [...] [and] Inhabitants' (I, i, 35–6), 'five Hundred Carpenters and Engineers' (I, i, 40), 'fifteen Hundred of the Emperor's largest Horses' (I, i, 40–1), 'an hundred thousand Inhabitants came out of the Town' (I, i, 42), 'ten Thousand [guards]', 'six Hundred Beds' and 'Domesticks' (I, ii, 47–8), 'Three Hundred Tailors' (I, vi, 92), 'three Thousand Foot [soldiers] and a Thousand Horse' (I, iii, 62), 'five Hundred Thousand Souls' in Mildendo (I, iv, 67), 'Eleven Thousand [Big-Endians] have suffered Death' (I, iv, 71), 'Thirty Thousand [...] Seamen and Soldiers' (I, iv, 72), 'seven Thousand Arrows' (I, v, 74), 'three Hundred Cooks' (I, vi, 93), 'Tallow of three Hundred Cows' and 'Carcasses of an Hundred Oxen and three Hundred Sheep' (I, viii, 109). The general effect of such numbers cuts several ways. As his Lilliputian name – Quinbus Flestrin or the Man Mountain – suggests, Gulliver can look down and comprehend entire crowds, fleets, armies, buildings, and herds of animals. His spectacles and pocket telescope aid his visual ability to see the whole at once. Yet this advantageous perspective oddly does not empower him. He sees widely yet remains a captive. In contrast, the Lilliputians do not understand objects, even familiar objects, that they cannot take in at a glance, as in their confused report of the contents taken from Gulliver's pockets. They do not recognise 'the Hyde of some prodigious Animal' (I, ii, 53) used in Gulliver's leather jerkin, although they have sheep and cows. They struggle to identify 'massy pieces of yellow metal', although they have gold coins and jewellery. They are baffled by a 'great black substance', although they wear hats. The play on perspective may entertain readers with its ingenious manipulation of detail, but in the final analysis, neither seeing in part or as a whole reliably overcomes the limits of human understanding.

Abstract and Concrete

The strategy of size emphasises the importance of the material world in which the variation of a fourteenth of an inch can make a difference, or in which a city of one square mile can house one hundred thousand little inhabitants. Swift is equally interested in the ramifications of what cannot be measured, in the power of concepts that affect human behaviour without reference to precise dimension or location. An important satiric strategy in Lilliput is the juxtaposition of abstract and concrete. What is more powerful in determining the fates of not only Gulliver but of whole people and nations – the force of bodies or of ideas? physical size and strength, or intangible concepts and beliefs perpetuated through law, custom, and religion? Some of the most memorable moments in Lilliput occur when these two means of exerting of power and authority collide.

Gulliver is twelve times as big and strong as the Lilliputians. He cuts down trees with his penknife (I, iv, 67), lifts passenger-filled carriages in his hands, places officers 'ready mounted and armed' on his handkerchief (I, iii, 59), and draws a fleet of Blefuscudian warships across the ocean (I, v, 75). He is confident of his physical prowess – 'so Prodigious a Creature as I must appear to them' (I, i, 37) – when troops marching between his legs gaze admiringly through his torn breeches, as well as when he pees out a raging fire in three minutes by 'void[ing] in such a Quantity, and applied so well to the proper Places' (I, v, 80). At the same time, Gulliver is no more powerful than the weakest Lilliputian because he is governed by abstract principles like respect, deference to rank, and friendship, and by constraints like laws, obligation, and oaths. He may feel the temptation 'to seize forty or fifty of the first [Lilliputians] that came within my Reach, and dash them against the Ground' but he desists. What restrains him? '[T]he Promise of Honour I had made them [...] soon drove out those Imaginations [...] I considered myself bound by the Laws of Hospitality to a People who had treated me with so much Expense and Magnificence' (I, i, 37). With the same reverence for royalty expected in Europe, he prostrates himself at the feet of six-inch monarchs and kisses their tiny hands. The disjunction between body and thought exposes the problems of each. In order to obtain his physical freedom of movement, Gulliver, who has been chained, must swear to a document of 'Articles and Conditions'. The required oath has a physical component, a conflation of concrete and abstract that ironically demonstrates how the contortions of the body mimic the twisted agreement of Gulliver's so-called liberty: 'I must swear', he says, while also required 'to hold my right Foot in my left Hand, to place the middle Finger of my right Hand on the Crown of my Head, and my Thumb on the Tip of my Ear' (I, iii, 63).

The problematic force of concepts on bodies undergoes further satiric exposure when Gulliver is elevated to the rank of Nardac 'which is the highest Title of Honour' bestowed by the Emperor after the capture of the

Blefuscudian fleet (I, v, 76). The title becomes a vehicle laden with irony because Gulliver draws attention to it so often and foolishly places so much substantive meaning in it. Faced with Flimnap's preposterous accusation of adultery, Gulliver does not refer to the irrefutable evidence of his body's bulk but relies on his superior social status: 'I had the honour to be a Nardac, which the Treasurer himself is not; for all the World knows he is only a Clumglum' (I, vi, 95). Swift's strategy of juxtaposing the abstract and concrete incites laughter but also raises questions with difficult answers. To what extent do the physical needs of the body – to eat, sleep, excrete, move about, propagate, seek pleasure, or simply survive – determine human behaviour? To what degree do intangibles – language, moral codes, concepts like justice, loyalty, respect, or even God – control human conduct? If the force of Nature requires Gulliver to disburden himself of stinking faeces and torrents of urine, the force of belief in monarchy requires him to bow down to a creature he easily could trample. Gulliver is not simply a gentle giant in Lilliput. He is a man caught between systems of measuring human accountability.

Expectation and Reversal

One of Swift's most effective satiric strategies works by arousing and then disappointing readers' expectations. Countermanded expectations force readers to reconsider the information Gulliver shares. An obvious reversal is the assumption that small things can be controlled by larger things. At first, Gulliver entertains the Lilliputians with feats of strength; he elicits their wonder along with their hard work to supply him with sufficient food and shelter. 'When I had performed these Wonders', he reports, 'they shouted for Joy, and danced upon my Breast'. When he gestures that he is thirsty, they respond with 'their largest Hogsheads' of wine (I, i, 37), and later 'three hundred Cooks to dress [his] Victuals' encamp around his house where he could take 'up twenty Waiters in [his] Hand' (I, vi, 93). But 'diminutive Mortals' turn out to have an enormous capacity for malice, cunning, ambition, and aggression that defies regulation. They secretly drug him. They develop elaborate plans for blinding him, exploiting and starving him to death, and cutting the flesh from his bones. Gulliver is fortunate to escape from Lilliput to Blefuscu, and more fortunate still to happen upon a boat large enough to carry him out to sea.

The strategy of reversal works in subtler ways as well. Many Lilliputian laws, customs, and learning are founded on admirable principles. The initial point seems to be that they are wiser than the English. What Gulliver calls 'very peculiar' has merit, and he reluctantly admits that 'if they were not so directly contrary to those of my own dear Country, I should be tempted to say a little in their Justification' (I, vi, 83). The narrative sets us up to admire Lilliputian courts and government. False accusers are 'put to an ignominious Death' while 'the innocent Person is quadruply recompensed for the Loss of his Time, for the Danger he underwent, for the Hardship of his Imprisonment, and for all the Charges he hath been at in making his Defense' (I, vi, 84). Fraud is a greater transgression than theft because property can be protected whereas 'Honesty hath no Fence against superior Cunning'. Ingratitude is a capital crime because 'whoever makes ill Returns to his Benefactor, must needs be a common Enemy to the rest of Mankind' (I, vi, 87). Lilliput's legal system not only punishes miscreants but actually rewards citizens who do no wrong by giving them money and upward class mobility (I, vi, 85). Moral virtues are valued over superior intelligence when 'chusing Persons for all Employments'. The Lilliputians astutely recognise that brainpower alone will not guarantee ethical actions. The most egregious abuses of power can be levied by an untrustworthy person of unusual ingenuity:

> They believe that the common Size of human Understanding, is fitted to some Station or other; and that Providence never intended to make the Management of publick Affairs a Mystery, to be comprehended only by a few Persons of sublime Genius [...] they suppose Truth, Justice, Temperance, and the like, to be in every Man's Power; the Practice of which Virtues, assisted by Experience and good Intention, would qualify any Man for the Service of his Country [...] they thought the want of Moral Virtues was so far from being supplied by superior Endowments of the Mind, that Employments could never be put into such dangerous Hands as those of Persons so qualified; [...] that the Mistakes committed by Ignorance in a virtuous Disposition, would never be of such fatal Consequences to the Publick Weal, as the Practices of a Man, whose Inclinations led him to be corrupt, and had great Abilities to manage, and defend his Corruptions. (I, vi, 86)

After persuading the reader of the superiority of these fine principles, Gulliver admits that they are routinely violated by 'the most scandalous Corruptions into which these People are fallen by the degenerate Nature of Man' (I, vi, 87). Swift offers readers a vision of sustainable morality before abruptly taking it away.

The fifth chapter provides another example of satiric reversal: its title seems to announce the coming of peace followed by the bestowal of a just reward: 'The Author by an extraordinary Stratagem prevents an Invasion. A high Title of Honour is conferred upon him' (I, v, 73). Gulliver believes that he is saving Lilliput from an attack by its arch enemy when he swims across the channel to Blefuscu, braves a barrage of arrows, and confiscates fifty warships. He is greeted as a returning hero: 'This great Prince received me at my Landing with all possible Encomiums' (I, v, 75–6). Such glory fades quickly as Gulliver discovers that the purpose of his 'great Adventure' was not peace but war and that the Lilliputian Emperor has been emboldened to colonise Blefuscu and enslave its inhabitants. Gulliver's finest moment is his protest that he 'would never be an Instrument of bringing a free and brave People into Slavery' (I, v, 76). But the height of his finest moment is also the beginning of his decline into disfavour and personal danger.

Saying Things Which Are Not

This chapter will consider one more narrative strategy that develops from Swift's lifelong interest in language, especially in its malleability. He quickly establishes that his protagonist Gulliver has a facility with foreign tongues, a facility that will be tested during his journeys. For the satirist, the capacity of statements to have more than one meaning is a source of both potential richness and potential danger because words can have consequences. Language can be expository, figurative, mistaken, false, or (the satirist's speciality) ironic. Its instability becomes an issue in Lilliput and never ceases to demand critical attention until the final pages of the *Travels* when Gulliver merges English with whinnies. Every nation – no matter if its inhabitants are small, gigantic, eccentric, or equine – has its particular system of communication that can unify or alienate people. Language, the eighteenth century believed, is the defining human trait.[4] As a complex system of symbols, language not only defines national groups; it shapes thought, facilitates relationships, preserves knowledge, organises society by laws and religion, and even can determine life and death. But it is not a stable symbolic system. The passage of time, regional differences, metaphor, sarcasm, and falsehood are among its destabilising permutations. A single signifier, as modern linguists would say, can generate many signifieds.[5] In the voyage to Laputa, Gulliver will encounter people whose anxiety about the discrepancy between words and reality silences them. They carry around

---

[4] See Deborah Baker Wyrick, *Jonathan Swift and the Vested Word* (Chapel Hill: University of North Carolina Press, 1988).

[5] Useful terms from semiotics first popularised by Ferdinand de Saussure in 1916; *Course in General Linguistics*, ed. George Bailly and Albert Reidinger, trans. Wade Baskin (New York: McGraw-Hill, 1959).

sacks full of objects to hold up in lieu of conversation. Or they close the gap between word and thing by inscribing information on edible wafers which they swallow in hopes of digesting and incorporating knowledge. In his fourth voyage to Houyhnhnm-land, Gulliver will discover creatures whose use of language is so purely expository that they never lie and have no word in their language for lying. They can only approximate the concept with the phrase 'saying the Thing which was not'. Gulliver, however, already has acquired experience with this concept in Lilliput.

Swift draws attention to language's multiple effects in several ways. He constructs the Lilliputian language with sound combinations that sit oddly in – and with rhythms that resist the iambic patterns familiar to – the ears of English speakers. The Emperor's long tongue-twisting name, contrary to Gulliver's deadpan recital, elicits readerly amusement rather than respect: 'GOLBASTO MOMAREN EVLAME GURDILLO SHEFIN MULLY ULLY GUE' (I, iii, 63). But language, no matter how arbitrary or alien its sounds, exerts force in the world. Gulliver, as noted above, invests a great deal of weight in the word Nardac and believes wrongly that his honorary title will protect him from harm. The written word is equally problematic. Two official documents – one proclaiming the terms of his liberty, and the other, his punishment for treason – are translated for the reader, 'the whole Instrument[s], Word for Word'. The Lilliputian authors of these decrees assume that by articulating the exact terms of Gulliver's freedom and subsequent impeachment, he can be controlled. They never doubt the power of the text over Gulliver: 'the Secretary will [...] read before you the Articles of Impeachment [...] whereby you are condemned to the Loss of your Eyes, which his Majesty's Surgeons will attend [...] by discharging very sharp pointed Arrows into the Balls of your Eyes, as you lie on the Ground' (I, vii, 103). Confidence in the straightforward use of language – for good or ill – is misguided.

Gulliver comes to understand that language's most powerful and disturbing effects come from saying one thing and meaning another. He learns (or perhaps is forced) to interpret, to recognise the deceptiveness of the apparent. His relationship to language parallels his relationship to the Lilliputians. They first appear delicate, attractive, and hospitable because his eyes cannot discern their flaws. On closer inspection, they prove to be coarse, repellent, murderous creatures, concealing plots and ulterior motives. They are not all bad, but they are bad enough. Similarly, Lilliputian language at first seems a means of clarity and new knowledge, a medium that Gulliver can translate 'Word for Word'. But eventually he becomes more astute (students of foreign languages know that 'getting' non-literal meaning takes time) and confronts their practice of concealing truth by saying the thing which is not:

> It was a Custom introduced by this Prince and his Ministry [. . .] that after the Court had decreed any cruel Execution [. . .] the Emperor always made a Speech to his whole Council, expressing his *great Lenity and Tenderness, as Qualities known and confessed by all the World.* This Speech was immediately published through the Kingdom; nor did any thing terrify the People so much as those Encomiums on his Majesty's Mercy; because it was observed, that the more these Praises were enlarged and insisted on, the more inhuman was the Punishment, and the Sufferer more innocent. (I, vii, 103)

Obfuscation denies but ultimately cannot suppress the import of the Emperor's speech. By drawing attention to the manipulation of words, Swift also draws attention to the larger paradox that frames his narrative and has led to centuries of critical debate about the meaning of *Gulliver's Travels*. If humans were prevented from (or incapable of) saying the thing which is not, there would be no falsehood. But there also would be no imaginary voyages. The instability of language contains both liabilities and opportunities. In Lilliput, Swift introduces a problem, even as he participates in the problem.

Swift's satiric techniques in Lilliput derive from the mutually reinforcing insights that result from the interaction between two narrative components: on one hand, the fantasy world of miniature and fixed measure (in which size is of paramount importance, and a drurr can never be anything but a fourteenth of an inch); on the other, the size-indifferent medium of language. The captivating fiction of an Englishman stepping cautiously through the streets of a little town, lifting its inhabitants gently into his hand, feeling embarrassment at his imposition of excretory waste onto their flowery landscape, trying to help with feats of strength and courage – this fantasy must be appreciated as a well-crafted and meticulously controlled effect of language, designed to contain the satirist's anger at the failures of the world. Language (Swift reminds us), the medium through which this world can be represented and critiqued, is tricky and potentially volatile. If signifiers and signifieds were truly stabilised, there would be neither satire nor irony. The satirist's frustration at the world would have no vent. Like Gulliver's occasional impulse to crush a fistful of 'diminutive Mortals' and dash them to the ground, violence lies just under the surface of Lilliput's most pleasing attributes, and also under the disarming strategies of the satirist's ironic language that dispels the deceptive charms of the small. By the end of the first voyage, readers have weathered painful truths, and are forewarned about the challenges of navigating journeys to come.

A Voyage to Brobdingnag

Nicholas Seager

Gulliver's second voyage reverses the difference of scale between the traveller and his hosts from his first voyage, and after residing in a land of miniature people engaged in momentous affairs he enters a world of giants occupied with trivial things. The satire in 'A Voyage to Brobdingnag' is more general than in 'A Voyage to Lilliput', yet the reflections on Brobdingnag's constitution and customs develop the narrative's earlier criticisms of English politics and society. The positive example of the King of Brobdingnag balances somewhat the almost entirely negative satire of Part I: there are, at least potentially, solutions to the political self-interest, venality, and vindictiveness that characterised Lilliput and, by association, England. Swift's focus remains on man in society, whereas in the third and fourth voyages his attention turns to human nature in the abstract. Gulliver's smallness in Brobdingnag is of course moral as well as physical. In Lilliput, he is a humanitarian hero who refuses to be an instrument of tyranny and maintains a wry attitude to the captious Lilliputians before falling victim to their jealousy and ingratitude. But in Brobdingnag Gulliver compensates for his littleness in ways the first voyage has preemptively condemned, with risible bravado and contemptible self-aggrandisement. He puffs himself up while Swift scales him down. His ignominious spell as a freak show is hardly improved upon when he again becomes that odious thing, a courtier. Gulliver's normative perspective is mostly restored in Part III, where again he is for the most part morally superior to the inhabitants of the worlds he visits; but our total alienation from his perspective in Part IV is anticipated by the ironic treatment accorded him in Part II, in which he is more the object than the agent of the satire. This chapter explains how Swift unsettles notions of human superiority within the order of creation, undercuts human dignity at the physical and moral levels, and extends his ideas about ineluctable human corruption to political systems.

'A Creature who had no sort of Consequence'

Towards the end of Part I, ship's surgeon turned Lilliputian courtier, military hero, improvisatory fireman, and political exile, Lemuel Gulliver, reports that once back in England he 'made a considerable Profit by shewing my Cattle to many Persons of Quality' (I, viii, 112). He refers to 'six Cows and two Bulls alive, with as many Yews and Rams', given him by the King of Blefuscu, which Gulliver imports to Britain and breeds (I, viii, 110). These acquisitions even aid Gulliver's credibility: rescued at sea after departing Blefuscu, he reports that the ship's captain 'thought I was raving, and that the Dangers I underwent had disturbed my Head; whereupon I took my black Cattle and Sheep out of my Pocket, which, after great Astonishment, clearly convinced him of my Veracity' (I, viii, 111). Before embarking on his second voyage – 'condemned by Nature and Fortune to an active and restless Life' (II, i, 117) – Gulliver sells this cattle, minus those he gives to the captain and one which is eaten by a rat, for 'six Hundred Pounds' (I, viii, 112). Gulliver, a veteran of trading voyages to the Levant and West Indies, where he would have witnessed slavery (I, i, 31–2), had casually asked the King of Blefuscu if he could take 'a Dozen of the Natives' back to England, but when his proposal to convert people into property and forcibly transport them across the globe is rejected, he settles for the livestock (I, viii, 110).

Among the giants, Gulliver, like his miniature sheep, is a commodity and exhibition item. He is perceived as 'a strange Animal', 'carried about for a Monster', 'exposed for Money as a publick Spectacle to the meanest of the People', and eventually sold to the Queen (II, ii, 136–7). Swift draws on contemporaneous accounts of popular freak shows, at which human 'prodigies' were put on display.[1] In Swift's view, these entertainments merely diverted an ignorant, prurient public and enriched the unscrupulous. As well as an indictment of modern commercialism, Gulliver's treatment probes the limits of the human because in Part II his species identity is cast in doubt, as it will be again in Part IV. Whereas the Lilliputians appeared as scaled-down humans to Gulliver, and they regarded him anatomically and legally as a person ('*Man* Mountain'), his diminutive size in Brobdingnagian eyes initially registers as a difference of species which sanctions maltreatment. His 'Master', the farmer, at first regards Gulliver as 'a small dangerous Animal', to be handled 'in such a Manner that it shall not be able either to scratch or to bite him; as I my

---

[1] Dennis Todd, 'The Hairy Maid at the Harpsichord: Some Speculations on the Meaning of *Gulliver's Travels*', *TSLL*, 34 (1992), 239–83.

self have sometimes done with a *Weasel* in *England* (II, i, 125). The farmer places Gulliver 'upon all four', assuming that this 'little Creature' plucked from a field is a quadruped (II, i, 126). Gulliver stands up, both to demonstrate that he is not a crawling creature and that he does not intend to run away, his first step towards domestication. Animal analogies then abound. The farmer's wife when she first encounters Gulliver 'screamed and ran back as Women in *England* do at the Sight of a Toad or a Spider', before she sees how 'tame and gentle' Gulliver is, 'and by Degrees grew extreamly tender of me' (II, i, 127; II, ii, 136). Paradoxically, Gulliver's re-establishment of his personhood, his right to a treatment better than that of a beast, requires total compliance – he becomes a 'Creature' that would 'do whatever it was bid' – which makes him a pet and even a 'Slave' (II, ii, 136; II, iii, 142).

Violence towards smaller, weaker species is normalised in Part II. Invoking tropes of savage cannibals derived from voyage literature, Gulliver fears being eaten as 'a Morsel in the Mouth of the first among these enormous Barbarians who should happen to seize me' (II, i, 124). However, the only adventure of this sort comes when the farmer's baby, regarding him as a new 'Play-thing', has a brief taste, which is Gulliver's comeuppance for the moment in Part I when he pretended to be about to eat a Lilliputian (II, i, 130; I, ii, 47). Later dropped in a bowl of cream, then wedged up to his waist in a marrowbone, Gulliver seems constantly in peril of being eaten by giants whose ingestion he describes so graphically. Notwithstanding his notion, confuted by his experiences, that 'human Creatures are observed to be more Savage and cruel in Proportion to their Bulk' (II, i, 124), wanton violence towards smaller species is as much a part of a mindset that the European traveller brings with him than what he actually encounters in Brobdingnag: a more systematic and commercially driven exploitation. He expects the farmer's son 'would dash me against the Ground, as we usually do any little hateful Animal' (II, i, 125), which is we recall how Gulliver was tempted to treat the Lilliputians, never mind English vermin. Assuming that children are 'naturally' cruel to 'Sparrows, Rabbits, young Kittens, and Puppy-Dogs', Gulliver adopts out of prudence a deferential attitude to stave off further malevolence when the farmer's son is chastised for aggressive behaviour: like an indulgent and benignant adult guest demonstrating magnanimity, the six-inch-tall Gulliver intervenes to avert the boy's punishment (II, i, 128). He is then gently stroked as a docile pet. His capacity for negotiation is part of Gulliver's gradual humanisation in Brobdingnag – his hosts (like those in Part IV) become convinced he is rational. His actions also differentiate

Gulliver from animals and consolidate species hierarchies: he shows no fear to a cat (domestic) and kills rats (vermin) and wasps (pests). Even humiliations such as the later monkey abduction affirm his humanity: it is funny to his companions because Gulliver is *not* a monkey, whereas the usually mirthless Houyhnhnms' laughter at Gulliver's assault by an amorous Yahoo originates in his denial of affinity with that species and its being proven by her attraction. His acceptance as a person in Brobdingnag makes the revelations of Part IV especially traumatic because Gulliver cannot assimilate to Houyhnhnm-land, as he does elsewhere, by learning the language of the dominant species and demonstrating a basic similarity of bodily form.

Before Gulliver establishes his personhood, however, his 'Master' realises that exhibiting him promises to be lucrative, and he is treated as an object, a clockwork automaton, toy, trinket, or miniature.[2] His robotic performance of a gruelling soldierly drill makes a mockery of his military heroics in Part I (II, ii, 138–9). His usage in these plebeian entertainments is on a continuum with that of a non-human animal. Gulliver gradually demonstrates that he is bipedal, rational, verbal, and that his clothes are manufactured rather than 'some kind of Covering that Nature had given me', as the Houyhnhnms will also assume (II, i, 126). Nevertheless, he still struggles for recognition as a person, with the attendant rights and dignities. The advertisement for his 'Hundred diverting Tricks' identifies Gulliver as 'resembling an human Creature', decisively not *being* one (II, ii, 138); he is touted as 'a strange Animal [. . .] exactly shaped in every Part like a human Creature; which it likewise imitated in all its Actions' (II, ii, 136). 'A Voyage to Brobdingnag' is in certain ways an 'it-narrative', the modern term for a subgenre of eighteenth-century fiction which critiqued consumerism and individualism by adopting the perspective of an object or animal: things, like Gulliver, which only resemble or mimic persons. It is ironic that Gulliver's first impulse is to give the farmer gold, a paternalistic gesture towards someone of lower social rank, but a transactional mentality that backfires because 'the more my Master got by me, the more insatiable he grew' (II, iii, 142). Gulliver's indignity in the Brobdingnagian freak shows is largely about social class: he objects to being gazed at by 'rude vulgar Folks' (II, ii, 137). Swift's satire is directed at a culturally impoverished society that values idle, vacuous spectacle over edifying intellectual pursuits. Gulliver is infected as well as victimised by this culture. Prompted by the same 'Curiosity' that

---

[2] Melinda Alliker Rabb, *Miniature and the English Imagination: Literature, Cognition, and Small-Scale Culture, 1650–1765* (Cambridge: Cambridge University Press, 2019), 61–2.

brought crowds to see him perform, he is a spectator at a public execution. Gulliver glibly compares the blood spurting from a decapitated body to 'the great *Jet d'Eau* at *Versailles*' (II, v, 169). It is another ostentatious and brutal entertainment devoid of moral edification.

But a more humanising aspect to Gulliver's experience in Brobdingnag is glimpsed in his relationship with his 'little Nurse' Glumdalclitch, who at nine years old is 'not above forty Foot high, being little for her Age' (II, ii, 135). With this infant, more than six times taller than him, Gulliver is for some of the time a living doll which she dresses and undresses, puts to bed, and tethers with 'Leading-Strings' (II, ii, 140). Gulliver avoids the fate of a lamb that her father previously gave to the girl before it went to the slaughter, partly because he demonstrates adequate difference from animals and partly because he exhibits ideal 'companion animal' traits that make him a pet – an animal not to be killed and consumed.[3] Glumdalclitch's ministrations humiliate Gulliver, and in this world to be susceptible to humiliation – a degradation based on knowledge of social norms like dignity and pride denied the individual in her or his treatment – is to be human. He reports his abasement in a typically disarming, matter-of-fact, even cheerful manner: 'This young Girl was so handy, that after I had once or twice pulled off my Cloaths before her, she was able to dress and undress me, although I never gave her that Trouble when she would let me do either myself' (II, ii, 135). The relationship is an eroticised vacillation between Gulliver's paternal and infantile attitudes toward the girl, and between compliance and compulsion. Like a child, Gulliver often resents and resists Glumdalclitch's protective 'Care and Affection' precisely until it is removed; when whisked away by an eagle he misses her more after 'one single Hour' than he apparently does his family back in England after months away (II, ii, 136; II, viii, 206). A relationship which threatens to strip Gulliver of his humanity actually affirms it.

'The Dignity of human Kind'

Overall, Gulliver recuperates his personhood in Brobdingnag, but whether the gain is worthwhile is questionable given the 'great foundation of Misanthropy' on which Swift professed his *Travels* is erected (*Correspondence*, III, 607). Gulliver ends up longing to be not human but Houyhnhnm, and even before his disenchantment with his own

---

[3] Ann Cline Kelly, 'Gulliver as Pet and Pet Keeper: Talking Animals in Book 4', *ELH*, 74 (2007), 323–49.

species in Part IV, people provoke immense disgust at the physical level in Brobdingnag.[4] The first two voyages are exercises in defamiliarising and deriding the human form, undercutting 'the Dignity of human Kind' that Gulliver invokes (II, viii, 203). The puny anatomies of the Lilliputians make ridiculous their pretensions to grandeur, and Gulliver is aware in Part I of his vulnerability – to penetration, mutilation, and privation. In Brobdingnag, Gulliver is even more alert to his physical fragility, and his struggle for social acceptance is repeatedly undercut because his size, married with his outsized pretensions, exposes him to 'ridiculous and troublesome Accidents' (II, v, 163). His being carried about by a spaniel, attacked by a kite, and ignored by smaller birds 'as if no Creature at all were near them' reinforces the fact that Gulliver has lost something of his position of precedence in the order of creation: to animals, he is prey or play, certainly no predator (II, v, 166). Gulliver's comical encounters with other species are either hushed up to preserve a dignity which does not seem worth the effort, or a creature that proved troublesome to him is executed to reinforce human superiority. Gulliver's bluster about defending himself, sword drawn, against a monkey 'as large as an Elephant', and which only wanted to coddle him anyway, provokes 'loud Laughter' among his Brobdingnagian hosts, leading Gulliver to 'reflect how vain an Attempt it is for a Man to endeavour doing himself Honour among those who are out of all Degree of Equality or Comparison with him' (II, v, 173–4). Gulliver pathetically affirms his identity as a 'Man'. The unfortunate monkey, meanwhile, is executed.

The satire is directed against bodies like Gulliver's and the dwarf's that are too small and against ones that are too large. Gulliver sees everyday objects and people as though through a microscope. Swift taps into contemporary satires directed against microscopists and, in another kind of objectification, makes Gulliver himself a kind of portable microscope akin to those carried around as 'toys' by fashionable folk in Swift's day.[5] By concentrating on the hero's acute perception of enlarged women's appearances, 'A Voyage to Brobdingnag' dovetails with Swift's poems that focus on the female body as a grotesque site of simultaneous attraction and repulsion. In *The Lady's Dressing-Room* (1732), for example, the prurient Strephon's invasion of Celia's closet is punished by his exposure to her dirty clothes, discarded cosmetics,

---

[4] Since the eighteenth century the charge has been levelled that Swift 'was unwilling to lose an opportunity of debasing and ridiculing his own species'. The accusation is usually levelled at Part IV, but Orrery's words here are directed against Part II. John Boyle, Earl of Orrery, *Remarks on the Life and Writings of Dr. Jonathan Swift, Dean of St. Patrick's, Dublin* (1752), 137.

[5] Deborah Needleman Armintor, 'The Sexual Politics of Microscopy in Brobdingnag', *SEL*, 47 (2007), 619–40.

and malodorous bodily residue. Like Strephon, Gulliver harbours unrealistic conceptions of women. He is particularly fixated on Brobdingnagian breasts, first when the farmer's baby is nursed with a 'monstrous Breast', which 'stood prominent about six Foot [. . .] so varified with Spots, Pimples and Freckles, that nothing could appear more nauseous', leading Gulliver to reflect on the importance of perspective in evaluations of beauty and the risk that instruments like 'a magnifying Glass' distort, and not merely enhance, perception (II, i, 130–1).

Swift's satire on empirical science and its optical technology, then, is directed against the female form; but as in *The Lady's Dressing Room* the satire also falls on the male voyeur who idealises the female body and ignores its materiality. Strephon's fright at the sight of Celia's 'magnifying glass' is caused by his own reflection – he is startled by 'the visage of a giant' – before the bizarre speculation about Celia using this mirror to pluck live worms out of her nose, an image belonging to the twisted male imagination rather than the reality of feminine beauty routines.[6] Gulliver's reactions to these huge bodies partly sound like a scientist looking for an analogy or system of measurement (he is, after all, a surgeon and benefactor of the Royal Society through his gift of giant wasp stings), and partly like a Freudian case study. At one point he records an odd fantasy of surreptitious immolation: 'There was a Woman with a Cancer in her Breast, swelled to a monstrous Size, full of Holes, in two or three of which I could have easily crept, and covered my whole Body' (II, iv, 159). The sexual potential in this is realised when the maids of honour at Court indulge 'the pleasure of seeing and touching me'; but even these younger, disease-free bodies nauseate Gulliver:

> They would often strip me naked from Top to Toe, and lay me at full Length in their Bosoms; wherewith I was much disgusted; because, to say the Truth, a very offensive Smell came from their Skins; [. . .] they would strip themselves to the Skin, and put on their Smocks in my Presence, while I was placed on their Toylet [dressing table], directly before their naked Bodies; which, I am sure, to me was very far from being a tempting Sight, or from giving me any other Motions [i.e. 'emotions' but with bawdy potential too] than those of Horror and Disgust. Their Skins appeared so coarse and uneven, so variously coloured when I saw them near, with a Mole here and there as broad as a Trencher, and hairs hanging from it thicker than Packthreads; to say nothing further concerning the rest of their Persons. (II, v, 166–8)

---

[6] Jonathan Swift, *The Lady's Dressing Room*, lines 59–68, in *The Complete Poems*, ed. Pat Rogers (London: Penguin, 1983), 450.

The trencher and pack-thread similes echo scenes of politicians performing absurd feats to secure preferment in Lilliput (I, iii, 57). What links these episodes is a lack of dignity associated with the body. Just as for Strephon, Gulliver's access to this feminine social space is a privilege that becomes a punishment: 'The handsomest among these Maids of Honour, a pleasant frolicksome Girl of sixteen, would sometimes set me astride upon one of her Nipples; with many other Tricks, wherein the Reader will excuse me for not being over particular' (II, v, 168). Gulliver, objectified now as an unwilling sex toy, is caught between compulsion to describe what he experiences and a reticence concerning what else ('many other Tricks') he is subjected to.

The satire on scientific speculation which becomes the essence of Part III is anticipated by the virtuosi who examine Gulliver in Brobdingnag:

> After much Debate, they concluded unanimously that I was only *Relplum Scalcath*, which is interpreted literally *Lusus Naturæ*; a Determination exactly agreeable to the Modern Philosophy of *Europe*: whose Professors, disdaining the old Evasion of *occult Causes*, whereby the Followers of *Aristotle* endeavour in vain to disguise their Ignorance; have invented this wonderful Solution of all Difficulties, to the unspeakable Advancement of human Knowledge. (II, iii, 146–7)

Designating Gulliver a 'freak of nature' in Latin may sound scientific but it is not scientifically sound. It is as much an evasion as the Aristotelian occultism that the modern philosophers deem ignorance. When in Glubbdubdrib Gulliver presents Aristotle's ghost with revisions to his system by 'moderns' like Descartes and Gassendi, the philosopher admits his mistakes, acknowledges that he, like all, proceeded on the basis of conjecture, not certitude, and prophecies a short shelf-life for the current crop of natural philosophers: 'New Systems of Nature were but new Fashions, which would vary in every Age; and even those who pretend to demonstrate them from Mathematical Principles, would flourish but a short Period of Time, and be out of Vogue when that was determined' (III, viii, 296). In the third voyage, Swift targets the self-assurance of the New Science, particularly the Royal Academy, as a manifestation of modern hubris. Whereas natural and moral philosophers in Brobdingnag limit themselves 'to what may be useful in Life' (II, vii, 195), the Laputans go to an extreme of abstraction and uselessness. The implication of his examination by the virtuosi, then, is that Gulliver is of zero use and so not worthy of more careful classification than 'freak'.

From the yokels who gawk at him on market day to the scientists who examine him, the Brobdingnagians' sense of the normal is unperturbed by the appearance on their shores of a man one-twelfth their height: to them, Gulliver is merely an oddity, initially classed as an animal and only gradually, equivocally, accommodated to the human. All in all, the Brobdingnagians seem oblivious, insulated, incurious. By contrast, Gulliver soon takes their outlook as normative, adopting their perspective again and again, seeing things through a giant's eyes, such as rating huge distances as small ('easy Journies of not above seven or eight Score Miles a Day' (II, ii, 140)). He is so immersed in their way of looking that even after nine months among people of his own size he sees his countrymen as pygmies when he finally arrives home. (In a similar manner, his sensitivity to smelly Yahoos is magically heightened after Part IV.) In light of how Gulliver reports on England while in Brobdingnag, exposing his homeland to the contempt of the King, his distorted perspective of the English as 'little' is entirely suitable.

'Thinking on poor *England*'

Gulliver's first two voyages enforce comparisons between the physical body and abstract qualities: authority, ambition, bravery, beauty, and so on. Most of these ideals can be made to appear ridiculous or repellent when magnified or miniaturised. As the King of Brobdingnag – 'a Prince possessed of every Quality which procures Veneration, Love, and Esteem' – says to Gulliver: 'How contemptible a Thing was human Grandeur, which could be mimicked by such diminutive Insects as I' (II, vii, 193; I, iii, 150). Reason and benevolence, embodied by the King, may be the only qualities that survive the process of enlargement without seeming ludicrous. Accordingly, the misuse of reason and misapplication or absence of benevolence are major themes of the third and fourth voyages. Embittered against his own kind at the end of the fourth voyage, Gulliver concedes that among human cultures 'the least corrupted are the *Brobdingnagians*, whose wise Maxims in Morality and Government, it would be our Happiness to observe' (IV, xi, 438). This is an equivocal compliment because the Brobdingnagians are only the best among corrupted Yahoos. It is also an insight that Gulliver missed when he debated statecraft with the King, finding his principles 'narrow' and dismissing the ethical system he encounters in Brobdingnagian literature, which, like *Gulliver's Travels*, 'treats of the Weakness of Human kind' and regards the species as inherently degenerate (II, vii, 193, 198–9).

In the dialogues with the King, Swift extends the idea of human fallibility and corruption to political institutions. He does so by exposing

the distortions of Gulliver's perspective, and so the level-headed, admirable
traveller of Part I becomes a true gull, a blinkered patriot, in Part II. Gulliver
takes the invitation to give an 'exact an Account of the Government of
England' as an opportunity to eulogise his homeland (II, vi, 179). His
descriptions of England are saturated with irony, such as the account of 'an
English Parliament' comprising Commoners '*freely* picked and culled out by
the People themselves, for their great Abilities, and Love of their Country';
bishops 'distinguished by the Sanctity of their Lives'; and Lords who were the
'Followers of their most renowned Ancestors, whose Honour had been the
Reward of their Virtue, from which their Posterity were never once known to
degenerate' (II, vi, 180–1). No wonder that Gulliver, still a lover of mankind at
this stage, dismisses the Brobdingnagian treatises on human degeneracy.
Similar condemnation of English politics via Gulliver's pygmy praise is
directed at standing armies, electoral fraud, financial dishonesty, and overseas
colonisation. *Gulliver's Travels* is a 'Country' satire written in opposition to
the Hanoverian Court, the prime minister Sir Robert Walpole, and the Whig
ascendancy over which Walpole and George I presided. Whereas 'A Voyage
to Lilliput' operated through topical allusions as 'parallel history', referring to
political events and figures in a manner easy for Swift to disavow,[7] 'A Voyage
to Brobdingnag' speaks directly about England, cleverly keeping its criticisms
general enough to avoid repercussions and using an obviously fictitious
outsider to voice them.

The King's scepticism about England is awakened by Gulliver's dis-
simulations and exaggerations – 'laudable Partiality', he terms it (II, vii,
190); 'an admirable Panegyrick', the King sneers (II, vi, 188). The King is
a searching inquisitor, alluding to the 'Answers I have with much Pains
wringed from you', whereas Gulliver admits reluctance even to report the
King's 'numberless Enquiries and Objections' as they nullify his claims
that the English polity is perfect (II, vi, 189, 184). Just after professing his
'extreme Love of Truth', Gulliver boasts that he 'artfully eluded many of
[the King's] Questions; and gave to every Point a more favourable turn by
many Degrees than the strictness of Truth would allow' (II, vii, 190).
Gulliver gives a similarly biased account of England to his Houyhnhnm
master in Part IV ('in what I said of my Countrymen, I *extenuated* their
Faults as much as I durst [. . .] and upon every Article, gave as *favourable*
a Turn as the Matter would bear' (IV, vii, 389)), again just after categorical
professions of his candour and veracity, and amidst praise for a species that
purportedly cannot dissemble. Gulliver has become a wholly unreliable

---

[7] J. A. Downie, *Jonathan Swift: Political Writer* (London: Routledge & Kegan Paul, 1984), 274–5.

narrator, a 'prostitute Flatterer', as Swift called him in a letter, 'whose chief Study is to extenuate the Vices, and magnify the Virtues of Mankind, and perpetually dins our Ears with the Praises of his Country, in the midst of Corruptions'.[8] It is significant that in this letter, Swift generalises Gulliver's bias to humanity as a whole, not just his own nation: the satire is topical, but it also targets Gulliver's ridiculous optimism about mankind. The King's faux naïve challenges to Gulliver's embroidered account are not party-specific, which is in keeping with his benign derision when he asks Gulliver whether he is a Whig or a Tory. We may say of the King, as Gulliver says of himself, that he 'meddle[s] not the least with any party' (IV, xii, 438). For instance, he asks 'What Qualifications were necessary in those who are to be created new Lords: Whether the Humour of the Prince, a Sum of Money to a Court-Lady, or a Prime Minister, or a Design of strengthening a Party opposite to the public Interest, ever happened to be Motives in those Advancements' (II, vi, 182–3). The King, motivated by a Swiftian mistrust of all 'Mystery, Refinement, and Intrigue' in politics (II, vii, 194), brings to this consideration a vigilance that would guard against corruption were it present in England. The particular referents for the enquiry about 'new Lords' are the creation of twelve peers on New Year's Eve 1711 by Queen Anne's Tory ministry, headed by Swift's friends Oxford and Bolingbroke, to overturn the Whig majority in the Lords ('I don't like the expedient', Swift confessed at the time (Journal to Stella, 358)), and more recently George I's creation of fourteen new peers to restore the Whig advantage after his succession in 1714. The political art of the satire is Swift's ability to mount a patently partisan attack on the present ministry as a succession of challenges to modes of government that any reasonable reader in 1726, Whig or Tory, would regard as misguided.

The King's interrogation of Gulliver is a condemnation of the political system under Walpole and he appraises the last century of English history as 'an Heap of Conspiracies, Rebellions, Murders, Massacres, Revolutions, Banishments; the very worst Effects that Avarice, Faction, Hypocrisy, Perfidiousness, Cruelty, Rage, Madness, Hatred, Envy, Lust, Malice, or Ambition could produce' (II, vi, 188). Political corruption is thus not just a particular set of modern circumstances but an expression of vitiated human nature in all places. Even Brobdingnag, despite flourishing under a benevolent monarch, is susceptible to 'the Weakness of Human kind' (II, vii, 197–8). The King's synopsis of the contention for power between the people, nobility, and crown in his own realm implies that a more detailed

---

[8] Swift to Henrietta Howard, 17 November 1726, Correspondence, III, 54.

account of Brobdingnag's recent past would replicate the bad qualities the King imputes to the English, 'the same Disease, to which the whole Race of Mankind is Subject' (II, vii, 200–1). Though free, unlike the English, from external enemies, the Brobdingnagians still need a sizeable army to preserve order at home, albeit modelled as a voluntary militia rather than a professional standing army. The King discerns in the English polity Gulliver describes 'some Lines of an Institution, which in its Original might have been tolerable; but these half erased, and the rest wholly blurred and blotted by Corruptions' (II, vi, 188). In Glubbdubdrib, Gulliver hears about cultural degeneracy in terms that suggest a cyclical view of civilisation (III, viii, 298–304). Brobdingnag is an ideal polity only because it is at the apex of the cycle. As a society, in many respects, it is a grubby, violent, tawdry, anti-intellectual place, and this fact frames the King's political idealism so as to compromise it, which makes the satire in Part II hardly more stable than that in Part IV. But anyone who thought problems in Lilliput were particular to that society, or the England it stands for, were forced to recognise in Brobdingnag that human corruption mars all human institutions.

Gulliver's attempts to ingratiate and distinguish himself at Court have so far been ridiculous (leaping cowpats, offering to wrestle a dwarf five times his height), entirely befitting the satire against courtiers in Part I and Part III. Gulliver boasts that he has 'become a great favourite', is 'known and esteemed among the greatest Officers', and maintains the absurd notion that he 'might live to do his Majesty some signal Service' (II, vi, 179). He has fallen into the servility condemned in 'A Voyage to Lilliput', but whereas then his rectitude was construed as disloyalty, now his proffered service is regarded as inhumane: he offers the King gunpowder. Gulliver refused in Lilliput to be 'an Instrument of bringing a free and brave People into Slavery' by spearheading an invasion of Blefuscu, but in Brobdingnag he tries to curry favour by offering the King the means to 'destroy the whole Metropolis, if ever it should pretend to dispute his absolute Commands' (II, vii, 192). The oppression of a populace through force anticipates the measures employed by the Emperor of Laputa, who weaponises the floating island to subjugate the Balnibarbians, not to mention the proposed extermination of the Yahoos. Gulliver, we have seen, spends large portions of Part II giving his disgusted responses to enlarged but intact and living bodies which he sees at close range; now he gives manic and gleeful descriptions of bodies mutilated by modern war machinery seen from afar. Swift conveys revulsion at the depersonalisation of war through technology that can produce rapid carnage: the pacifist king is 'struck with Horror' at Gulliver's proposals and thus 'humanity' resides with a race of giants whose ruler regards actual humans as 'little odious Vermin' (II, vi, 189).

Gulliver's repeated classification by Brobdingnagians as an animal risks returning his speciological class to 'non-human', an ontological threat that his conversation with the King staved off. Their exchange of cultural values arrogates to Gulliver not just human status but an exalted standing as a kind of ambassador at Court, someone trusted to report the norms of a distant land. All this is shattered when the murderous and tyrannical ideology of Gulliver's own culture provokes the King's horror, and Gulliver goes from being perceived and addressed as a little man to being labelled, along with his whole species, as an 'impotent and grovelling [. . .] Insect' (II, vii, 192). The colonial gaze is turned on the technologically more advanced European. However, so is the colonial experience: Gulliver comes to feel again the dehumanising effects of his predicament when the King speculates that he could be bred (like the Blefuscudian livestock). Gulliver's response, despite all the ways in which he has been derided in the voyage, is genuinely pathetic because it is the product of recent experience in the freak show: 'I think I should rather have died than undergone the Disgrace of leaving a Posterity to be kept in Cages, like tame Canary Birds; and perhaps in time sold about the Kingdom to Persons of Quality for Curiosities'. This prospect 'ill became the Dignity of human Kind', says Gulliver (II, viii, 202). The anti-slavery sentiment of Gulliver's words, as well as at the famous fulmination against the '*modern Colony*' in Part IV (IV, xii, 441), is negated neither by Gulliver's forgetting his own plan to take Blefuscudians home nor the improbable biology of his 'leaving a Posterity' in Brobdingnag. At the close of Part II, there is still just about such a thing as human dignity, predicated on a human–animal polarity and hierarchy which is threatened but affirmed in 'A Voyage to Brobdingnag'. This sets up its more radical explosion in Part IV.

CHAPTER 12

A Voyage to Laputa, Balnibarbi, Luggnagg, &c.

Barbara M. Benedict

Part III of *Gulliver's Travels* stands as a comprehensive yet compressed satire of the abuses of Modern learning. It encompasses natural philosophy; impotent and antisocial virtuosi; British tyranny and the oppression of Ireland and the colonies; British political, cultural, and social corruption; antiquarianism; Modern education; and the vanity of human wishes. In the character of Lord Munodi, Swift sketches himself, the despised outsider who maintains the old ways; in the anagram of Tribnia, he ropes the reader into complicity with the mad wordsmithery of Modern literature. Through a chain of five journeys that Gulliver takes from one magical island world to another, Swift lambasts the entire Whiggish project to improve on the natural world given by God and the cultural world built by the Ancients.

Whiggish and secular religious abuses open and close Part III. Captured on a trading expedition by pirates, Gulliver encounters an English-hating, blasphemous Dutchman and his honourable Japanese Captain. This contrast between the Protestant but impious Dutch and the merciful, pagan Japanese reintroduces the themes of xenophobia, prejudice, and religious factionalism that appear in the Lilliput court and will dominate Houyhnhnm-land. Swift's emphasis on trade over morality also reinscribes the motif of exploitative and soulless colonialism that studs the book, notably in the convention of 'trampling upon the Crucifix' demanded by the Japanese from the willing Dutch as a condition of trade, and in Luggnagg, Japan's trading partner, where Gulliver must crawl 'upon my Belly' and '*lick the Dust*' before the King (III, xi, 324; III, ix, 306–7). These incidents link Whiggish greed with political corruption.

However, once released, off Gulliver ventures in a small canoe with a sail, paddles, and eight days' worth of provisions, a journey that resembles Robinson Crusoe's trip around the Island of Despair and foreshadows Gulliver's banishment from Houyhnhnm-land in a Yahoo-skin canoe at the end of the *Travels*. The voyages proper begin.

The Voyage to Laputa: Politics and Virtuosi

Laputa, the first inhabited place that Gulliver encounters, satirises both British imperial tyranny, particularly over Ireland, and the quantifying bent of Modern philosophers. Swift sees these as related because both entail an arrogant autocracy. Fully three-fifths of Part III take place on the island of Laputa and the continent of Balnibarbi below it, and thus Modern natural philosophy draws the lion's share of Swift's satire. The island city of Laputa, a sheer, shining, flat-bottomed constellation, manufactured from diamond, floats above the continent of Balnibarbi (Figure 12.1). The Balnibarbian workers toil the land, subordinate to the whims of the Laputans above and subject to Laputan punishment, since the Laputans can manipulate Laputa at will to hover over Balnibarbi and block sun and rain should the oppressed Balnibarnians attempt insurrection. From below, the Laputans receive 'Wine and Victuals' while the people send up 'Petitions', strung on weighted threads that the Laputans lower from their literally superior Island (III, ii. 233). In literalising the cliché of oppression – force from above on the hapless beneath – Swift employs the satirical technique he uses throughout *Gulliver's Travels* of rendering metaphors physical: for example, by making the petty King of Lilliput as tiny in size as in soul, and the big-hearted King of Brobdingnag huge. This technique also inspires many of Swift's images: the 'Globes and Spheres and Mathematical Instruments' that litter the King's table, for example, symbolise both the Laputans' otherworldly preoccupations and the diversion of political attention from the state to abstract matters literally above the heads of mere plebs.

Laputa is peopled by fanatical mathematicians representing the Modern philosophers whom Swift saw as reducing the Ancients' moral and social values to numbers, figures and fractured facts. Habited in clothes embroidered with celestial and musical images, these mathematicians build by theory not practice; their garments represent their quantifying obsessions with the cycle of the spheres and the abstract relations of music. Superstitious and fractious, the Laputans believe in astrology, although 'they are ashamed to own it publickly', and suffer constant apprehension that a comet will incinerate the earth, or that 'Effluvia' will encrust the sun and turn it dark (III, ii, 235–6). This mockery of astrological prediction and unmoored imagination revisits Swift's impish Bickerstaff papers (1709), in which he impersonates an astrologer, and stems from Swift's association of science with a mechanical, deistic displacement of God. Here, the secret astrological 'Faith' of the Laputan mathematicians indicates their absence of a moral centre (III, ii, 235).

Swift also represents as physical traits the Laputans' intellectual obsessions, ranging from the self to the spheres. Gulliver reports, 'Their Heads were all reclined either to the Right, or the Left; one of their Eyes turned inward, and the other directly up to the Zenith' (III, ii, 226). With one eye sunk in self-contemplation, and the other surveying the stars, they cannot see what is before them. As with the microscopic Lilliputians and the telescopic Brobdingnagians, distorted perspective indicates moral distortion. Scorning the ways of the Ancients and mesmerised by mathematical formulations, the Laputans cut their food into geometrical shapes – a fine example of their doomed attempt to force physical nature into ideal shapes. Similarly, when they make clothes for Gulliver, they calculate them by abstract navigational and mathematical formulae instead of by a plain tape-measure, so that the clothes do not fit. Again, they design their houses by theoretical 'Instructions [. . .] too refined for the Intellectuals of their Workmen', instead of by 'practical Geometry; which they despise as vulgar and mechanick': predictably, the buildings are all off-kilter (III, ii, 234). The Laputans' 'intense Speculations' result in a collapse of social context and consequent practical dysfunction (III, ii, 227).

Indeed, so detached are these philosophers from empirical and social reality that they 'neither can speak, nor attend to the Discourses of others' without the help of 'Flappers' (III, ii, 227). These are servants who prompt them to sociability by batting them gently with pea-filled bladders on their mouths when they are to speak, their ears when they are to listen, and their eyes when they are to see to walk:

> This *Flapper* is likewise employed diligently to attend his Master in his Walks, and upon Occasion to give him a soft Flap on his Eyes; because he is always so wrapped up in Cogitation, that he is in manifest Danger of falling down every Precipice, and bouncing his Head against every Post; and in the Streets, of jostling others, or being himself jostled into the Kennel. (III, ii, 228)

This portrait of Laputan distractedness recalls depictions of the speculative philosopher, a stereotypical figure of fun, especially since Thomas Shadwell invented the boasting, buffoonish Sir Nicholas Gimcrack in his comedy *The Virtuoso* (1676). Lost in theory, the Laputans are baffled and even endangered by 'the common Actions and Behaviour of Life': while imagining that they are mastering nature's laws, they fail to register the immediate reality (III, ii, 234). By describing the Laputans' clumsiness, competitiveness and self-absorption as they shoulder each other into the gutter, Swift represents literally the jostling for position of members of the

Royal Society. Laputans also argue constantly: Gulliver observes that, 'They are very bad Reasoners, and vehemently given to Opposition' for its own sake (III, ii, 234). Here, Swift targets the autodidactic quarrelsomeness of members of the Royal Society, notably the inflammable antiquarian and naturalist Dr John Woodward, whose irascibility was made notorious by his public insults. This disputativeness reappears in the learned disagreements about Gulliver's species by the Brobdingnagian natural philosophers.

Symptomatic of this intellectual abstraction and social detachment is the Laputans' sexual naiveté. This recalls another stereotypical trait of the virtuoso: the perversion – or diversion – of sexual appetite into compensatory intellectual fiddling. The result is a dysfunctional marital life:

> The Women of the Island have Abundance of Vivacity; they contemn their Husbands, and are exceedingly fond of Strangers, whereof there is always a considerable Number from the Continent below, attending at Court [. . .] but [these] are much despised, because they want the same [intellectual] Endowments. Among these the Ladies chuse their Gallants: But the Vexation is, that they act with too much Ease and Security; for the Husband is always so wrapped in Speculation, that the Mistress and Lover may proceed to the greatest Familiarities before his Face, if he be but provided with Paper and Implements, and without his *Flapper* at his Side. (III, ii, 237–8)

Frustrated and lustful, the women escape to the land below (literally and figuratively) for their pleasures. Gulliver illustrates this with the anecdote of the wife of the Laputan prime minister, the 'richest Subject in the Kingdom' and a loving husband, who escaped to Balnibarbi and took up with 'an old deformed Footman' (III, ii, 238). Although he beat her and reduced her to rags, she fled back to him even after being rescued, forgiven and affectionately treated by her husband. 'This may perhaps pass with the Reader rather for an *European* or *English* Story, than for one of a Country so remote', observes Gulliver limpidly, 'But he may please to consider, that the Caprices of Womankind are not limited by any Climate or Nation; and that they are much more uniform than can be easily imagined' (III, ii, 238). While this episode specifically echoes Gulliver's reputed affair with the wife of the Lilliputian Treasurer in Part I, it also alludes to two Ancient beliefs: in women's fabled promiscuity and in the universality of humans' irrational nature.

This broad satire on women sounds a familiar Swiftian note of misogyny. Gulliver characterises women as sexually insatiable, addicted to physical pleasures and incapable of intellectual ones. His own revulsion reprises Swift's persistent critique of women's bodies, desires, and frivolity. This critique runs throughout Swift's work, notably in the grotesque descriptions of the female Brobdingnagians in Part II, who play with Gulliver as a sex toy on their hideously enlarged nipples, and in the besotted female Yahoo who howls for Gulliver in Part IV. Only when seen from a far distance, as Gulliver sees the Lilliputian ladies, do women appear fair. Yet in the mechanistic world of Laputa, women supply the only note of humanity.

The Voyage to Balnibarbi: Natural Philosophy and Modern Languages

Like Laputa, Balnibarbi dramatises the difference between a laudable science that improves the human condition and the fantastical, theoretical science that wastes resources, violates nature, and ignores common sense. Prominent is the implied comparison between derelict Ireland and novelty-mad England. In Barnibarbi's metropolis of Lagado, Gulliver notes the decrepit housing, the city-dwellers who 'walked fast, looked wild, their Eyes fixed, and [. . .] generally in Rags', and a myriad of labourers working the fertile but uncultivated soil in accordance with Modern notions of farming (III, iv, 251). The desperate, half-mad people represent the Irish under British rule, and their soil Ireland under the management of absentee British landlords. In contrast, the estate of the admirable Lord Munodi (signifying 'I hate the world' in Latin and adding a touch of Swiftian self-parody), which employs traditional building and farming methods, is lush and productive. However, even Lord Munodi must bow to Lagado, a code word for London: he confesses that he will have to conform to the Modern method, 'unless he would submit to incur the Censure of Pride, Singularity, Affectation, Ignorance, Caprice; and [. . .] his Majesty's Displeasure' (III, iv, 254). Here, Swift refers to his own exile to Ireland and banishment from political influence under George I. The rhetorical technique of amplification provides a litany of near-synonymous nouns, each denoting a specific vice specifying the particulars of his topic; it also appears in the Brobdingnagian King's excoriating lecture on British vices. The technique works to enlarge and emphasise the subject. Balnibarbi shows that tyranny, modernity, and obstinate innovativeness beggar nature and corrupt culture.

The futility of an ignorant natural philosophy rooted in arrogant new ideas also informs the experiments in the Academy of Projectors in Lagado. Modelled on the Royal Society for the Advancement of Learning that opened in 1660, this Academy of experimentalists was founded by a group of Lagadians who became converted in Laputa to ill-understood mathematics, returned full of contempt for the conventional practices of Balnibarbi, and 'fell into Schemes of putting all Arts, Sciences, Languages, and Mechanicks upon a new Foot' (III, iv, 255). Their experiments range from improving nature to systematising culture. One side of the Academy is devoted to practical science, the other to speculative learning. Despite the variety of the Projectors' practical experiments, all share a basic flaw: each reverses nature, instead of following it; each replaces common sense with contorted reasoning. One attempts to extract 'Sun-Beams out of Cucumbers', another to build houses from the roof down, another 'to calcine Ice into Gunpowder'; still another adjusts a sun dial to a weathercock in order to recalibrate the earth's and moon's orbits to turn with the wind (III, v, 260–3). Their attempts to regularise art similarly employ inappropriate methods and agents: a blind man has his apprentices mix paint colours; an artist strives to make silk from cobwebs. The core problem Swift finds in Modern projects like these is their aim to correct, outdo, or even replace the Creator, God. One Projector epitomises this proud ambition. Called *the universal Artist*, he 'had been Thirty Years employing his Thoughts for the Improvement of human Life', and has fifty men at work in 'two large Rooms full of wonderful Curiosities' (III, v, 265). Their experiments mimic those of the Royal Society: liquefying air, softening marble for pillows, petrifying living horses' hooves to prevent lameness, sowing land with chaff, and breeding naked sheep.

Naturalist Projectors concern themselves with the human body. One, himself projecting a foul stench, receives weekly a pot of 'Ordure' for his work 'to reduce human Excrement to its original Food', and another delivers reverse enemas with 'a large Pair of Bellows' to cure digestive problems (III, v, 260–1; 264). These experiments link thematically with Gulliver's minute descriptions of his own defecation in Part I and the odiferous bodies of the Brobdingnagian women in Part II. They also resonate with the scheme of the 'ingenious Doctor' in the Academy of Projectors who, observing 'a strict Universal Resemblance between the natural and the political Body', proposes to cure political megrims with digestive potions and nostrums (III, vi, 275–6). These experiments express Swift's fascination with human physicality and especially scatology, evident in his 1730s Dressing Room poems. The greater targets, however, are the absurdity of mankind's pride in the human body or in human beauty, which Swift finally eviscerates in the grotesque humanoid Yahoos in Part IV, and, more generally, the secular emphasis on physical, material reality characteristic of the Moderns.

Linguistic improvements, literature, and language itself form a prominent theme throughout the *Travels*. Not only does Gulliver boast of his linguistic prowess, but in each of the voyages he takes note of some particular

vocabulary or usage unique to that culture. This emphasis on the idiosyn-
crasies of modern languages targets Modern education, which replaced
ancient Greek and Latin with Continental tongues. Further, Swift suggests
that the decay of literature was its result. Indeed, in the half of the Academy
of Projectors devoted to speculative science, Gulliver describes several experiments designed to organise literature and language by scientific principles.

In the most ambitious linguistic project, Swift represents visually the
Modern method of turning sense into nonsense by breaking sentences into
words. Here, a Professor aims to improve 'speculative Knowledge by
practical and mechanical Operations' (III, v, 266). Foremost among them
is a device that replaces the 'laborious [. . .] usual Method of attaining to
Arts and Sciences' and enables 'the most ignorant Person at a reasonable
Charge, and with a little bodily Labour, [to] write Books in Philosophy,
Poetry, Politicks, Law, Mathematicks and Theology, without the least
Assistance from Genius or Study' (III, v, 268). This mechanism consists
of a huge, wooden frame strung with wire on which are suspended random
words in rows, written on paper, 'in their several Moods, Tenses, and
Declensions, but without any Order' (III, v, 268). At the Professor's
command, the students then give the rows a quick rotation so that 'the
whole Disposition of the Words was entirely changed'; they pore over the
results until they find 'three or four Words together that might make Part of
a Sentence', which are collected in 'several Volumes in large Folio', ultimately to be pieced together 'to give the World a compleat Body of all Arts
and Sciences' (III, v, 268–9). By illustrating this three-dimensional
Scrabble-like contraption with the only pictorial image in the book – aside
from maps – Swift dramatises the breakdown of literature into formula.
Indeed, the Professor tells Gulliver, 'that he had emptied the whole
Vocabulary into his Frame, and made the strictest Computation of the
general Proportion there is in Books between the Numbers of Particles,
Nouns, and Verbs, and other Parts of Speech' (III, v, 269). The word frame
embodies the Modern enterprise to reduce art to material, to quantify
cultural expression, to drain inspirational creativity and social meaning out
of literature, and so to render it mechanical chance: meaning as roulette.
Gulliver's fascinated precision in describing the device exposes his Whiggish
preoccupation with novelty, invention, and improvement, and reflects his
own, literalistic rhetoric.

In a further linguistic satire of the Moderns, Swift targets the Royal
Society's theory, advocated by its first historian Thomas Sprat, to literalise
and purify language by eschewing metaphor in favour of simple description in plain English. To improve the Balnibarbi language, the Academy's

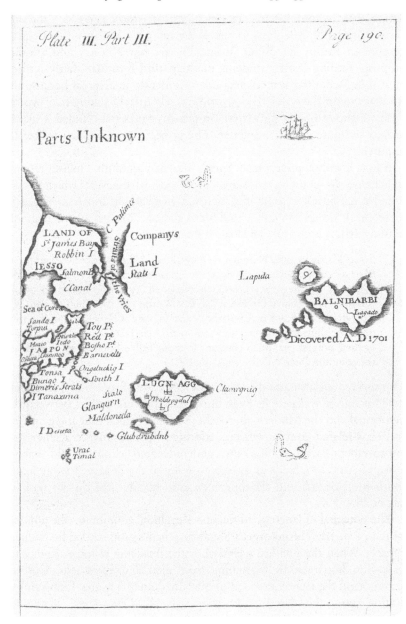

Figure 12.1 Laputa and Balnibarbi, from *The Works of J. S, D.D, D.S.P.D.*, 4 vols. (Dublin: George Faulkner, 1735), volume 3, Bodleian Library, University of Oxford (Bodl. Radcl. e.233)

nationalistic School of Languages includes three more projects. One suggests 'cutting Polysyllables into one, and leaving out Verbs and Participles; because in Reality all things imaginable are but Nouns', and another proposes feeding fasting students mathematical formulae 'fairly written on a thin Wafer' with medicinal ink – evidently ineffectual because the students vomit the wafer (III, v, 270, 273). By literally eating their words, these students embody the material-minded, or material-blinded, Modern project to figure culture as matter. The project, Swift implies, is literally disgusting.

A final linguistic project takes Sprat's ideal ad absurdum. Gulliver reports, 'a Scheme for entirely abolishing all Words whatsoever', which would improve the people's health and lifespans, and abolish unnecessary speech; moreover, it would establish a 'universal Language' to facilitate international relations (III, v, 270, 273). The logic is materialistic:

> Since Words are only Names for *Things*, it would be more convenient for all Men to carry about them, such *Things* as were necessary to express the particular Business they are to discourse on. And this Invention would certainly have taken Place [. . .] if the Women in conjunction with the Vulgar and Illiterate had not threatned to raise a Rebellion, unless they might be allowed the Liberty to speak with their Tongues, after the Manner of their Forefathers: Such constant irreconcileable Enemies to Science are the common People. (III, v, 271)

This project encapsulates the Projectors' rejection of sociability, its preference for things over people. Swift also represents this conflict between the traditional and the Modern approaches to social interaction as a gendered and class-related contest: whereas educated men approve efficiency and improvement, women and the undereducated cling to old habits. However, as often, Swift satirises both poles of the debate: if women and commoners chatter and clamour, men and the educated do not want to talk at all.

The potential of language to foment 'Rebellion' adumbrates the political satire in Part III. This informs a linguistic scheme propounded by Gulliver himself. When the political scientists in the Academy propose diagnosing traitorous Statesmen by examining their diets and excrement, Gulliver recommends the techniques used in the Kingdom of Tribnia. Using amplification again, he describes its people as all 'Discoverers, Witnesses, Informers, Accusers, Prosecutors, Evidences, Swearers [. . .] all under the Colours, the Conduct, and pay of Ministers', who attempt to gain power by libelling rivals (III, vi, 281). Their method is to manufacture hidden meanings in their opponents' correspondence through acrostics and anagrams, or transposing letters to twist ordinary sentences into 'political Meanings' and thus to discover 'Plots and Conspiracies against the Government' (III, vi, 284, 280). 'Artists' employed by these agents interpret denotative plain nouns as metaphors, so that, instead of critiquing the state, art becomes subject to its corruption.

Attentive readers of the *Travels* will already have detected 'Britain' anagrammed in 'Tribnia', and thus have become complicit in the meaning-mongering Swift indicts. Still, Gulliver supplies examples that offer further opportunities for reading meanings into words through a litany of glorious metaphors:

> These papers are delivered to a Set of Artists very dextrous in finding out the mysterious Meanings of Words, Syllables and Letters. For Instance, they can decypher a Close-stool to signify a Privy-Council; a Flock of Geese, a Senate; a lame Dog, an Invader; the Plague, a standing Army; a Buzard, a Minister; the Gout, a High Priest; a Gibbet, a Secretary of State; a Chamber pot, a Committee of Grandees; a Sieve a Court Lady; a Broom, a Revolution; a Mouse-trap, an Employment; a bottomless Pit, the Treasury; a Sink, a C —— t; a Cap and Bells, a Favourite; a broken Reed, a Court of Justice; an empty Tun, a General; a running Sore, the Administration. (III, vi, 282–3)

This plethora of cyphered synonyms constitutes a blistering indictment of British politics that the reader must decode. At the same time, it triumph-antly proclaims the power of metaphor to combine designation and opin-ion: 'a standing Army' as 'the Plague', for example, articulates the age-old popular protest against the expense and intimidation of a perpetual, state-funded force, and 'a Sieve, a Court Lady' expresses the common complaint against the tattling women. By using these metaphors, Swift also under-scores the need for such coded language in a corrupt and paranoid state where 'a Court of Justice' is nothing but a 'broken Reed', a pen without a point. Balnibarbi illustrates the errors of Modern science.

The Voyage to Glubbdubdrib: Antiquarianism and History

In Glubbdubdrib, 'the Island of *Sorcerers* or *Magicians*' who can summon the dead, Swift extends his satire on learning to Modern distortions of history (II, vii, 286). Here, the King invites Gulliver to question anyone from the beginning of time to the present, being sure that they will tell the truth, since 'Lying was a Talent of no Use in the lower World' (III, vii, 289). Gulliver uses the opportunity to revisit trivial obsessions, such as what killed Alexander the Great, whether Hannibal really dissolved the Alps with vinegar, and how the

Romans dressed dinner. As a Modern, Gulliver seeks the wrong lessons from history. However, his interests give way to Swift's own historical vision when Gulliver compares the 'Assembly of Heroes and Demy-Gods' of the ancient Roman senate with the 'Knot of Pedlars, Pick-pockets, Highwaymen and Bullies' of the modern Parliament, and praises Brutus, Socrates, Sir Thomas More and other luminaries who fought against tyranny (III, vii, 291). This episode not only refigures the issues at stake in the clash between the King of Brobdingnag, a giant of the past, and the small-minded Gulliver on the knowledge of modern gunpowder, but it also anticipates the ambiguity of the flawed but quasi-classical world of the Houyhnhnms.

Aristotle provides the case in point. He emblematises the contrast between Modern historians' petty, materialistic interests and the moral perspective of the Ancients that provides history's real lessons. Tellingly, in the halls of the dead, Modern commentators on ancient sources, conscious of their distortions, shirk both Aristotle and Homer. However, Swift does not roundly applaud Aristotelian science. Rather, he shifts the central point from the details of scientific theories to the long view of time. When Aristotle, easily conceding his errors, listens with scepticism to Gulliver's accounts of the Modern ideas of René Descartes and Pierre Gassendi, he observes that 'new Systems of Nature were but new Fashions, which would vary in every Age; and even those who pretend to demonstrate them from Mathematical Principles, would flourish but a short Period of Time, and be out of Vogue when that was determined' (III, viii, 296). It is Aristotle's philosophical perspective that demonstrates the superiority of the Ancients, rather than his specific system of knowledge: he himself models Ancient virtue.

Modern distortions extend beyond textual errors to genealogical ones as Gulliver discovers that blue blood is not what historians represent it to be. Himself 'a great Admirer of old illustrious Families', Gulliver finds, when he summons these families' ancestors, instead of a queue of honourable grandees, a jumble of social types: one family alone boasts 'two Fidlers, three spruce Courtiers, and an *Italian* Prelate', and another, 'a Barber, an Abbot and two Cardinals', in contrast to the simple and honest '*English* Yeomen of the old Stamp' (III, viii, 297, 303). Gulliver detects the heritage of stupidity, knavery, cheating, decrepitude, and syphilis that has resulted in familial decay, concluding, 'Neither could I wonder at all this, when I saw such an Interruption of Lineages by Pages, Lacqueys, Valets, Coachmen, Gamesters, Fidlers, Players, Captains, and Pick-pockets' (III, viii, 298). This record of promiscuity and slumming indicts the pretensions to superiority based on lineage in place of accomplishment or virtue. Moreover, Gulliver finds modern history a parade of injustices, vices and misrepresentations, which commends cowards, ascribes wisdom to fools, 'Sincerity to Flatterers, *Roman* Virtue to Betrayers of their Country, Piety to Atheists', and death to 'many innocent and excellent Persons' (II, viii, 298). Enfolded in this attack on learning is an attack on Whiggish ideas of 'progress' that also informs Gulliver's ill-advised jingoistic boasts to the King of Brobdingnag. Glubbdubdrib demonstrates the regression of Modern Britain.

The Voyage to Luggnagg: The Vanity of Human Wishes

Swift's critique of Whiggish history and historians concludes with Gulliver's imaginary ascent to Godhood through his account of the Struldbruggs, or Immortals, a tiny population unique to Luggnagg. This lambasts the Modern naïve belief in improvable human nature. Confessing that he has often mused on what he would do were he 'a King, a General, or a great Lord', the entranced Gulliver launches into an enthusiastic fantasy of how he would live were he immortal:

> I would first resolve by all Arts and Methods whatsoever to procure myself Riches: In the Pursuit of which, by Thrift and Management, I might reasonably expect in about two Hundred Years, to be the wealthiest Man in the Kingdom. In the second Place, I would from my earliest Youth apply myself to the Study of Arts and Sciences, by which I should arrive in time to excel all others in Learning. Lastly, I would carefully record every Action and Event of Consequence that happened in the Publick, impartially draw the Characters of several Successions of Princes, and great Ministers of State; with my own Observations on every Point. I would exactly set down the several Changes in Customs, Languages, Fashions, Dress, Dyet and Diversions. By all which Acquirements, I should be a living Treasury of Knowledge and Wisdom, and certainly become the Oracle of the Nation [...] I would entertain myself in forming and directing the Minds of hopeful young Men, by convincing them from my own Remembrance, Experience and Observation, fortified by numerous Examples, of the Usefulness of Virtue in publick and private Life. (III, x, 312–13)

In this passage, Gulliver reveals more of his character than anywhere else in Part III. Blind to his greed, vanity, and pride, as to the possibility of his own corruption, he dreams of witnessing the discovery of the secrets of the earth and skies; he sees himself as a moral touchstone, issuing 'Memorials' informing the people of 'the Gradations by which Corruption steals into the World', and 'giving perpetual Warning and Instruction to Mankind' (III, x, 313). Clearly, he has learned nothing about human nature from his exploits. Moreover, his dream of being another creature foreshadows his doomed longing to be Houyhnhnm in Part IV.

Furthermore, he exposes his own historical ignorance, forgetting (despite his Cambridge education) the classical tale of Tithonus, to whom the gods granted eternal life but not eternal youth. The omission underscores the limits of a merely modern education that does not teach lessons from history or classical literature. Gulliver also unwittingly exposes his own Whiggish desires, as well as the injustice of the current economic system, by estimating that it would take as long as 200 years to grow as rich as he desires, which is as rich as the King and richer than anyone else. His idealism and ambition appear in his blithe assumption that his experience and character would qualify him as historian, politician, and cultural guide.

Gulliver is soon set straight, and in correcting the errors into which he has fallen 'through the common Imbecility of human Nature', the Luggnuggians expose humanity's basic weaknesses (III, x, 315). Growing ever older and more infirm, the Struldbruggs represent mankind stripped of the restraints imposed by the fear of death: 'Envy and impotent Desires' rend them; they resent the young, misremember the past, hoard their land and possessions, lose their ability to delight in physical pleasure, and lose touch with the evolving language so that they cannot communicate with new generations (III, x, 317). Considered 'dead in Law' after eighty, outcast and despised, they are mere skeletons of humanity, living lessons of the folly of wishing for what God has denied (III, x, 318). The Struldbruggs' world contains neither heaven nor hell: it is a pagan vision that Swift will explore more fully in Part IV.

Conclusion

Bookended by brief encounters with generous Japanese and irreligious Dutchmen, each episode in Part III represents an error-filled aspect of Modern learning. As a whole, it mounts a comprehensive attack against Whiggish frenetic innovation and rudderless improvement, and Modern ideas of human and physical nature, of the past and the present. In the process, it also illustrates Gulliver's weaknesses and flaws. In the Academy of Projectors, Gulliver believes he can belong, for 'My Lord was pleased to represent me as a great Admirer of Projects, and a Person of much Curiosity and easy Belief; which indeed was not without Truth; for I had my self been a Sort of Projector in my younger Days' (III, iv, 258). This revealing aside illuminates the physician Gulliver's own Whiggish, credulous, quantifying bias, evident in his linguistic pride and rosters of dreary navigational details, and foreshadows the desire for power and influence exposed in his fantasy of being a Struldbrugg. Underlying the satire in Part III is a nostalgia for the Ancient values of Classical learning, humanity, morality, and sociability, and for a return to a world with a moral core. The Part is a granular return to the quarrel satirised in Swift's *A Tale of a Tub* and *The Battle of the Books* (both 1704).

The unusual form of this Part seems to break with the generic conception of the *Travels* as a coherent novel. Despite the unity Gulliver's perspective provides, each island world exists independently, connected by theme and tone, episodic rather than narrative. Unlike the other three Parts, it possesses a disconnected structure that interrupts the progressive account of the development (or deterioration) of Gulliver's personality as it unfolds through Voyages I and II and IV. Moreover, Part III is not a single adventure tale, and Gulliver mainly plays the role not of adventurer but of observer, serving to illuminate scholarly misconceptions, vanities, and vices. This seems inconsistent, even jarring, in the context of the other three voyages.

However, this disunity also enables a different kind of unity in the *Travels*. The panoply of individual topics embodied by the peoples in Part III echoes the themes and motifs in the other Parts. These include the unreliability and distortions of perspective; the dangers of cultural solipsism; man's natural love of violence and argument; the vanity of human wishes, embodied in Gulliver himself; and a critique of British politics, culture, and institutions. Part III thus contributes to Swift's overarching and encyclopaedic satire of British society. Like the other Parts, it targets the way current culture supports abusive class hierarchy and political corruption. Furthermore, the variety of human types in Part III, from scientist to philosopher, from the immortal to the dead, opens up Swift's satire from a simple Lilliputian-Brobdingnagian comparison to a more comprehensive portrait of man's flaws and vices: it shows how Modern learning perverts humanity and sets the tone for the final blistering Yahooisation of man in Part IV. This enchanting and enchanted medley of discrete, diverting episodes presents a smorgasbord of incidents that cohere to the multi-generic and inclusive form of the early novel. Part III belongs in *Gulliver's Travels*.

CHAPTER 13

A Voyage to the Land of the Houyhnhnms

Judith Hawley

'an Odd Adventure'

Towards the end of his sojourn in the Land of the Houyhnhnms, Gulliver relates what he calls 'an odd Adventure' (IV, viii, 400). One day when he is out with his 'Protector the Sorrel Nag', the weather is so hot, he asks the Nag for permission to cool off in a nearby river. When he strips and enters the stream, he is seen by 'a young Female Yahoo' who, 'inflamed by Desire, as the Nag and I conjectured, came running with all Speed, and leaped into the Water within five Yards of the Place where I bathed. [. . .] She embraced me after a most fulsome Manner'. When Gulliver 'roared' to alert his equine protector to frighten her away, 'she quitted her Grasp, with the utmost Reluctancy, and leaped upon the opposite Bank, where she stood gazing and howling all the time I was putting on my Cloaths' (IV, viii, 400–1). A crucial turning point for Gulliver, this traumatic sexual assault is an arresting moment for the reader, not least because it overturns expectations in numerous respects. This grotesque reworking of Ovid's tale of the encounter between Acteon the hunter and the chaste goddess Diana involves an eleven-year-old girl attacking an older man who is then defended by an equine chaperone. The horses then humiliate Gulliver: 'This was Matter of Diversion to my Master and his Family, as well as of Mortification to my self. For now I could no longer deny, that I was a real Yahoo, in every Limb and Feature, since the Females had a natural Propensity to me as one of their own Species' (IV, viii, 401). Male and female, young and old, human and animal change place. Gulliver's apparently misogynistic if not racist revulsion at the desire of the Female Yahoo is also transformed into self-disgust when he realises that he 'was a real Yahoo, in every Limb and Feature'. What are we to make of Gulliver's final and most disturbing voyage? Is Part IV a free-standing animal fable, or is it the climax and éclaircissement that delivers the moral of the whole satire: that man is a brute beast? Or is Swift, as he said to Pope, aiming 'to vex the world'?

For support and advice during the preparation of this chapter, I am grateful to Olivia Horne, John Regan, Anne Varty, and my colleagues in Write Club.

So many people found the last part of *Gulliver's Travels* both unfathomable and distasteful that it was frequently omitted from nineteenth- and early twentieth-century editions, especially those intended for children. Part III suffered the same fate. Neither book seems to fit with Swift's imaginatively appealing tales of little and large people. Yet it is likely that he conceived all four parts to work as a whole and this is strongly suggested by the fact that he completed Part IV before III but placed it last. Swift also constructed links and parallels with earlier books. For example, Gulliver discharges his urine on the imperial palace of Lilliput (I, v, 79–80) and the Yahoos discharge their excrement on him (IV, i, 335); a monkey in Part II takes him to be 'a young one of his own Species' (II, v, 172), like the young female Yahoo (IV, viii, 401); his physical disgust in the latter incident is perhaps also foreshadowed in his description of the naked Brobdingnagian Maids of Honour (II, v, 167–8); equally, the kindness he receives from Glumdalclitch parallels the solicitude of the sorrel nag and both anticipate the good Portuguese Captain (IV, xi, 430–2).

The question remains whether or not these links concatenate and lead up to Part IV as both termination and conclusion of an argument. There are binary structures at work in *Gulliver's Travels*: Parts I and II set up a series of contrasts between little and large, petty and gross, pernicious and monstrous; Part IV also depends on oppositions between natural and civilised, bestial and rational. However, I will argue that Swift does not resolve this thesis and antithesis into a neat synthesis. Like Part III which disturbs the pattern of opposition by introducing a range of different targets, Gulliver's voyage to the land of the Houyhnhnms disturbs and destabilises the reader by repeatedly defying expectations. Rather than being the spot of solid ground onto which the shipwrecked reader can crawl and from there look back over the rest of the text to find it resolves itself into an order that points at one clear meaning, Part IV leaves many readers baffled and discomforted – and that is the point.

Since its publication, disagreement about what Swift intended by his final allegory has been widespread. For some, the rational Houyhnhnms represent Swift's positive ideal. His friend Thomas Sheridan thought they were the picture of perfection, but only of the nobler aspects of humanity, just as the Yahoos represent 'all the passions and the evil propensities of man's nature'.[1] Another friend, the Earl of Orrery, found 'the picture, which he

---

[1] Thomas Sheridan, *The Life of the Rev. Dr Jonathan Swift* (1787), quoted in *On Gulliver Among the Houyhnhnms*, ed. Milton P. Foster (New York: Thomas Y. Crowell, 1970; 1st printing 1961), 76–80; George Sherburn largely agrees in 'Errors concerning the Houyhnhnms', *MP*, 56 (1958), 92–9, quoted in Foster, *On Gulliver*, 258–66.

draws of the Houyhnhnms, [not] inviting or amusing. [. . .] It is cold and insipid. [. . .] They are incapable of doing wrong, therefore they act right'.[2] F. R. Leavis qualifies this remark by arguing that Swift's 'Augustan positives', Reason, Truth and Nature, were not 'solidly realized', rather 'The clean skin of the Horses, in short, is stretched over a void; instincts, emotions and life, which complicate the problem of cleanliness and decency, are left for the Yahoos with the dirt and the indecorum'.[3] Swift's depiction of the 'the dirt and the indecorum' of the Yahoos suggested to Orrery that 'Swift has indulged a misanthropy that is intolerable'. His conclusion that 'In painting the Yahoos, he becomes one himself' became common in the nineteenth and much of the twentieth century when critics sought the source of Swift's satiric vision in his diseased psyche, even though he was not to descend into madness for at least another decade.[4] Nonetheless, the novelist and critic William Makepeace Thackeray created a lingering vision of Swift's supposed state of mind when he wrote his final voyage: 'It is Yahoo language, – a monster gibbering shrieks and gnashing imprecations against mankind; tearing down all shreds of modesty, past all sense of manliness and shame; filthy in word, filthy in thought, furious, raging, obscene'.[5]

'I was a real Yahoo'

Let us begin, then, with the language of the Yahoo. The origin and meaning of the name are uncertain and 'Yahoo' might just be an exclamation. It perhaps, however, originates in unreliable accounts of Coptic Christian and Semitic tribes in West Africa whose name might be derived from YHWH, a Hebrew name of God. So 'Yahoo' in its usage in Africa might have signified 'Jew' and designated highly civilised people who had degenerated under subjection to other tribes.[6] This etymology suggests that Swift might have

---

[2] John Boyle, 5th Earl of Orrery, *Remarks on the Life and Writings of Dr. Jonathan Swift* (1751), quoted in Foster, *On Gulliver*, 71, 73.
[3] F. R. Leavis, 'The Irony of Swift', in *The Common Pursuit* (New York: George W. Stewart, 1952), 84–7, quoted in Foster, *On Gulliver*, 204, 205.
[4] Boyle, *Remarks*, quoted in Foster, *On Gulliver*, 73.
[5] W. M. Thackeray, 'Swift', in *Thackeray's English Humorists of the Eighteenth Century*, ed. J. W. Cunliffe and H. A. Watt (Chicago: Scott, Foresman, 1911), 35–64.
[6] J. R. Moore, 'The Yahoos of the African Travellers', *N&Q*, 195 (1950), 182–5. Frank Kermode, 'Yahoos and Houyhnhnms', *N&Q*, 195 (1950), 317–18 suggested that, while browsing through travel literature, Swift might have come across the Yaios of Guiana. The founders of the web services provider Yahoo! apparently chose the name because to them, in 1990s Californian, the name meant 'rude, unsophisticated, uncouth'. They then coined a 'backcronym' so that the name designates the initial letters of the phrase: 'Yet Another Hierarchically Organized Oracle' (William Safire, *The Right Word in the Right Place at the Right Time* (New York: Simon and Schuster, 2004), 397).

been drawing on contemporary travel literature. His description of the physical appearance of a Yahoo could place them anywhere in the Tropical imaginary: 'the Face of it indeed was flat and broad, the Nose depressed, the Lips large, and the Mouth wide'; it also has nails like claws, dark skin and profuse hair (IV, ii, 342). Swift read discussions of supposedly savage peoples and their relations to humanoids; such racist attitudes were given even greater weight in Edward Long's *History of Jamaica* (1774), as Claude Rawson details in *God, Gulliver and Genocide*, his intricate study of the hinterland and afterlife of *Gulliver's Travels* from Columbus to the Nazis. Yet, as Rawson points out, despite the possible African derivation of the name, Swift locates the Yahoos in the South Pacific.[7] Furthermore, although travel writers were wont to compare Africans to apes, the only animals Gulliver specifically compares them to are goats and squirrels (IV, i, 333, 334).

It is likely that Swift was thinking not only of distant lands but the people he lived among, the native Irish. English commentators often assimilated the Irish with the Indian Other, an identification further complicated by the fact that the term 'Indian' already conflates various racially distinct groups.[8] Swift's depiction of the Yahoos echoes hostile accounts of Gaelic Irish peasants. Tradition maintained that the Irish were descended from the Scythians, nomadic people from the Eurasian steppes who were described as cannibals by the ancient Greeks.[9] Commentators such as Edmund Spenser and Fynes Moryson, who had an interest in exaggerating the supposed barbarism of the Irish in order to justify their suppression by the English, were appalled by the diets of the Irish; though the result of starvation, they resembled the eating habits of 'savage' people.[10] Gulliver's Master

---

[7] Claude Rawson, *God, Gulliver and Genocide: Barbarism and the European Imagination, 1492–1945* (Oxford: Oxford University Press, 2001), 147.

[8] Rawson, *God, Gulliver and Genocide*, 3 and passim.

[9] Herodotus, *The Persian Wars, Volume II: Books 3–4*, trans. A. D. Godley, Loeb Classical Library (Cambridge: Harvard University Press, 1938), IV, 70; Strabo, *Geography, Volume III: Books 6–7*, trans. Horace Leonard Jones, Loeb Classical Library (Cambridge: Harvard University Press, 1917), VII, iii, 7; *Volume II: Books 3–5*, IV, v, 4. Swift repeated this claim, with irony, in *An Answer to a Paper, Called a Memorial of the Poor Inhabitants, Tradesmen, and Labourers of the Kingdom of Ireland* (1728): 'I know very well that our ancestors the *Scythians*, and their posterity our kinsmen the *Tartars*, liv'd upon the Blood, and Milk, and raw Flesh of their Cattle, without one Grain of Corn; but I confess myself so degenerate, that I am not easy without Bread to my Victuals' (*Irish Political Writings after 1725*, 33).

[10] Edmund Spenser, *A View of the Present State of Ireland* (1596); Fynes Moryson, *An Itinerary . . . Concerning His Ten Yeeres Travel through the Twelve Dominions of Germany . . . Scotland and Ireland* (1617). See also William Camden, *Britannia* (1586; 1st English translation, 1610) and John Temple, *The Irish Rebellion; or An History of the Beginning and First Progresse of the Generall Rebellion Raised within the Kingdom of Ireland* (1646). Such views were still being voiced while Swift was composing *Gulliver*; see, for example, Viscount Molesworth, *Considerations for the Promoting of Agriculture, and Employing the Poor* (1723). Swift's friend Thomas Sheridan drew sympathetically on Moryson's

avers that 'There was nothing that rendered the *Yahoos* more odious, than undistinguished Appetite to devour every thing that came in their Way' (IV, vii, 393). Swift's depiction of the Yahoos also alludes to other elements of the deliberate and offensive stereotyping of the Catholic Irish: their supposed depraved sexual appetites, drunkenness, casualness about parenting, laziness, and fondness for squalor.[11]

Swift did not experience warm and fuzzy feelings about the Catholic Irish. His fear and loathing are well attested, even though he was embraced as a champion of liberty for his efforts in overturning the British government's imposition of a debased system of coinage with his series of pamphlets known as *The Drapier's Letters* (1724–5). Yet, when he expressed his hatred of Ireland in his published texts and even in his private correspondence, he did not, to my knowledge, depict the Irish as racially inferior, though he certainly saw them as lesser beings. He also maintained that the Irish were reduced to slavery and beggary by the impositions of English overlords who treated Ireland virtually as a colony, the land and people theirs to exploit. 'A great cause of this nation's misery', thundered the Dean from his pulpit in 1728, 'is that Ægyptian bondage of cruel, oppressing, covetous landlords'.[12] It is significant, then, that it is the Houyhnhnm Master who is most disgusted by the Yahoos' diet and, when Gulliver reports that he witnesses some Yahoos 'feeding upon Roots, and the Flesh of some Animals', he notes that 'They were all tied by the Neck with strong Wyths, fastened to a Beam' (IV, ii, 341–2) as if in 'Ægyptian bondage'. At the same time, Swift held the Irish, the Gaelic poor especially, morally responsible for their own degradation, believing them to be enslaved to their own appetites. Though critical of the rule of the Lord Lieutenant of Ireland, he summarily dismisses the Irish as 'stupid, slavish, complying beasts'.[13] Critique rather than sympathy is Swift's primary response.

account of cannibalism in *The Intelligencer*, 18 (1728), a paper in a journal he co-wrote with Swift. See Jonathan Swift and Thomas Sheridan, *The Intelligencer*, ed. James Woolley (Oxford: Clarendon Press, 1992), 197–203. For a fuller discussion, see Rawson, *God, Gulliver and Genocide*, esp. 17–91. See also Donald T. Torchiana, 'Jonathan Swift, the Irish, and the Yahoos: Their Case Reconsidered', *PQ*, 54 (1975), 195–212.

[11] See for example the Master's account of the Yahoos' behaviour and qualities in IV, vii, 388–97. A useful starting point for an exploration of Swift's attitudes to Ireland and the Irish is *Swift's Irish Writings: Selected Poetry and Prose*, ed. Carol Fabricant and Robert Mahoney (Basingstoke: Palgrave Macmillan, 2010). See also Joseph McMinn, *Jonathan's Travels: Swift and Ireland* (Belfast: Appletree Press, 1994), 86; James William Kelly, 'A Contemporary Source for the Yahoos in *Gulliver's Travels*', *N&Q*, 45 (1998), 68–70.

[12] *A Sermon on the Causes of the Wretched Condition of Ireland* (dated late 1720s-early 1730s? by Fabricant and Mahony). He maintained the same line in his correspondence: for example, Swift to Charles Wogan, 10 August 1732, *Correspondence*, III, 514–15.

[13] Swift to Edward Harley, 28 April 1730, *Correspondence*, III, 307.

Nonetheless, Gulliver recognises himself as Yahoo. In a reversal both of the myth of Narcissus and of Swift's own dictum that '*Satyr is a sort of Glass, wherein Beholders do generally discover every body's Face but their Own*'[14] he declares: 'When I happened to behold the Reflection of my own Form in a Lake or Fountain, I turned away my face in Horror and detestation of my self; and could better endure the Sight of a common Yahoo, than of my own Person' (IV, x, 420). Moreover, this is not just an instance of self-loathing, for when he thinks of the

> human Race in general, I considered them as they really were, *Yahoos* in Shape and Disposition, perhaps a little more civilized, and qualified with the gift of Speech; but making no other Use of Reason, than to improve and multiply those Vices, whereof their Brethren in this Country had only the Share that Nature allotted them. (IV, x, 420)

As Rawson argues, we can let Swift off the charge of racism only by convicting him of misanthropy.[15]

The State of Nature

Just as the stature of Gulliver gains meaning when contrasted with that of both the Lilliputians and the Brobdingnagians, the nature of Gulliver gains meaning in relation to both Houyhnhnm and Yahoo. In setting them against each other, Swift is restaging debates about the nature of man and the relation of man to nature. If the Yahoos are 'like brute beasts without understanding', a phrase Dean Swift would have used when conducting the marriage service from the *Book of Common Prayer*, are they, then, like man in a state of nature? Philosophers in the long eighteenth century rehearsed a thought experiment about what humans were like before society developed in order to consider what shape society should take. According to Thomas Hobbes, primitive humans lived in a state of warfare until they accepted the need for a powerful authority to keep them in check. Horrified by this bleak vision and keen to heal divisions as Britain recovered from civil war, Shaftesbury developed a moral philosophy which insisted that humans were innately benevolent, while John Locke developed a political philosophy in which he maintained that, even in a state of nature, humans were governed by the law of nature, 'and that law is reason'. Nature and reason school everyone to respect the life, liberty and

---

[14] Jonathan Swift, Preface of the Author, to *Battle of the Books*, in *Tale*, 142.
[15] Rawson, *God, Gulliver and Genocide*, 171.

property of others.[16] These more abstract debates are entangled with classical and literary traditions about natural simplicity in an imagined Golden Age Arcadia. Some versions of history provided evidence of ways of living a virtuous life in harmony with nature. The example of Lycurgus, the lawgiver of Sparta, became the model for schemes for ideal societies from Plato, to Thomas More and Swift's mentor, William Temple. The Yahoos perhaps represent Hobbesian savage man and, in many respects, the behaviour and social organisation of the Houyhnhnms is modelled on that of the quasi-legendary Spartans. Their unsentimental attitudes to children, their rigorous scheme of education for both boys and girls, their political councils, simple diets, and scorn of luxury are all reflected in the habits of the Houyhnhnms, as are their selective breeding programmes, preference for oral culture, distrust of lawyers, and lack of passion.[17]

'the Perfection of Nature'

In many ways, then, the Houyhnhnms are the opposite of the Yahoos. Yet, what satirical point Swift intends – or the reader receives – through this opposition takes some working out. Physically, the Houyhnhnms are, as near as dammit, horses. They look exactly like horses, though they have some physical adaptations which allow them to undertake some human activities. An adaptation to 'the hollow part between the Pastern and the Hoof of their Fore-feet' greatly increases their fine motor skills, enabling them to do everything from milking cows to threading a needle. Coupled with their innate class system, these adaptations mean that Houyhnhnm society resembles the social and gendered divisions of eighteenth-century Europe: 'the *Bay*, the *Dapple grey*, and the *Black*' elite sit on their haunches talking while 'the *White*, the *Sorrel*, and the *Iron-grey*' lower orders perform manual labour (IV, vi, 385). Surely there is a comical as well as a satirical dimension to these talking horses.

---

[16] These ideas are set out in Thomas Hobbes, *De Cive* (1642), *Leviathan* (1651), Anthony Ashley Cooper, 3rd Earl of Shaftesbury, *Characteristics of Men, Manners, Opinions, Times* (1711), and John Locke, *Second Treatise on Civil Government* (1689). For the wider context to this debate, see K. Widerquist and G. McCall, *Prehistoric Myths in Modern Political Philosophy* (Edinburgh: Edinburgh University Press, 2017).

[17] For accounts of the Spartans, see Plutarch, *Life of Lycurgus* and Plato, *Republic*. Sources for Swift's ideas of virtuous societies also include Thomas More's *Utopia* (1516), Montaigne's essay 'Of Cannibals', and various essays by Swift's patron, William Temple. See *GT*, 545 and William H. Halewood, 'Plutarch in Houyhnhnmland: A Neglected Source for Gulliver's Fourth Voyage', *PQ*, 44 (1965), 185–94.

So, let us consider the name they give themselves in their language of expressive neighs. Critics agree that Houyhnhnms is pronounced 'whinnims', evoking the whinnying of a horse. But what are they saying? Could it be the word 'human'? If so, that would suggest that although Gulliver repeatedly asserts that humans are really all Yahoos, Swift is holding out the possibility that some of us might be or become Houyhnhnm. 'The Word *Houyhnhnm*, in their Tongue', Gulliver learns, 'signifies a *Horse*; and in its Etymology, *the Perfection of Nature*' (IV, iii, 350). This definition raises further questions about what the Houyhnhnms signify. The phrase 'perfection of nature' is used by others in ways that suggest that human perfectibility might be problematic as well as impossible. Thomas Sprat in his *History of the Royal Society*, urges man to acquire complete knowledge of nature and thus to command the world which, he argues, 'must needs be the utmost perfection of *humane Nature*'.[18] The hubristic attitudes of the Royal Society as represented by Sprat are the target of much of Swift's satire in Part III. The clergyman Swift might also have had in mind one of the central tenets of the Church of England, that is 'Christ did truly rise again from death, and took again his body, with flesh, bones, and all things appertaining to the perfection of Man's nature'.[19] The implication is that the perfection of man's nature is not possible on this side of death. A third usage also suggests a chastening of human pride. Stoic philosophers urged man to commit himself to perfecting his nature by the exercise of rational control. Yet Epictetus taught that self-extinction might be the only route to self-perfection: 'a Man had better die from Want, and preserve his Mind from immoderate Fear and Concern, and by that means attain to the peculiar Perfection of his Nature, than live in continual Perplexity'.[20]

'a reasonable Animal'

The Anglican clergyman Swift would not have counselled suicide, but Stoical philosophy, especially its emphasis on the exercise of reason to control the passions, is one of the major sources for Swift's conception of the Houyhnhnms. Reason is one of those complex terms whose meaning was particularly contested in the eighteenth century, especially in the fields of philosophical or scientific method. Its meanings range from scholastic logic,

[18] Thomas Sprat, *The History of the Royal Society*, 2nd ed. (1702), 110–11, quoted in *GT*, 553.
[19] Article IV of the Thirty Nine Articles, quoted in *GT*, 551. For an elucidation, see Edgar C. S. Gibson, *The Thirty-Nine Articles of the Church of England Explained* (London: Methuen, 1896), 187.
[20] *Epictetus His Morals, with Simplicius His Commentary*, trans. George Stanhope, 4th ed. (1721), 105, quoted in *GT*, 553.

to empiricism, induction and deduction and common sense. Repeatedly, Swift satirised the ratiocination of metaphysical disquisitions and the wrangling of modern natural philosophy. The Houyhnhnms laugh at disputes in natural philosophy, so what kind of reason do they profess and practise? Reason, explains Gulliver, is not 'among them a Point problematical as with us, where Men can argue with Plausibility on both sides of a Question; but strikes you with immediate Conviction; as it must needs do where it is not mingled, obscured, or discoloured by Passion and Interest' (IV, viii, 401). This kind of mental process is less akin to logic and closer to common sense: 'That which is reasonable or sensible; that which appeals to or is in accord with instinctive understanding or sound judgement; *esp.* (in earliest use) written or spoken discourse that is reasonable or sensible'.[21] Gulliver's master tells him: 'Nature and Reason were sufficient guides for a reasonable Animal, as we pretended to be, in shewing us what we ought to do, and what to avoid' (IV, v, 36). In effect, the idea is that reason consists in bringing your mind in alignment with things as they are. This idea is a central tenet of Lycurgus and the Stoic Seneca and strongly recommended by several thinkers who are elsewhere favoured by Swift, including More, Montaigne, and Temple.[22]

Swift employs their arcadian innocence to criticise the fallen nature of civilised man. They cannot understand Gulliver's use of clothes or books, nor can they understand how humans make war because they reason only from the form of their own bodies (IV, ii, 343; IV, iii, 348; IV, v, 365–6). The Brobdingnagians similarly do not understand things outside their ken (II, iii, 143–4). The problem is, as A. D. Nuttall observes, the Houyhnhnms appear to be quite stupid: 'They are sages who never philosophise'.[23] Whether or not Swift intended this as an irony at their expense, it is certainly the case that the price of their innocence is an ignorance which means that, unlike Gulliver, they are unable to learn and change. As well as being imperfect, they are also inconsistent. Famously, Houyhnhnms cannot lie; they do not say '*the Thing which is not*' (IV, v, 366). However, on two occasions, Gulliver's Master deliberately conceals the full truth. (He agrees to conceal from the

[21] *OED*, s.v. Common Sense, 2. A special meaning of common sense developed later in century in the Scottish philosophical tradition: *OED* 4 c 'The innate or instinctive human capacity to recognize as self-evident certain fundamental truths about the world. Also: the fundamental truths (held to be) so recognized, as attested by the common consent of mankind'.

[22] See *GT*, 545–6. A. D. Nuttall quotes from Seneca's Moral Epistle 'On the God Within Us', *Epistulae Morales*, 41.8–9, in 'Gulliver Among the Horses', *The Yearbook of English Studies*, 18 (1988), 51–67 (64).

[23] Nuttall, 'Gulliver', 62.

Houyhnhnms the fact that Gulliver wears clothes (IV, iii, 352) and conceals from Gulliver the decision of the general assembly concerning his fate (IV, x, 421).) Yet, it is likely that here, as elsewhere, Swift sacrifices the kind of coherence that is valuable in creating novelistic characters for the sake of the localised effects necessary to satire. A more problematic inconsistency occurs in Gulliver's account of the Houyhnhnms' general assembly. He relates that the logical corollary of their dependence on the conformity of language to fact is that debate in council is unknown. There is no point arguing 'because no Person can disobey Reason, without giving up his Claim to be a rational Creature' (IV, x, 422).[24] However, they actually keep returning to 'their old Debate' at their General Assembly: 'Whether the *Yahoos* should be exterminated from the Face of the Earth' (IV, x, 408). Not only is this an example of the sorts of 'Controversies, Wranglings, Disputes' (IV, x, 402) they supposedly avoid, it is a sign that reason and nature do not tell us what to do in every case.

The Problem of Evil

The Houyhnhnms' ability to pose this appalling question casts doubt on their sweet reasonableness. Surely this debate, while it exhibits the extension of a sequence of logic which might run: 'the Yahoos are evil therefore getting rid of them would be good', is boosted by an emotional charge based on one of the few passions the Houyhnhnms feel: a visceral revulsion for the Yahoos. Undoubtedly, the Yahoos are dangerous and malign brutes and an 'evil' in the sense of something that causes harm (*OED*). But how does one deal with the problem of evil in a way that is not in itself wicked? This debate brings into intense focus issues which disturb readers throughout this voyage: what is Swift saying about human nature and what are we supposed to do about it? Does he genuinely condemn humanity? Or does he wish us to consider some sort of Christian or Stoical middle ground whereby we exterminate the Yahoo portion of ourselves in order to refine the Houyhnhnm within? These alternative interpretations are sometimes dubbed 'hard' and 'soft' readings.[25] But such a simplifying division mischaracterises both groups

---

[24] William Godwin recommends the council of the Houyhnhnms as a model for government and particularly admired the use of '*Hnhloayn*' or exhortation to convince the delegates of the reasonableness of the measures proposed. 'Of Legislative and Executive Power', in *Political Justice* (1793), ed. F. E. L. Priestley (Toronto: University of Toronto Press, 1946), facs of 3rd ed., Vol II, Book V, 209, n.

[25] See *GT*, xciii–xcv.

of critics and overlooks valuable nuances in their arguments. It also falls into a binary pattern which the topsy-turvy tropes and structure of *Gulliver's Travels* both instantiate and critique. Moreover, the focus on Swift's intention overlooks the responsibility the reader bears to work through the complexities and conundrums of the text.

While the prose and narrative of the *Travels* are lucid, the morality is anything but; there is an offset of ethics and style. The text confounds readers' expectations and keeps them in a state of unease as the Houyhnhnms and Yahoos are not completely stable in their signification. In depicting the Houyhnhnms as rational beings, Swift inverts expectations as horses had traditionally been used as symbols of uncontrolled passion.[26] He also presents them as simple and natural beings, yet the same terms could be used – with very different connotations – of the Yahoos. Similarly, the Yahoos who bear the features 'common to all savage Nations' (IV, ii, 342) are treated with contempt but later, in his attack on the imperial project, Gulliver turns his anger towards the 'execrable Crew of Butchers' who forcibly colonise 'harmless People' (IV, xii, 441). If we are tempted to rely on Gulliver as our guide, we soon discover he is an unreliable witness. In his first two voyages, Gulliver is disoriented by abrupt shifts of scale; in the third he is dizzied by being whirled from one place to another, each more confounding of expectations than the last. In his fourth and final voyage he is presented with a stark choice of identifying himself with either savage humans or superior animals; the dilemma drives him mad. The journeys he has taken to reach these destinations have confronted him with the dangers of the world and the evils of man. If *Gulliver's Travels* were a Bildungsroman or another form of realistic novel, we might expect that these experiences had shaped his character, tracing an arc from innocence and gullibility to experience and horrified enlightenment. However, *Gulliver's Travels* is not a novel but a satire; Gulliver is not a rounded character but a multifaceted device which presents different aspects as the valency of Swift's satire demands. He is variously a mouthpiece for Swift's satire (when, for example, he condemns the pride of men riddled with physical and moral deformity (IV, xii, 443–4)) and the butt of the joke (when, for example, he permits his wife to dine with him 'at the farthest End of a long Table' (IV, xii, 443)). Swift's ironic method obliges the reader to work hard to distinguish the point of the satire moment by moment.

[26] See *GT*, IV, iii, 347, n 2.

'to vex the World'

His correspondence with his friends provides tantalising commentaries on Swift's satire. One letter to his friend and fellow satirist, Alexander Pope, furnishes several much-quoted dicta about Swift's misanthropic attitudes including the following: 'the chief end I propose to my self in all my labors is to vex the world rather then divert it'; 'I hate and detest that animal called man, although I hartily love John, Peter, Thomas and so forth'; 'I have got Materials Towards a Treatis[e] proving the falsity of that Definition animal rationale; and to show it should be only *rationis capax*. Upon this great foundation of Misanthropy (though not in Timons manner) the whole building of my Travells is erected'.[27] While all of these statements might represent Swift's thinking, they are also part of a bantering playful conversation with particular readers whose presuppositions Swift anticipated and pandered to. Pope had suggested that they meet not 'to vex our own or others hearts [. . .] but to divert ourselves, and the world too if it pleases'.[28] Swift's reply demonstrates that he was not ready to put down the lash and also that he was capable of vexing Pope with his irony. Surely his claim that he hates 'that animal called man' but loves named individuals is an example of that logical absurdity called an 'Irish bull' in that the individuals are examples of the species and therefore objects of Swift's hatred? His treatise purporting to overturn the commonplace logical definition of man as 'a rational animal' by demonstrating that he was merely capable of reason ('*rationis capax*') was not written in stone for when Pope immediately wrote to attempt to moderate his misanthropy, Swift replied, 'I do not hate Mankind, it is vous autr[e]s who hate them because you would have them reasonable Animals, and are Angry for being disappointed'.[29] Thus his misanthropy is qualified. He hates and does not hate mankind at the same time.

His friends appreciated the black humour of the fourth voyage and entered into Swift's joke. Henrietta Howard signed a letter to Swift: 'Your most humble Ser^r Sieve Yahoo', coupling the code name for a court lady with Swift's beastly creature.[30] Pope wrote a poem in the voice of Gulliver's wife Mary, jealously enquiring 'What mean those Visits to the *Sorrel Mare?*'[31]

---

[27] Swift to Pope, 29 September 1725, *Correspondence*, II, 606–7.
[28] Pope to Swift, 14 September 1725, *Correspondence*, II, 597. See *GT*, lxxvii about vexation as a key term in Swift's satirical theory.
[29] Swift to Pope, 26 November 1725, *Correspondence*, II, 623. See also *GT*, IV, iii, 346, n 2 and Long Note 34, 558–60.
[30] Howard to Swift, 10 November 1726, *Correspondence*, III, 50; cf. *GT*, III, vi, 283.
[31] 'Mary Gulliver to Capt. Lemuel Gulliver; An Epistle', in *GT*, 583. It is one of a collection of verses by Pope and Gay in the voices of Swift's characters which was printed in Motte's 'second Edition', 1727.

When Gulliver retreats to his stable to live among horses, he is clearly mad. Yet, given what he has learnt about the nature of the human, he is also not wrong. At the same time, we might see Swift himself as implicated in his own satire. The fact that the Houyhnhnms countenance genocide as if it were a form of pest control might imply a critique of the destructive energies of satire itself. The Houyhnhnms' proposition is an echo of God's judgement on his creation. When he sees how wicked the human race has become, God declares: 'I will wipe from the face of the earth the human race I have created – and with them the animals, the birds and the creatures that move along the ground – for I regret that I have made them'.[32] Swift is no doubt aware of the hubris involved in a satirist alluding to divine retribution and equally aware that Noah persuaded God to preserve a select few from destruction.

---

[32] Genesis 6:7. See Rawson, *God, Gulliver and Genocide*, 267–9, 299, 311, n 3 on this point.

PART IV

Afterlives

CHAPTER 14

Critical Reception

Jack Lynch

We have been reading *Gulliver's Travels* for nearly three hundred years, and we have been arguing about it just as long. The history of the critical reception of Swift's masterpiece begins as soon as the book was published.

Travels into Several Remote Nations of the World appeared in London bookshops on 28 October 1726, identifying itself as the work of one 'Lemuel Gulliver, First a Surgeon, and then a Captain of Several Ships'. Swift's name was nowhere to be found in the book, and on first glance it may have looked like an authentic book of travels. Some may even have bought it without realising it was fiction. Those who read it, though, were rarely taken in by the ruse. Swift tells of a bishop who said that the 'Book was full of improbable lies, and for his part, he hardly believed a word of it',[1] and Swift's friend John Arbuthnot 'lent the Book to an old Gentleman, who went immediately to his Map, to search for Lilly putt'.[2] But most readers were savvy enough to realise they were reading fiction, and that Gulliver was not an author but a character. The book rapidly became the talk of literary London. 'From the highest to the lowest', John Gay wrote to his friend Swift just weeks after the book appeared, 'it is universally read, from the Cabinet-council to the Nursery'.[3]

Vexing the World

Gay was right that the book created a sensation, but not all the chatter was positive. The book had been out only a few weeks when a pamphlet complained of the 'gross Words, and lewd Descriptions' in *Gulliver's*

---

[1] Swift to Pope, [27?] November 1726, *Correspondence*, III, 56.
[2] Arbuthnot to Swift, 8 November 1726, *Correspondence*, III, 45.
[3] Gay and Pope to Swift, [7] November 1726, *Correspondence*, III, 47.

Travels. The anonymous author tore into the book for affronting decency itself:

> [Swift] spares neither Age or Sex, neither the Living or the Dead; neither the Rich, the Great, or the Good; the best of Characters is no Fence, the Innocent are the least secure; even his Majesty's Person is not sacred, the Royal Blood affords no Protection here [...][4]

And so on, for more than twenty pages. Samuel Johnson, the most important critic of the century, was more moderate, but still he shocked a friend by grumbling, 'When once you have thought of big men and little men, it is very easy to do all the rest'.[5]

But *Gulliver's Travels* was an immediate bestseller, and dozens of editions appeared over the next few decades. The first part, the voyage to Lilliput, was the popular favourite, and even today, people who know nothing else about the *Travels* know that the hero travels to a land of tiny people. 'The voyage to Lilliput', wrote Lord Monboddo, 'in my judgment, is the finest of them all [...] I think I do not go too far when I pronounce it the most perfect work of the kind, antient or modern, that is to be found'.[6] The second part, the voyage to Brobdingnag, was admired nearly as much. The second half of the book, though, got mixed reviews. Nearly everyone agreed that the third part, including the voyage to Laputa, was artistically the least effective, probably because it was the most miscellaneous. And the voyage to the Houyhnhnms quickly became notorious. The anonymous pamphleteer quoted above called Part IV 'tedious', adding, 'a Man grows sick at the shocking Things inserted there; his Gorge rises; he is not able to conceal his Resentment; and closes the Book with Detestation and Disappointment'.[7]

The Scottish critic James Beattie summed up the split verdict delivered by many eighteenth-century readers. He thought Swift's 'fable [plot] is well conducted' and said the style 'has not been exceeded by any thing in our language'. But Beattie had to draw a line somewhere: 'I must not be understood to praise the whole indiscriminately', he insisted.

[4] *A Letter from a Clergyman to His Friend, with an Account of the Travels of Capt. Lemuel Gulliver* (1726), 6, 12.
[5] James Boswell, *The Life of Samuel Johnson, LL.D.*, ed. G. B. Hill, rev. L. F. Powell, 6 vols. (Oxford: Clarendon Press, 1934–64), II, 319.
[6] James Burnet, Lord Monboddo, *Of the Origin and Progress of Language*, 6 vols. (Edinburgh, 1773–92), III, 196.
[7] *A Letter from a Clergyman to His Friend*, 7.

The last of the four voyages [. . .] abounds in filthy and indecent images [. . .] the general tenor of the satire is exaggerated into absolute falsehood; and [. . .] there must be something of an irreligious tendency in a work, which, like this, ascribes the perfection of reason, and of happiness, to a race of beings, who are said to be destitute of every religious idea.[8]

Gulliver's Travels was condemned for teaching us to hate humankind itself.

A few readers tried to defend Swift from this charge of misanthropy. Swift's godson and biographer Thomas Sheridan maintained Part IV 'is evidently designed to shew in what the true dignity and perfection of man's nature consists, and to point out the way by which it may be attained'.[9] But most readers, even habitual supporters of Swift, found the story of the Houyhnhnms and the Yahoos hard to take. Swift's ideal beings, the Houyhnhnms, lead rational, emotionless lives, and have achieved perfect contentment, free from all the vices that afflict human beings. We are supposed to see ourselves and all human beings in the Yahoos, the filthy, violent, lustful creatures who deserve all the punishment the Houyhnhnms can dish out. That is hard for us to take, and it seems to bear out Swift's declaration to his friend Alexander Pope that he intended to 'vex the world rather then divert it'[10] – to torment us rather than to entertain us. Even one of Swift's friends, the Earl of Orrery, wrote that in Part IV 'Swift has indulged a misanthropy that is intolerable. The representation which he has given us of human nature, must terrify, and even debase the mind of the reader who views it. His sallies of wit and humour lose all their force, nothing remaining but a melancholy, and disagreeable impression'. Swift had become as unhinged as his most appalling creation: 'In painting Yahoos he becomes one himself'.[11]

Throughout the eighteenth century, *Gulliver's Travels* remained hugely popular. A new edition, adaptation, or abridgement appeared on average once a year, along with translations into French, Italian, Spanish, Portuguese, German, Dutch, Polish, Russian, Danish, and Swedish. Eighteenth-century readers did not want to like it, but they did in spite of themselves. It was too offensive to read, but too compelling to ignore.

[8] James Beattie, *Dissertations Moral and Critical* (Edinburgh, 1783), 514–16.
[9] *The Works of the Rev. Dr. Jonathan Swift, Dean of St. Patrick's, Dublin*, ed. Thomas Sheridan, 17 vols. (1784), I, 503.
[10] Swift to Pope, 29 September 1725, *Correspondence*, II, 597.
[11] John Boyle, 5th Earl of Orrery, *Remarks on the Life and Writings of Dr. Jonathan Swift, Dean of St. Patrick's Dublin* (Dublin, 1752), 183–4, 188.

A Brain Not Wholly under Control

This paradoxical attitude towards the *Travels* only intensified in the nineteenth century. Sir Walter Scott praised it, but he found Part IV 'the basest and most unworthy part of the work' because 'It holds mankind forth in a light too degrading for contemplation [...] no good could possibly be attained by the exhibition of so loathsome a picture of humanity'.[12]

The metaphors critics used show us just how offensive they found the account of Gulliver among the Houyhnhnms and the Yahoos: we hear of sinfulness, impurity, rage, contempt, horror, monstrosity, shrieking, filth, disgust, even nausea. The novelist William Makepeace Thackeray, writing in 1853, for instance, praised the voyage to Lilliput – 'What a surprising humour there is in these descriptions! How noble the satire is here! how just and honest! How perfect the image!' – but his tone changed as he turned to the Houyhnhnms. 'As for the humour and conduct of this famous fable', he wrote, 'I suppose there is no person who reads but must admire'. The moral, though, is another story: 'I think it horrible, shameful, unmanly, blasphemous; and giant and great as this Dean is, I say we should shoot him'. He had a hard time with the Yahoos defecating from the trees:

> The reader of the fourth part of Gulliver's Travels is like the hero himself in this instance. It is Yahoo language; a monster gibbering shrieks, and gnashing imprecations against mankind, – tearing down all shreds of modesty, past all sense of manliness and shame; filthy in word, filthy in thought, furious, raging, obscene.[13]

How to account for Swift's revolting portrait of his own species? Some sought to explain the least palatable parts of Swift's work with reference to his biography. Swift's health problems – including his chronic Ménière's disease and the strokes he suffered at the end of his life – gave the impression that he had lost his mind and had fallen prey to 'madness' or 'lunacy'. This made it possible to explain his misanthropy as the product of a diseased mind. Houyhnhnmland was medicalised and pathologised. Most commentators today would agree that Swift suffered from nothing we would classify as a mental illness, and in any case he wrote *Travels* at the height of his intellectual powers, with nineteen years of life left. But for many readers the temptation was too strong: *Gulliver's Travels* was misanthropic because

---

[12] *The Works of Jonathan Swift, Dean of St. Patrick's, Dublin*, ed. Walter Scott, 2nd ed., 19 vols. (London: Bickers and Son, 1883), XI, 10.

[13] William Makepeace Thackeray, *The English Humourists of the Eighteenth Century*, 2nd ed. (London: Smith, Elder, and Co., 1853), 36, 40.

Swift's mental faculties were damaged. The book was less satire than symptom.

The habit goes back at least to the Earl of Orrery, who read episodes in *Travels* in light of what he knew about Swift's mental life. By the nineteenth century notions of Swift's madness had hardened into conventional wisdom. Scott, for instance, advised readers to make allowance 'for the soured and disgusted state of Swift's mind, which doubtless was even then influenced by the first impressions of that incipient mental disease which, in his case, was marked by universal misanthropy'.[14] By the end of the nineteenth century, it was unquestioned dogma. As Edmund Gosse, one of the critical giants of the late Victorian era, put it in 1889, the voyage to the Houyhnhnms showed 'the darker side of Swift's genius [. . .] exemplified to excess', and he explains the change by noting 'His vertigo became chronic, and so did his misanthropy [. . .] there is something which suggests a brain not wholly under control'.[15]

Gulliver's Travels never lacked readers. Vast numbers continued to read the original, and adaptations and condensations grew ever more popular. One kind of adaptation, in fact, managed to avoid the arguments over misanthropy altogether: starting in the 1770s, *Gulliver's Travels* became a children's book. Most of those children's versions not merely excised Gulliver's quick thinking in extinguishing the fire in the empress's rooms and the 'pleasant frolicksome Girl of sixteen' who 'would sometimes set me astride upon one of her Nipples' (II, v, 168). They also usually just omitted the third and fourth parts altogether. Expurgation let readers enjoy the enchantment without ever confronting the ugliness. But the debates over madness and misanthropy continued to dominate grownup discussions.

Multiple Lines of Enquiry

The picture began to change early in the twentieth century as literary criticism became a professional enterprise, the work not of gentleman amateurs but of professional scholars.

One enterprise that kept them busy was source-hunting. People had commented on older writers' influence on Swift before, but in 1923 William A. Eddy first approached the question systematically, ranging over ancient and modern literature for works that Swift may have drawn on. He considered the *Travels* as a 'philosophic voyage', and traced the

[14] Scott, *Works*, XI, 10.
[15] Edmund Gosse, *A History of Eighteenth Century Literature (1660–1780)* (London: MacMillan and Co., 1889), 161.

genre from Lucian's second-century *True History* through the seventeenth-century French writer Cyrano de Bergerac's imaginary voyages. He put Swift's work in the context of classical and modern satires, 'oriental tales', and beast fables. Even the playing with perspective that marks the 'big men and little men' in Parts I and II was traced back to the philosopher George Berkeley's *New Theory of Vision*.[16] The work Eddy began has continued ever since.

Others looked not for sources but for political parallels. Swift's first readers would have spotted parallels between the Lilliputian politics and real-life British politics, as Scott explained:

> The Voyage to Lilliput refers chiefly to the court and politics of England, and Sir Robert Walpole is plainly intimated under the character of the Premier Flimnap [...] The factions of High-Heels and Low-Heels express the factions of Tories and Whigs, the Small-Endians and Big-Endians the religious divisions of Papist and Protestant; and when the heir-apparent was described as wearing one high heel and one low, the Prince of Wales, who at that time had divided his favour between the two leading political parties of England, laughed very heartily.[17]

But how far to take the comparisons? Is *Gulliver's Travels* reducible to political allegory? – is it profitable to track down every allusion to a minor government minister? Writing in the 1970s and 1980s, Phillip Harth and F. P. Lock urged caution in depending on political allegories, making the case that the book's concerns are more general than specific figures in eighteenth-century British politics.[18] Others suggested that the political contexts were essential, but were much more than simple one-to-one correspondences between the book's characters and actual politicians. Z. S. Fink worked to explicate the 'political theory' that informed Swift's work, focusing on the way the division of political power among different factions protects against tyranny.[19] In recent decades, Swift's politics have continued to attract scholars, including those thinking of him in a specifically Irish political context.

Others have contextualised *Gulliver's Travels* not in party politics but in intellectual history. Many critics have seen the *Travels* as a way to gain insight into eighteenth-century philosophical, theological, and scientific thinking. T. O. Wedel, writing in 1926, saw a rivalry between philosophers Thomas Hobbes and John Locke playing out in *Gulliver's Travels*.[20] Because many

[16] William A. Eddy, *'Gulliver's Travels': A Critical Study* (Princeton: Princeton University Press, 1923).
[17] Scott, *Works*, I, 306–7.
[18] Phillip Harth, 'The Problem of Political Allegory in *Gulliver's Travels*', *MP*, 73 (1975–6), 540–7; F. P. Lock, *The Politics of 'Gulliver's Travels'* (Oxford: Clarendon Press, 1980).
[19] Z. S. Fink, 'Political Theory in *Gulliver's Travels*', *ELH*, 14 (1947), 151–61.
[20] T. O. Wedel, 'On the Philosophical Background of *Gulliver's Travels*', *SP*, 23 (1926), 434–50.

thought of the eighteenth century as an 'age of reason', Gordon McKenzie offered a close reading of the word *reason* as it appears throughout Swift's works.[21] *Gulliver's Travels* has been read as both a celebration and a critique of the movement known as the Enlightenment. Samuel Holt Monk, for instance, points out that '*Gulliver's Travels* was written at the height of that phase of European civilisation which we know as the Enlightenment, and the Enlightenment was the first clearly defined manifestation of modernity – the modernity of which our age may be the catastrophic conclusion'. *Gulliver's Travels*, he maintains, was written 'in opposition to the Enlightenment and as an enemy of "modernism"'.[22]

Philosophy shades easily into religion. Irvin Ehrenpreis argued in 1956 that 'the Houyhnhnms represent in general (though not wholly) what he considered to be a deistic view of human nature' – that is, the belief that the world was created by God, but He did not interfere in the daily operation of the universe.[23] George Sherburn, though, was equally confident the Houyhnhnms have nothing to do with Deism: 'Ehrenpreis is not alone in misunderstanding the Houyhnhnms, but I think he is the first to suggest the impossible notion that, in the Houyhnhnms, Swift is satirising deism. To Ehrenpreis deists apparently are simply people who glorify reason'.[24] If we are to understand the book's religious contexts, we will need to be exceptionally clear in defining our terms.

One consequence of exploring the intellectual contexts for *Gulliver's Travels* is that Part III – which, though never the most hated, has historically been the least read part – became newly interesting. When, in 1937, Marjorie Hope Nicolson and Nora Mohler demonstrated that nearly every crazy 'project' under investigation at the Academy of Lagado could be traced to a publication in the scientific journals of Swift's day, they showed that the bizarre experiments involving extracting sunbeams from cucumbers and turning excrement back into food were not mere flights of fancy but topical satire.[25] As historians of science, and scientific modes of understanding, have grown more sophisticated and more sensitive to nuance, Part III of *Gulliver's Travels* has become ever richer.

[21] Gordon McKenzie, 'Swift: Reason and Some of Its Consequences', in Bertrand Bronson et al., *Five Studies in Literature* (Berkeley: University of California Press, 1940), 101–29.
[22] Samuel Holt Monk, 'The Pride of Lemuel Gulliver', *Sewanee Review*, 63 (1955), 48–71 (50).
[23] Irvin Ehrenpreis, 'The Origins of *Gulliver's Travels*', *PMLA*, 72 (1957), 880–99 (889).
[24] George Sherburn, 'Errors Concerning the Houyhnhnms', *MP*, 56 (1958), 92–7 (92).
[25] Marjorie Hope Nicolson and Nora M. Mohler, 'The Scientific Background of Swift's *Voyage to Laputa*', *Annals of Science*, 2 (1937), 299–334.

Swift's complex medical history, combined with the widespread assumption that he succumbed to dementia, made him the favourite of many armchair physicians and psychologists throughout the nineteenth century. In the twentieth, when the theories of Sigmund Freud dominated psychology, the professional analysts got involved. In 1926 Sándor Ferenczi, an associate of Freud and a recent president of the International Psychoanalytical Association, read a paper on 'Gulliver Phantasies', treating Lilliput as the location of Swift's wish-fulfilment regarding his own 'genital inadequacy'.[26] It was the first of many Freudian readings. Soon Swift's scatological obsessions – including the armies of Lilliputians charged with carrying out Gulliver's bowel movements in wheelbarrows and the Yahoos who 'discharge their Excrements on my Head' – were interpreted as signs of the author's 'anal fixation'.[27]

For the Freudians, the misogyny apparent in *Gulliver's Travels* was symptomatic of the author's frustrated sexuality – many noted that we have no clear evidence of any sexual relationships in Swift's life. Not everyone, though, wanted to explain the misogyny with reference to Swift's own psychopathology. Feminist scholarship came late to *Travels*, but in the 1980s critics began to reckon with how women figure in both Swift's work and its critical reception. Ruth Salvaggio, for instance, turned a sceptical eye on the Freudian tradition and argued that 'the whole controversy about whether Swift was neurotic or healthy may have something to do with the masculine perspective that dominates the question – in other words, with the masculine framework of psycho- and literary analysis that governs our reading'.[28] Felicity Nussbaum too was attentive to the role women play in Swift's satire, and Susan Bruce read Part III in connection with the notorious Mary Toft, the woman who in 1727 convinced many people she gave birth to rabbits.[29]

Others have read *Gulliver's Travels* through postcolonial lenses. Swift was born in Ireland and spent much of his life there, and became a hero among many Irish for standing up to some of the British government's policies. Critics like Carole Fabricant and Clement Hawes have written

[26] Sándor Ferenczi, 'Gulliver Phantasies', *The Psychoanalytic Review*, 19 (1932), 226–31.
[27] See especially Norman O. Brown, *Life against Death: The Psychoanalytical Meaning of History* (Middletown: Wesleyan University Press, 1959).
[28] Ruth Salvaggio, 'Swift and Psychoanalysis, Language and Woman', *Women's Studies*, 15 (1988), 417–34 (418).
[29] Felicity A. Nussbaum, 'Gulliver's Malice: Gender and the Satiric Stance', in *Gulliver's Travels: Complete, Authoritative Text with Biographical and Historical Contexts, Critical History, and Essays from Five Contemporary Critical Perspectives*, ed. Christopher Fox (London: Palgrave Macmillan, 1995), 318–34; Susan Bruce, 'The Flying Island and Female Anatomy: Gynaecology and Power in *Gulliver's Travels*', *Gender*, 2 (1988), 60–76.

about this Irish colonial context.[30] Others, meanwhile, have taken the book's form as a travel narrative seriously, and connected it with the larger eighteenth-century colonial project.[31] Swift's Houyhnhnms treat the Yahoos as slaves, which resonates differently when we remember Britain was at that time a leading player in the international slave trade.[32]

Rhetoric and Genre

Despite all these diverse critical approaches, though, the old concern about misanthropy has refused to go away. *Gulliver's Travels* may tell us about eighteenth-century epistemology and political theory; we may learn about the workings of the psyche and the complex legacy of Britain's colonial project – but should we spend any time on it? Much critical ingenuity has been devoted to redeeming a book readers want to love but cannot approve of. Unlike the nineteenth-century readers who simply condemned the book, most modern critics have seen the book's misanthropy not as something to be blamed or excused, but as something to be understood.

How, though, to get a grip on the notoriously slippery text? Many in the mid-twentieth century turned their attention to exactly how the book's irony functions. The so-called New Criticism of the mid-twentieth century convinced many that sufficient attention to irony would settle some literary conundrums once and for all. Samuel Holt Monk, for instance, went straight to the heart of the problem of misanthropy in Part IV by insisting that it is simply not misanthropic. 'To conclude that *Gulliver's Travels* expresses despair', he wrote, 'or that its import is nihilistic is radically to misread the book'.[33] The book *contains* a misanthropist – by the end of Part IV Gulliver is certainly disgusted by humanity – but, he insisted, Swift was not, and he resorted to capital letters to make his point:

> All of this Gulliver is; but let us notice carefully what he is NOT. He is NOT Jonathan Swift. The meaning of the book is wholly distorted if we identify the Gulliver of the last voyage with his creator, and lay Gulliver's

---

[30] Carole Fabricant, *Swift's Landscapes* (Baltimore: Johns Hopkins University Press, 1984); Clement Hawes, 'Three Times Round the Globe: Gulliver and Colonial Discourse', *Cultural Critique*, 18 (1991), 187–214.

[31] Jessica Durgan, 'Souvenirs of the South Seas: Objects of Imperial Critique in Jonathan Swift's *Gulliver's Travels*', in *Eighteenth-Century Thing Theory in a Global Context: From Consumerism to Celebrity Culture*, ed. Ileana Baird and Christina Ionescu (Farnham: Ashgate, 2013), 289–305.

[32] Ann Cline Kelly, 'Swift's Explorations of Slavery in Houyhnhnmland and Ireland', *PMLA*, 91 (1976), 846–55.

[33] Monk, 'The Pride of Lemuel Gulliver', 48.

misanthropy at Swift's door. He is a fully rendered, objective, dramatic character, no more to be identified with Swift than Shylock is to be identified with Shakespeare.[34]

Any reader should be able to see that Gulliver at the end of the book – unable to bear human company, spending all his time in the stables – is not enlightened but absurd.

But when we analyse irony it is much easier to discuss what authors *don't* mean than what they *do*, and satire tells us more about what they dislike than what they admire. As a result, the critics who have paid attention to irony are usually much better at attacking others' interpretations than defending their own. It is easy to go too far in invoking irony: any time an admired author says something we dislike, we can explain it away by declaring the author is speaking ironically, and if we like what we see we assume they are being direct. As Wayne C. Booth put it, too many

> critics, unable to believe that an author could really contradict their own beliefs, conclude that he is being ironic. Pious authors cannot possibly have meant their piety, defenders of authority must have been kidding. In the fourth book of *Gulliver's Travels,* Swift cannot possibly have approved of the rationality of the Houyhnhnms because it is so obviously – by some standards of this century – absurd.[35]

Because Swift offends *our* sensibilities, he cannot have meant what he said. This is a bad critical method, so we must be very conscientious in citing evidence that any given sentence is offered either ironically or sincerely.

If the answer to the problem of Swift's misanthropy is not to be found in attention to irony, maybe an answer can be found in genre. What kind of *thing* is *Gulliver's Travels?* It is a long fictional prose narrative, so we may want to discuss it with the other long fictional prose narratives of the day. But the most influential account of that form in the eighteenth century, Ian Watt's *Rise of the Novel* (1957), does not even mention *Gulliver's Travels.* Why not? Watt and his successors who told the story of the early novel focused especially on what he called 'formal realism' and on the depth and coherence of the characters' psychology, and by that measure *Gulliver's Travels* can hardly be called a novel. Contrasting *Gulliver's Travels* with contemporary novels, though, helps us pay attention to the places where Swift departs from the realistic depiction of the world, and

---

[34] Monk, 'The Pride of Lemuel Gulliver', 56.
[35] Wayne C. Booth, *A Rhetoric of Irony* (Chicago: University of Chicago Press, 1974), 82.

especially to the shallowness and inconsistency of Gulliver as a character. In Christopher Fox's words,

> Gulliver is not a character, or even a narrator, in the usual sense – certainly not in the way a character operates in a typical novel. He does not grow, develop, change, or 'learn' from his experiences [...] and he displays no consistency of attitude or, despite his protests, integrity of character. He is pretty much whatever Swift wants or needs him to be at any given point in the narration.[36]

Most critics agree *Gulliver's Travels* is not a novel, but when pressed to identify its genre, the usual answer is 'satire'. But not everyone agrees that the word *satire* refers to a genre at all. Satire studies has been divided into two schools of thought. One treats satire as a genre, derived from the 'formal verse satires' of the ancient Roman satirists Horace, Juvenal, and Persius. The other thinks of satire as a 'mode', a kind of critical spirit that can be found in any genre. We might say it comes down to whether we focus on the noun *satire* or the adjective *satirical*. There can be no question that *Gulliver's Travels* is often satirical: Swift ridicules hypocrisy, greed, pride, philosophies, religious conflicts, economic and linguistic theories, lawyers, scientists, priests, and a thousand other things. But can we say *Gulliver's Travels* is 'a satire'? – what assumptions are we making when we classify it that way?

Others have suggested different genres might make sense of the book. Many critics have considered it as part of a tradition of utopian writing, stretching from Plato's *Republic* to Thomas More's *Utopia*. The floating island has shown up in discussions of the prehistory of science fiction. W. B. C. Watkins, in *Perilous Balance*, granted that most of *Travels* is a satire, but maintained that in Part IV the book deviates into tragedy. John F. Ross, writing in 1942, went in the opposite direction, arguing that even the most corrosive and Juvenalian passages contain a lot of comic, Horatian satire.[37] And Swift's playful style, his ironic misdirections, and the inconsistency of his narrative voice have encouraged some readers to think of him as a proto-modernist or proto-postmodernist author, a precursor to his fellow Irishman James Joyce.

---

[36] Christopher Fox, 'A Critical History of *Gulliver's Travels*', in *Gulliver's Travels*, ed. Fox, 226–7.
[37] W. B. C. Watkins, *Perilous Balance: The Tragic Genius of Swift, Johnson, & Sterne* (Princeton: Princeton University Press, 1939); John F. Ross, 'The Final Comedy of Lemuel Gulliver', *University of California Publications in English*, 8 (1941), 175–96.

Hard, Soft, Spongy, Soggy

Still the question remains: is Part IV misanthropic? Is Gulliver's position at the end of the book, convinced all human beings are repulsive Yahoos unable to live up to the standards of the gloriously rational Houyhnhnms, also Swift's position, and should it be ours? Or is the misanthropic Gulliver ridiculous at the end of the book, and is Swift telling us that the Houyhnhnms are not ideals at all?

James L. Clifford gave us the terms in which this discussion has been held ever since: 'hard' and 'soft' readings. He defines them succinctly: 'By "hard" I mean an interpretation which stresses the shock and difficulty of the work, with almost tragic overtones, while by "soft" I mean the tendency to find comic passages and compromise solutions'.[38] Both readings present problems.

The 'hard' reading 'stresses the shock and difficulty of the work', and if we take the Houyhnhnms seriously as ideals, there is plenty of shock and difficulty. The rational Houyhnhnms are emotionless – are we supposed to believe this is an ideal? Because they cannot conceive of lies they have no fiction, surely a problem for a writer like Swift. Maybe worst of all, they advocate wiping out Yahoo-kind completely. Swift's contemporaries had no word for this mass execution, but we do: genocide. Some readers went out of their way not to think about the Houyhnhnms' proposed Yahoo genocide in terms of the twentieth century's real-world genocidal projects, the Holocaust above all. But others asked whether that was really necessary. If the Holocaust is part of what genocide means today, why should we not see it in *Travels*?[39]

Concerns like these – the belief that Swift cannot have wanted us to be on the side of the Houyhnhnms – led many critics in the middle of the twentieth century to join Team Soft. But the tide turned in the late 1950s, as hardliners insisted the Houyhnhnms' apparent flaws are merely on the surface. For advocates of the hard reading, there is nothing funny about Gulliver's fate: he winds up not a figure of fun but a pathetic emblem of human inadequacy. It is hard to take, but why should we expect the truth to be pleasing? And just as soft-school critics invoked the Holocaust as evidence that Swift cannot have been a supporter of genocide, the hard-school critics

---

[38] James L. Clifford, 'Gulliver's Fourth Voyage: "Hard" and "Soft" Schools of Interpretation', in *Quick Springs of Sense: Studies in the Eighteenth Century*, ed. Larry S. Champion (Athens: University of Georgia Press, 1974), 33–49 (33).

[39] See Claude Rawson, *God, Gulliver, and Genocide: Barbarism and the European Imagination, 1492–1945* (Oxford: Oxford University Press, 2001).

in the wake of the Second World War looked at civilisation's smoking ruins and thought that despair and contempt toward humankind might be perfectly justified.

The choice between 'hard' and 'soft' need not be binary. As Clifford put it, 'Inescapably there continues to be a variety of interpretations. Some of them, while not strictly "soft," could be called "spongy" or "mushy," or even "soggy," although others could more fairly be termed "firm" or "hard of center"'.[40] We can ask about Swift's intentions in several ways, and sometimes slight differences in framing the question lead to different answers. We might ask, for instance, whether and when Gulliver speaks for Swift: is Gulliver's disgust at humanity really Swift's disgust at humanity? Or we can ask whether the Houyhnhnms are truly ideal: might they too be the targets of satire? We can think about whether Houyhnhnm-land really constitutes a utopia, or whether it is actually a dystopia packaged in utopian form. Finally, we can ask whether human beings are nothing more than Yahoos – or, more pointed still, whether *we* are nothing more than Yahoos. This is the lesson Gulliver learns, but is it what Swift teaches us? Are we supposed to think of Yahoos as only a part of us that we might hope to transcend, or are we truly nothing more than the debased, fallen creatures that provoke so much disgust?

There is always the danger that the misanthropy debate over Part IV will crowd out all other discussions of the book – it has been the case since the eighteenth century. Leo Damrosch puts it well: 'The Fourth Voyage will always be controversial, because it forces us to question our deep, self-flattering assumptions about that animal called man'.[41] Whatever answers we arrive at, Swift promises to leave us profoundly uncomfortable. After three centuries, *Gulliver's Travels* continues to vex the world.

---

[40] Clifford, 'Gulliver's Fourth Voyage', 38–9.
[41] Leo Damrosch, *Jonathan Swift: His Life and His World* (New Haven: Yale University Press, 2013), 378.

CHAPTER 15

Further Voyages

Daniel Cook

Despite Swift's complaints (in character) about the 'Libels, and Keys, and Reflections, and Memoirs, and Second Parts' loaded up on *Gulliver's Travels*, including a fraudulent *Volume III* (1727), secondary authors gleefully expanded the world of Lemuel Gulliver through multiple fifth voyages, spinoffs, mock-treatises, verse exchanges, and much more, for many more years to come (*GT*, 11). They still do. Using Jeanne K. Welcher and George E. Bush Jr's eight-volume collection of pre-1800 Gulliveriana as a guide, we can identify close to two hundred imitative or supplementary works that were produced and reproduced between late 1726 and 1730 alone, and well over a hundred in each of the following two decades, the 1730s and 1740s. In 1726, we find twenty-six Gulliver-related publications – remarkable, considering that Swift's book appeared in October. For 1727 the figure leaps to sixty-eight items.

Representing a multimedia, word-and-image (and sometimes wordless) body of materials, 'Gulliveriana' must remain a broad term, even if we can easily discount loose reworkings, nominal homages, or incidental references. (In what follows I focus on print-based prose and verse; essays elsewhere in this collection, by Jones and Menzies, consider Gulliver's afterlives on screen and across visual culture.) Some Gulliveriana is Gulliveriana in name only. In 1730 and 1731 six writings under the pseudonym Martin Gulliver and one under Martinus Gulliverianus appeared in Dublin. There is also an alleged brother, Ephraim Gulliver. There have been many Lemuel Gulliver Juniors too. Most Gulliveriana nevertheless signals a formal connection with *Travels*, whether it revisits old settings, fills in perceived gaps in the narrative, or provides additional material. To take a familiar example, *Modern Gulliver's Travels* (1796) opens with an account of the infamous traveller's romance with a Blefuscudian lady, which, we learn, was omitted from the prior book on the grounds of decency. Filling this omission, the new author seizes on a small hint in the original, thereby legitimising his endeavours. *An Account of the State of Learning in the Empire of Lilliput* claims on its title page to be

Faithfully Transcribed out of Captain LEMUEL GULLIVER*'s General Description of the Empire of Lilliput, mention'd in the 69th Page of the First Volume of his Travels* (1728), which marks out its affiliation with the original publication as precisely as possible.

With John Arbuthnot (the most likely author of *Account*) and Alexander Pope (author of Lilliputian poems) and other members of Swift's circle in mind, Welcher distinguishes between complicit Gulliverian writers and opportunists: 'His friends caught his spirit of self-imitation, echoed it for his delight, passed it on. The genuine alter egos of Swift entered into mock complicity with Gulliver. The fake ones functioned as Gulliver clones'.[1] A distinction between 'genuine' alter egos and 'fake' clones is problematic, but it does capture a curious conundrum within the study of Gulliveriana and, by extension, allographic sequels (that is, texts not written by the original author): to what extent is the field shaped by the authors, whether primary or secondary, whether outsiders or complicit, or by the consumers? To what extent is complicity akin to professional status? Welcher and Bush Jr acknowledge over sixty significant responses to *Travels* that endeavour 'to reproduce something of its style, intent, and design'.[2] This definition is also problematic because it fails to accommodate partisanship, or anti-Swiftian, contra-Swiftian, and de-Swiftian responses, and it would rely on a narrow consensus on what the original intentions and targets are. Tone and topicality aside, we might limit our focus to technicalities. For Nicholas Seager, Gulliverian sequels are 'prose fictions that accept the fictional world detailed in Swift's original, and which supplement it in some way – accretive, rather than analogous works'.[3]

We might factor in plot and character. Would the new Gullivers have to fall in line with their prototype? Would the same logic apply to other, less prominent characters, such as Mary Gulliver (née Burton)? Does *Travels* even have a replicable plot? Reflecting on the wide appeal of *Travels* for secondary authors, David A. Brewer considers the plotlessness of the original: 'There is no actual story behind the bulk of Gulliver's plot. Or rather, there are as many stories as there are readers'. All they need to do, he continues, 'is not to contradict the *Travels* themselves too egregiously'.[4] But

[1] Jeanne K. Welcher, 'Gulliveriana: Ways of Reading *Gulliver's Travels*', in *Approaches to Teaching Swift's Gulliver's Travels*, ed. Edward J. Rielly (New York: MLA, 1988), 96–101 (97).
[2] *Gulliveriana*, ed. Jeanne K. Welcher and George E. Bush, Jr, 8 vols. (Gainesville: Scholars' Facsimiles & Reprints, 1970–99), I, v.
[3] Nicholas Seager, '*Gulliver's Travels* Serialized and Continued', in *Münster* 6, 543–62 (551).
[4] David A. Brewer, *The Afterlife of Character, 1726–1825* (Philadelphia: University of Pennsylvania Press, 2005), 39.

what would the protected characteristics be? Gulliveriana is not necessarily tethered to Gulliver's voyages. Gulliveriana does not even need a Gulliver – we might call Gulliver-less imitations 'Gulliveriads'. Some unannounced Gulliveriads thrive on a more substantial engagement with Swift's materials than some explicit Gulliveriana, where the action might be slight, or the satire less severe, even if the original time period, characters, setting, and the like are retained. Having established some common terms and issues, let us explore some notable examples. First, we will look at different ways in which authors have filled in and filled out Gulliver's world in his name. The second section explores proleptic continuations attributed to Gulliver's offspring, time-forwarded Gullivers, and other, non-Gulliverian authors.

Innumerable Passages

In a letter included in the first and subsequent editions of *Travels*, the fictive print agent Richard Sympson claims that this volume 'would have been at least twice as large, if I had not made bold to strike out innumerable Passages' (*GT*, 16). If Sympson can destroy unwritten material that only existed in a fictional universe, such material could be restored, rewritten (that is, written), either by the author himself or appropriators. The vagueness of the phrase 'innumerable Passages' even goads adapters into counterfeiting the seemingly missing pieces in any form they wished. Sympson also gestures towards the prevailing culture of abridgement, which had latched onto *Travels* as early as 1727. Omitting the third and fourth voyages, Francis Newbery's *The Adventures of Captain Gulliver* (1772) remained in print for the next thirty years before being phased out in favour of further low-cost abridgements. While textual cuts could be characterised as pragmatic, some alterations were ideological. As Julian Fung has shown, many condensers softened Part IV.[5] Different versions of *Travels* attracted different readerships. Many abridgements were aimed at English-speaking children. Some were foreign-language retellings attuned to local interests.

Many of the fifty-five child-friendly versions examined by M. Sarah Smedman, published between 1727 and 1985, simplify the language and syntax.[6] Twelve switch to third-person narration – just like Newbery's

[5] Julian Fung, 'Early Condensations of *Gulliver's Travels*: Images of Swift as Satirist in the 1720s', *SP*, 114 (2017), 395–425 (423).

[6] M. Sarah Smedman, 'Like Me, Like Me Not: *Gulliver's Travels* as Children's Book', in *The Genres of Gulliver's Travels*, ed. Frederik N. Smith (Newark: University of Delaware Press, 1990), 75–100. For a more recent study, see Haifeng Hui, 'The Changing Adaptation Strategies of Children's Literature:

popular version. Many add material, seemingly to make Gulliver more heroic, as in Edith Robart's *Gulliver in Lilliput* (1909). Other authors created Gulliverian spinoffs for young audiences, such as 'Lilliputius Gulliver' (Richard Johnson), who edited into ten volumes *The Lilliputian Library*, among other things. Not all abridgements merely reduce the original text. Some add new material, to smooth out the joins if nothing else, or rework specific elements. Then there are murderous continuations that seek to obscure the original by claiming the true authority or 'correcting' mistakes. On 26 August 1727, *The British Journal* advertised the imminent publication of a book by a certain Captain Alexander Smith, an authorial figure known for a bestselling history of the lives of modern criminals.[7] The latest book would overturn the recent *Travels* written by an imposter 'who falsely usurps the Name, Stile and Title, of Capt. Gulliver'. No such book has been found yet, but it speaks to the complex ways in which a market-focused model of adaptation theory might prove useful for understanding the motives driving different types of Gulliveriana. In particular, Linda Hutcheon's notion that an adapted text provides a 'reservoir of instructions' rubs against the more cynical treatment of adapters as 'raiders'.[8] One such raider is Samuel Richardson, who in the same month he printed the first abridged version of *Travels* for J. Stone and R. Long, attached an unauthorized *Volume III* to *Travels*. *Volume III* adopts the structural pattern of Swift's book, the reservoir of instruction. Despite appearances, the text Richardson raids most egregiously is in fact Denis Vairasse's *History of the Sevarites or Sevarambi* (1675), which had not been reprinted in English since 1700.[9]

Part I of *Volume III* starts with an imitation of the original second voyage to Brobdingnag, which comprises about two chapters. The extensive plagiarism from Vairasse comes as early as page 51 and occupies the rest of Part I. Part II is almost entirely derivative, though none of it is a straightforward lifting. Rather, it abridges Vairasse, which, says Seager, 'shows some care'. With regards to the Gulliverian material, which includes a return to worlds and characters created by Swift, Richardson's narrative is the first to extend the story chronologically beyond where the first two volumes end. After embarking from Brobdingnag,

Two Centuries of Children's Editions of *Gulliver's Travels*', *Hungarian Journal of English and American Studies*, 17 (2011), 245–62.
[7] *A Compleat History of the Lives and Robberies of the Most Notorious Highway-men, Foot-pads, Shop-lifts, and Cheats, of Both Sexes, in and about London and Westminster* reached a fifth edition as recently as 1719. Captain Smith had disappeared from the print market by 1726.
[8] Linda Hutcheon with Siobhan O'Flynn, *A Theory of Adaptation*, 2nd ed. (2006; London: Routledge, 2013), 84, 88.
[9] Nicholas Seager, 'Samuel Richardson and the Third Volume of *Gulliver's Travels*', *SStud*, 28 (2013), 128–36.

Gulliver finds (to him and most if not all of his readers) new lands: Sporunda
and Sevarambia. Adhering to an author-as-owner model, Walter Scott was not
alone in dismissing *Volume III* as a mere imposition. But such impositions
lingered. French, Dutch, and German versions appeared in 1728. There were
more than a dozen printings of all three volumes together across Europe as one
work before 1740. As late as the 1790s, the first Spanish version of *Travels* still
included *Volume III*. No mere book-historical anomaly, *Volume III* should also
be read as 'a re-envisioning of Swift's *Travels*'.[10] It is at once a forgery and
a 'genuine' continuation, as Welcher puts it (*Gulliveriana*, III, x). Wittily, the
introduction to *Volume III* outlines a motivation driving the continuation that
becomes a commonplace in Gulliver's afterlives, the fear of being forgotten: 'I
am terribly afraid some more fortunate Mortal will tread the Paths I have gone
before'. More than that, the author fears being over-written when the new
traveller renames 'the Countries I have discover'd'.[11]

Richardson even prolongs Gulliver's quarrel with his fictive print agent,
Sympson (here Simpson, a friend rather than a cousin). Claiming the 'Editor
of my former Volumes' now avoids him, he references the alleged bulkiness
of the original, which 'would be considerably increas'd, if he had printed my
Course of Sailing, and many Sea-Terms' (*Vol. III*, 6). That is, Richardson the
author endorses Swift's belated paratextual joke about superfluous, unwritten materials. As a sequelist, Richardson also extends the ending of *Travels*.
We had left Gulliver in the company of his horses. By *Volume III* his respect
for his 'Companions in the Stables' has 'augmented daily'. After a lengthy
account of his attempts to educate his horses (now named Lmnfrimpnmo
and Trtpmpfnic), Gulliver realises he must take them to Houyhnhnm-land.
The new adventure, via 'A Second Voyage to Brobdingnag', bolts onto the
old one. But unlike Swift, Richardson practically kills off Gulliver at the end
of the book, where, now widowed, the eponymous hero awaits the inevit-
ability of death. Published at around the same time, *Memoirs of the Court of
Lilliput* (1727) builds on Swift's property in a markedly different way: the
title page calls it 'omitted' material. The Preface also hints that there are yet
more scandalous supplements waiting to be published, from Gulliver's time
in other lands: '*I publish at present but that part which relates to* Lilliput, *and
shall proceed gradually with the Memoirs of the several Kingdoms he resided at in
their due order*'.[12] Read as a legitimate extension of *Travels*, *Memoirs* consoli-
dates the unsettling threat of further, perhaps unmasked satiric swiping.

---

[10] Seager, '*Gulliver's Travels* Serialized and Continued', 557–8.
[11] *Travels into Several Remote Nations of the World* (1727), III, 2–3.
[12] *Memoirs of the Court of Lilliput* (1727), vi.

It also introduces new characters and settings, and even newly engages familiar Swiftian targets (projectors, legal inequalities, and the like). Like *Volume III*, *Memoirs* implies a familiar relationship with the original author-character, as well as with Gulliver's print agent. In fact, *Memoirs* adds a further paratextual character, its alleged publisher Lucas Bennet, who claims he received '*the original Papers under Mr.* Lemuel Gulliver'*s own Hand*' from Sympson. But it eschews any semblance of being an autographic sequel. An anti-Swiftian parody by proxy, in its mockery of prominent members of his circle, *Memoirs* was associated with Eliza Haywood in Pope's *Dunciad*.[13] Judged as an illegitimate extension, moreover, it inverts the values of *Travels* while filling in its apparent redactions. Gulliver becomes gossipy, and the focus shifts to private intrigues not public-office failures. While Swift's account includes coy if boastful remarks about Gulliver's exposed penis in Lilliput, the new author (still in the voice of Gulliver) lingers over the romantic intrigues of the Lilliputian ladies. Written instead in the voice of an unknown author, *A Cursory View of the History of Lilliput* (1727) challenges Gulliver's account outright. In the words of the editor: '*I must observe to the Reader, that in those Places where my Friend and Mr.* Gulliver *differ, I am of opinion the latter was mistaken*' (*Gulliveriana*, V, 110).

Some 'corrections' are whimsically benign and, from a narratorial perspective, even welcome. Whereas the original Gulliver identifies only two kingdoms which Lilliputians called the two great empires of the world, the new author 'has often assured me, there were divers other Monarchies and Republicks composed of the same sort of Men'. Other changes speak to Whiggish principles. Swift's fictional equivalent of the future George II plays to both Whigs and Tories, as signified by his hobbling gait (one high heel, one low), but *A Cursory View* dismisses this as an error of interpretation. Corrections notwithstanding, the new pamphlet assumes no prior knowledge ('The *Lilliputians* [. . .] are Men about six Inches high'), suggesting it can stand apart from the original. Often attributed to a member of Swift's literary circle, John Arbuthnot, *An Account of the State of Learning in the Empire of Lilliput* (1728), modifies Gulliver's authorial property more explicitly. Like *Memoirs*, it revisits familiar targets, though it addresses them more blatantly than we see in *Travels*. Here, the pedantic librarian Bullum, who is clearly modelled on the Royal Librarian Richard

---

[13] On Haywood's authorship see Seager, '*Gulliver's Travels* Serialized and Continued', 552. For deattribution see Leah Orr, 'The Basis for Attribution in the Canon of Eliza Haywood', *The Library*, 7th series, 12 (2011), 335–75 (374).

Bentley, frustrates Gulliver's research: 'Bullum, as I heard afterwards, was in great Wrath, and loaded me with many opprobrious Names, for refusing to hear his Speech out, and daring to treat a Man of his Learning with so little respect' (*Gulliveriana*, V, 194).

Amusingly, as Seager notices, the 'greater Work' filled in by *Account* amounts to thirty-seven pages: 'The joke here is *against* the desire for more'.[14] And a substantial part of the mini-account, as highlighted on the title page, is given to an improbable biography of Bullum. Promised five hundred books – an erroneous 'Interpolation' in the Emperor's order, the librarian claims – Gulliver receives only five. Amid generic titles (such as 'A Collection of Poetry') we have titillating callbacks to Swift's most celebrated scenes ('A Dissertation upon Tramescans and Slamescans, or High-heel'd and Low heel'd Shoes' and 'A Bundle of Controversies concerning the primitive way of breaking Eggs'). Because the Lilliputian context seems extraneous, we might dismiss *Memoirs* for hijacking the popularity of *Travels*. *Account*, meanwhile, happily deposits supplementary material into the Gulliverian archive while appropriating the smallness conceit to make Swiftian jokes against vainglorious scholars. Intertextually, it even expands the Lilliputian language to include such words as Glomflastru and Mulro. Mercenary motives, and even literary merit, aside, one consistent way to judge Gulliveriana would be to consider the contribution it makes to Swift's heterocosm. *Account* at once fills in and fills out the first part of *Travels*. *Memoirs* repurposes it. *Volume III* embellishes and then closes it. *A Cursory View* reboots it.

Other early Gulliveriana borrowed Gulliver's voice but largely neglected his voyages. *The Anatomist Dissected, or the Man-Midwife finely brought to Bed* (1727) appeared a matter of months after *Travels*. Hailed as Surgeon and Anatomist to the Kings of Lilliput and Blefuscu, and Fellow of the Academy of Sciences in Balnibarbi, Gulliver weighs in on a bizarre real-life hoax involving Mary Toft, who purportedly gave birth to a litter of rabbits. Gulliver the neglectful family man becomes the ironic author of *The Pleasures and Felicity of Marriage* (1745). Poets ventriloquised Gulliver, his wife, and other characters. As with the prose works explored above, often these poems expanded the scope of *Travels* by returning to old scenes. Others were entirely ornamental. An unlikely balladist, the ship surgeon is the alleged author of *An Excellent New Ballad on the Wedding of Pritty Miss S–ly to Jolly Old J–o* (1730), a fairly conventional piece of street verse that addresses a common theme in the period: age-inappropriate

[14] Seager, '*Gulliver's Travels* Serialized and Continued', 554.

relationships. Conscripted to Edmund Curll's army of hacks, Captain Gulliver is given *The Totness Address Transversed* (1727), itself a loose appropriation of an anonymous and entirely Gulliver-less satirical poem printed for H. Whitridge. Credited as Poet Laureate to the King of Lilliput, Lemuel Gulliver leads Henry Fielding's early squib, *The Masquerade, A Poem* (1728). Unlike the Curllian piece, the latter makes explicit reference to *Travels*, though it does not reboot, rework, or even revisit it in any extended way.

The most blatant sequel is simply titled *Sequel to Gulliver's Travels* (1830), which the editor claims is based on an unpublished epilogue (or a eulogy, in their words) from the end of *Travels*. Having 'hinted' at the end of the ninth chapter of the fourth voyage (in Swift's text) that 'I should in a short time publish a whole volume by itself upon the manners and virtues of this excellent people', namely the Houyhnhnms, Gulliver now resolves to 'redeem' his promise.[15] Rather than extending the narrative, *Sequel* fills out the description of the Houyhnhnms – it is an elliptic continuation. More recent ventriloquisations of Gulliver include Conrad Peregrinus's (Kurt Friedlaender) *A Voyage to Springistan* (1972), from a German translation of a manuscript in Swift's hand 'recovered' from an Irish castle, and John Paul Brady's *A Voyage to Inishneefa* (1987), which had been 'discovered' in Swift's writing desk in Saint Patrick's Hospital in Dublin. Offering a suggestive parallel with Swift's Struldbruggs, Justus Franz Wittkop's *Gullivers letzte Reise* (*Gulliver's Last Voyage*, 1941) takes the protagonist to the Island of the Mortals, whose inhabitants live for only thirty days. Matthew Hodgart's *A New Voyage to the Country of the Houyhnhnms* (1970), another 'Fifth Part', mimics the typography of the original (capitalisation, italicisation) and brings back old characters (Yahoos, Houyhnhnms); it is at once an appropriation and an extension. The Sorel Nag claims 'things are different now', but the New Yahoos, now likened to modern-day college students, are no less scatological.[16]

By the end of *A New Voyage*, Gulliver's misanthropy has descended into madness: 'I have crept into a Bin, that formerly held Oats, and I have pulled the Cover over my Head; and now I sit in the Dark, scribbling, scribbling . . . ' (91). The final ellipsis ingeniously captures the unwritten, or yet-to-be-written, Gulliveriana that lay ahead. This Gulliver, though, is silenced. Brady's Gulliver ends more peaceably: 'A man could live a secure and contented life in England as nowhere else on the globe'.[17] We find precedent for a happier

---

[15] *Sequel to Gulliver's Travels: An Eulogy* (London: J. Jaques, 1830), 3–4.
[16] Matthew Hodgart, *A New Voyage to the Country of the Houyhnhnms* (New York: G. P. Putnam's Sons, 1970), 32.
[17] John Paul Brady, *A Voyage to Inishneefa* (Santa Barbara: John Daniel, 1987), 103.

hero in *Gulliver's Last Voyage, describing Ballymugland, or the Floating Island* (1825), in which the protagonist declares in closing that he is ready 'to set out, on the ensuing spring, in quest of new discoveries'.[18] Alison Fell's *The Mistress of Lilliput or The Pursuit* (1999) comes back to the site of the first voyage but instead radically refocuses the point of view to that of Mary Gulliver. Lauren Chater takes this refocalisation further in her lengthy novel *Gulliver's Wife* (2020), where Mary's life independent of and with her husband is extensively filled out. As early as 1727, the abandoned Mrs Gulliver had aired her grievances in Pope's 'Mary Gulliver to Capt. Lemuel Gulliver', one of five poems added to the second edition of *Travels*.[19] Desperate to reunite with her husband, she is willing to indulge his hippophilia and other habits: 'I'd call thee *Houyhnhnm*, that high sounding Name, / Thy Children's Noses all should twang the same' (*GT*, 586). In the modern novels, Mary tracks down her husband, at once exploring new yet familiar ground. Textually, as Ruth Menzies shows, Gulliver's original tirade against colonialism, among other things, is 'inserted' into the secondary narrative by Fell.[20]

In form and tone, Pope's epistle and Fell's *Mistress* recalibrate the barely sketched relationship between the Gullivers in starkly different ways. Fell's Mary now gains agency, overseas; Pope's merely demands to be heard at home. Although written in the third person, *Mistress* contains free indirect discourse and extensive dialogue, allowing for emotional insights or dramatic exchanges between the Gullivers as needed. Begging affection from her husband ('What, touch me not? what, shun a Wife's Embrace?'), in a one-way verse conversation, Pope's Mary becomes a figure of fun. As Brewer observes, the poem 'recasts Gulliver's misanthropic repulsion toward his wife as bawdy farce'.[21] In the purview of anti-Gulliver Gulliveriana, alternatively, Mary exposes her husband's dereliction of duty: 'to see / The *Groom* and *Sorrel Mare* preferr'd to me!' (*GT*, 584). Despite their formal differences, Fell's and Pope's texts expand, and comment on, the sexlessness of the original Gullivers. While overtly engaging with Swift's material, the Lilliputian ode enjoyed a lengthy afterlife of its own, aesthetically (as part of a wider poetics of transgression that prioritised an oxymoronic compound of high and low

---

[18] *Gulliver's Last Voyage, Describing Ballymugland, or the Floating Island* (London: William Cole, 1825), 79.

[19] Contra Faulkner, modern scholars usually follow Norman Ault's attribution of all five poems to Pope: *New Light on Pope* (1949; Hamden: Archon Books, 1967), 231–42.

[20] Ruth Menzies, 'Re-writing *Gulliver's Travels*: The Demise of a Genre?', *E-Rea*, 3 (2005), https://doi.org/10.4000/erea.613.

[21] Brewer, *The Afterlife of Character*, 36.

art) and materially (beyond the pages of *Travels*).[22] Not long after adding them to his reset *Travels*, Benjamin Motte issued the poems in a separate collection, *Several Copies of Verses on Occasion of Captain Gulliver's Travels* (1727), in a large print run. Pirated reprints quickly circulated in Dublin.

Two Lilliputian Odes (1727) soon followed. The first, the bawdy ode 'On the Engine with which Captain *Gulliver* extinguish'd the Flames in the Royal Palace', replays an infamous scene in Swift's Lilliput, while the second, 'Inviting a Bookseller to a Coffee-House, where the Author was', explicitly adopts the authorial persona of one of Pope's paratextual poems – 'Sure as I am Titty Tit', Lilliput's Poet Laureate. Members of Swift's circle revelled in the prosodic absurdity of the form, beyond the prose-shaped *Travels*. 'Whereas the wits of the town are mightily taken with the Lilliputian measure, and have shrunk their verses to two syllables in a line', writes Arbuthnot, 'the author is preparing for the Press an ODE, which shall contain but a Syllable and a half in a Line'.[23] But what would half a syllable sound like? Outsiders used the mini-genre against Swift. Jonathan Smedley smuggled into *Gulliveriana* (1728), his patchwork attack on his rival cleric-poet, 'A Lilliputian Ode; In Imitation of, and humbly Inscrib'd to, Captain Gulliver', in which he mockingly conflates Swift's littleness conceit (taken from *Travels*) with his scatological style (as exhibited in his poetry):

> *Eccho* too!
> Nasty Verse!
> Things so *true*
> To rehearse.[24]

Most early Lilliputian and Brobdingnagian verse has an incidental connection to *Travels*. Exceptions include the five poems by Pope, which enhance the perspectives of Gulliverian characters, such as the Lilliputians' mind-bending awe in Titty Tit's 'To Quinbus Flestrin the Man-Mountain': 'Can our Eyes | Reach thy Size?' (*GT*, 574). 'The Words of the King of Brobdingnag', conversely, considers the opposite point of view: 'In Miniature see *Nature's* Power appear' (*GT*, 587). 'The Lamentation of Glumdalclitch for the Loss of Grildrig', a mock-pastoral, captures the young giantess's extreme distress: 'She wept, she blubber'd, and she tore her Hair' (*GT*, 576). In *Dreams in Lilliput* (1790), a collection of instructive verses for children, and *Lilliput Lyrics* (1899) alike, references to *Travels* are barely noticeable. The same can

[22] See Thomas Van der Goten, 'The Lilliputian Ode, 1726–1826', *American Notes and Queries*, 28 (2015), 94–104.
[23] Quoted in Welcher and Bush, *Gulliveriana*, VI.I, lxxii.
[24] *Gulliveriana: Or, a Fourth Volume of Miscellanies* (1728), 266.

be said of the plentiful prose works for young audiences, such as *The Lilliputian History* (1800). *The Lilliputian Library, or Gulliver's Museum* (1782) poses a more complex case. In a medley of lectures, poems, fables, and jokes, Lilliputius Gulliver reworks his kinsman's materials while adding copious items to the Gulliverian archive, usually by appropriating Aesop and other familiar authors. Within a section on voyages, he rewrites the first two parts of *Travels* in a simplified, third-person format: it is a reboot from within.

The post-*Travels* story of Gulliver's 'little nurse' from Brobdingnag makes up Leo Sonderegger's *Glumdalclitch* (2000), where she grows into womanhood, marries Harlbruug (a new character), creates a Gulliver museum, and is saved from the villainous Skraagnok (another new character) by a crew of English sailors who have retraced Gulliver's steps. Lilliput or relocated Lilliputians have long featured prominently in children's Gulliveriana, most memorably in Henry Winterfeld's *Castaways in Lilliput* (1960) and T. H. White's *Mistress Masham's Repose* (1946), where Maria finds them exiled on the lakes of Malplaquet. Jamie finds them, later, in Andrew Dalton's homage to White, *The Temples of Malplaquet* (2005). Gulliver does make an appearance in Sam Gayton's *Lilliput* (2013) – as a malevolent giant who imprisons the heroine. Usually, nominally condensed versions of *Travels* for children render Gulliver's character benign and sketch him in pastel colours. At each extreme, we find a different but entirely plausible iteration of Swift's principal character.

Gulliver's Clones

Arguably the most persistent form of Gulliveriana concerns not a period-appropriate Lemuel Gulliver but his fictional clones, whether nominal offspring or time-forwarded travellers who share his name. Some were self-proclaimed descendants, such as Philip Hippophil (a great-grandson on the father's side) in Walter Copland Perry's *The Revolt of the Horses* (1898), a war-torn and relocated extension of the story of the Houyhnhnms. The most famous clone appeared early, in Pierre-François Desfontaines's *Le Nouveau Gulliver* (1730), which John Lockman translated into English a year later as *The Travels of Mr. John Gulliver, Son to Capt. Lemuel Gulliver*, and which responded to Desfontaines's loose translation of the original, *Les Voyages de Gulliver*.[25] Lemuel Gulliver, Jun. is also the pseudonymous author of

[25] See Paul-Gabriel Boucé, 'Gulliver's Frenchified Travels to Blefuscu: The First Two Translations', in *Münster* 4, 379–86.

Modern Gulliver's Travels, where he finds Lilliput almost a century after his father had discovered it. Yet another Gulliver the Younger 'retraces' (his word) his father's steps in *Voyage to Locuta* (1818), though he opts to proceed 'still farther', just beyond Laputa, to explore another island in a similar setting – this is repetition with a difference.[26] By 1979, Lemuel Gulliver Jr had found innumerable new worlds, as in Esmé Dodderidge's SF retelling, *The New Gulliver; or, The Adventures of Lemuel Gulliver Jr in Capovolta*, though this offspring is a namesake only.

Desfontaines's narrator is apparently the same John mentioned in *Travels* as the son of Mary and Lemuel before the latter undertook his ill-fated voyage in 1696. Less plausibly, the younger Gulliver of *Modern Gulliver's Travels* is the illegitimate issue of a Blefuscudian nun. Conceived between 1703 and 1705, if we stick with the dates established in *Travels*, he lives to write his autobiography well into his nineties. (Deliberately skewed logic aside, a precedent for time-forwarded clones had been set.) The French editor's preface insists on the originality of the work while relying on the readers' prior experience with *Travels*: 'as the public have made the philosophical, and bold ideas of Capt. *Lemuel Gulliver* familiar to them; they would be less surpriz'd at those of *John Gulliver* his son [. . .] for tho' the fictions are very different, there yet is a kind of analogy between them'.[27] Inadvertently or not, the editor invites comparison around absurd juxtaposition, subverted binaries, and other techniques common to both texts. The Letalispons, 'a people, who return to the bloom of youth at a certain age, and enjoy a long life', are anti-Struldbruggs ('The French Editor's Preface', I, 7). He may find different worlds, but John Gulliver believes himself to be a carbon copy of the first Gulliver ('I can say that I take very much after my father, not only with regard to the exterior qualities, but also those of my mind').[28]

Expanding our set of clones to include non-Gullivers, we have *A Trip to the Moon* (1728). Murtagh McDermot, the authorial pseudonym, dedicates the work to the 'Worthy, Daring, Adventurous, Thrice-renown'd, and Victorious Captain Lemuel Gulliver', and displays a similar mix of aptitude and ignorance as he recounts his fantastical voyages. In the final forty-odd pages of *A Voyage to Cacklogallinia* (1727), Samuel Brunt similarly journeys to the moon, a blatant departure from *Travels* but an endorsement of the

---

[26] *Voyage to Locuta: A Fragment* (London: J. Hatchard, 1818), 9.

[27] *The Travels of Mr. John Gulliver, Son to Capt. Lemuel Gulliver*, trans. John Lockman, 2 vols. (1731), 'The French Editor's Preface', I, 2–3.

[28] *The Travels of Mr. John Gulliver*, 'The Travels of John Gulliver, &c.', I, 2. The pagination begins again after 'The French Editor's Preface'.

early trend for lunar Gulliveriana. However, the bulk of *Cacklogallinia* parallels Gulliver's earth-bound voyages, not least of all its avian utopia of sorts, which resembles Houyhnhnm-land in scope. Its principal figure, Captain Brunt, whom the Cacklogallians dub *probusomo* ('Monster of Nature'), recalls the Brobdingnagian depiction of Gulliver as a *lusus naturae* ('freak of nature'). Both author-explorers have an idealised vision of England, display advanced language-learning skills, and view their respect-ive hosts, Cacklogallians and Lilliputians, as bickering societies in decline. Some other character connections in the period seem forced, as in Baron Munchausen's claim to be Gulliver's appointed heir in a revised edition of Eric Raspe's Lucianic *Singular Travels* (1785–7).[29] Evidently, the borrowed fame worked: the new version rapidly ran to eight editions as *Gulliver Revived*. Published around this time, *A Fable Founded upon Fact* (1784) is based on a manuscript 'found' in an unnamed castle apparently written by an unnamed great-grandson of Gulliver. The borrowed fame had less effect here: only one short print run took place.

A more substantial work, *The Adventures of Gulliver Redivivus* (1881) by Joseph Orme immediately signals, in the opening sentence if not the title, who the actual hero is: the non-Gulliverian Christopher Columbus Smythe. Some characters have the name Gulliver thrust upon them, such as young Omar in Michael Morpurgo's *Boy Giant* (2019), whom the gleeful Lilliputians dub the Son of Gulliver when he crashes on their coast ('What "Gulliver" meant I had no idea').[30] In addition to Gulliver's nominal descendants, and para-Gullivers with no explicit connection, a third grouping comprises far-flung figures who share Gulliver's name and wanderlust. Among the most famous such works are Frigyes Karinthy's *Voyage to Faremido* (1916) and *Capillaria* (1921), as they are commonly known in English, and Sándor Szathmári's *Voyage to Kazohinia* (1941).[31] *Faremido* is labelled as a fifth voyage, and its Gulliver is apparently the original who remembers his experiences in Lilliput, Brobdingnag, Laputa, and Houyhnhnm-land. But the year is 1914, and world war the occupation. A sequel to the sequel, *Capillaria* pushes the Gulliver clone into further fantastical worlds. Szathmári moves his Gulliver to the 1930s. Set in the context of protests against the Vietnam War, Felix Gasbarra's *Schule der Planeten* (*School of the Planets*, 1968) takes Lemuel Gulliver and Jonathan Swift (now

[29] See Welcher and Bush, *Gulliveriana*, IV, xxiii–xxvii.
[30] Michael Morpurgo, *Boy Giant* (London: HarperCollins, 2019), 57.
[31] See Gabriella Hartvig, 'Hungarian Gulliveriads: *Gulliver's Travels* in Faremidó, Capillária, and Kazohinia', in *Münster* 5, 519–31.

a character) on an interstellar voyage to the land of the Yahoo-like Mnus and the Houyhnhnm-like Mecs.[32]

Using the term 'clone' figuratively here, we might note that human cloning exists elsewhere in modern Gulliveriana: Ariazad's *Gulliver in Cloneland* (2000). Like the Hungarian-made Gullivers, this narrator draws on established experience; unlike them, he remains in his own century, though the science belongs to ours. Michael Ryan's *Gulliver* (1993) radically reboots *Travels*, at turns reinscribing or outright rejecting the original. In the fourth and final voyage, the narrator – a twenty-second-century spaceship's surgeon – lands in Ecologia, where intelligent dogs, pigs, and horses marvel at the talking human. Treated like an inferior creature, though, this Gulliver refuses to stay. Adam Roberts's *Swiftly* (2008) jettisons the four-voyage structure entirely, as well as the setting and style of *Travels*. Not unlike *Memoirs*, *Account*, and other early Gulliveriana, Roberts's novel ingeniously explores the logic of Swift's fictional world when propelled forward into Victorian society. It is an extension, a refocalisation, and a reimagining all at once.

Coda: Fanfiction

While the main production line of Gulliveriana and Gulliveriads has slackened in recent years, more continue to appear, and will appear in greater numbers as we reach the three-hundredth anniversary of the first publication of *Travels*. New online fanfiction fora, such as Archive of Our Own, offer quick opportunities for growth. Since 2007, twenty-eight separate stories related to the Lilliputians and other figures have appeared there. Literary technology may have changed, but the scope of Gulliveriana has not. Circulated privately throughout the second half of the eighteenth century, Horace Walpole's Gulliverian tales are fanfictions *avant la lettre*.[33] Among these diverse materials we find an SF fairy tale set in the year 2000096 and an epistolary account of newly discovered giants that, according to the author, is not 'some political allegory' or a 'new-vamped edition of Swift's Brobdignags [*sic*]'. Since the beginning, as we have seen, Gulliveriana has traversed a range of worlds and time periods. Genre and form have proven to be no impediment either.

---

[32] See Astrid Krake, Hermann J. Real, and Marie-Luise Spieckermann, 'The Dean's Voyages into Germany', in *The Reception of Jonathan Swift in Europe*, ed. Hermann J. Real (London: Thoemmes Continuum, 2005), 93–141 (132).

[33] See Jeanne K. Welcher, 'Horace Walpole and *Gulliver's Travels*', *Studies in Eighteenth-Century Culture*, 12 (1983), 45–57.

CHAPTER 16

Visual Culture

Ruth Menzies

When it was initially published in 1726, *Gulliver's Travels* contained various images: Motte's first edition included four maps (one per voyage), a plan showing the motion of the flying island of Laputa, and a diagram of the Lagadan writing machine. These remained in all Motte's reprints and were reengraved for Faulkner's 1735 edition and further complete editions of the *Travels* published in the eighteenth century. From the outset, they underscored the ambiguity inherent to Swift's travel tale: the maps, in particular, ostensibly provided geographical and cartographic substance authenticating Gulliver's account, yet were so vague as to do nothing of the kind. This blurring of boundaries between reality and fiction was also enacted through the inclusion of frontispiece portraits of Lemuel Gulliver which varied through the different imprints and editions (Figures 9.1 and 9.2) – so much so that, rather than providing readers with a definitive or enduring visual image of the traveller, they contributed to the deliberate uncertainty surrounding his identity and the authorship of his narrative.[1]

Swift's satire soon prompted other images: the Dutch translation published in January 1727 was the first edition to contain a significant number of illustrations depicting scenes from the narrative, and Motte's 1727 second edition also contained several plates (Figure 16.1). The publisher clearly intended to include more in future editions, for he wrote to Swift asking which scenes he wished to see portrayed. Swift replied that he had purchased woodcuts of various episodes from his work, including Gulliver in a Brobdingnagian bowl of cream, and he indicated numerous incidents from the second, third, and fourth voyages that he considered

---

[1] See Janine Barchas, 'Prefiguring Genre: Frontispiece Portraits from *Gulliver's Travels* to *Millenium Hall*', *Studies in the Novel*, 30 (1998), 260–87; Ruth Menzies and Sandhya Patel, 'Transparency and Truth: Prefatory Material in Fictional and Non-Fictional Eighteenth-Century Travel Writing', *XVII–XVIII*, 70 (2013), 265–84; Peter Wagner, *Reading Iconotexts: From Swift to the French Revolution* (London: Reaktion, 1995).

Figure 16.1 Illustration (artist unknown) from Benjamin Motte's 1727 2nd ed. of *Gulliver's Travels*. Reproduced with kind permission of the Department of Special Collections, University of Wisconsin-Madison Libraries (PR3724 G7 1731)

worth illustrating (*Correspondence*, III, 149), although little came of his suggestions.[2]

As *Gulliver's Travels* grew in popularity, chapbooks, abridgements, and other adaptations appeared: some, such as the first surviving chapbook edition (c.1750), contained illustrations,[3] although others, like the 1727 Stone and King abridgement, dispensed even with the maps, diagrams, and portrait from the first edition, doubtless to cut costs. Where illustrations were introduced, they inevitably framed and formed readers' mental

[2] See Robert Halsband, 'Eighteenth-Century Illustrations of *Gulliver's Travels*', in *Münster* I, 83–112.
[3] A 1776 chapbook *Gulliver's Travels* can be seen online at: www.bl.uk/collection-items/the-adventures-of-captain-gulliver, accessed 3 June 2022.

representations of Lemuel Gulliver, the remote countries he visited, and key episodes in the narrative. However, they also contributed to some of the changes undergone by Swift's satire following its initial publication. The relationship between *Gulliver's Travels* and visual culture is a vast field of study: this chapter will provide an overview of the ways in which imagery from Swift's text is used in illustrated editions, graphic novels, and comics, paintings and portraiture, caricatures and cartoons, and advertising and merchandising.

Illustrated Editions of the *Travels*

Gulliver's Travels is characterised by its generic instability and borrows freely from traditions which are themselves hybrid or overlapping, such as travel writing, imaginary voyages, utopias, anti-utopias, satire, and allegory. Over the years, episodes and characters from the text gradually became disconnected from their original context, which was identifiably, albeit not exclusively, that of philosophical and political satire. This process was facilitated by the production of images outwardly associated with Swift's text, but which bore little connection to it. By around 1730, for instance, 'Lilliputian Figures' began appearing. These sets of some dozen figures, often on twelve pages mapping the calendar year, depicted human faults also highlighted in *Gulliver's Travels*. While some included representations of Lemuel Gulliver, their links to Swift's work were tenuous, sometimes limited to the word 'Lilliputian'. Terminology found in the text thus slithered away from it, acquiring new meaning and symbolism, including on a visual level.

This drift away from satire was probably accelerated by the publication of the Newbery edition, entitled *The Adventures of Capt. Gulliver, in a Voyage to Lilliput and Brobdingnag*, which was advertised in the *Middlesex Journal* in 1772 (the earliest extant copy is dated 1776). The Newbery edition, the first known adaptation of the *Travels* specifically for children, excised Laputa and Houyhnhnm-land, setting the tone for many such editions. It contained nineteen woodcuts, eleven of which illustrate episodes from Lilliput (including one reproduced from Motte's 1727 edition), while seven represent scenes from Brobdingnag; the frontispiece illustration appears unconnected to the narrative. Adorning abridged and bowdlerised editions, illustrations like these contributed to focusing attention on differences in scale, which gradually came to overshadow other aspects of *Gulliver's Travels*. Reiterating themes from popular tales, such as *Jack and the Giant Killer* or *Jack and the Beanstalk*, they introduced generations of readers to a story of adventure and danger – often with a dramatic emphasis on voyages, storms, and shipwrecks – which diverged more or less appreciably from Swift's satire, in which the travel narrative is both pretext and target. The first two voyages were also included in picture books alongside traditional rhymes and stories,[4] an editorial choice that exemplifies the *Travels*'s unstable generic status and confirms – to misquote Pope and Gay – that although Swift's satire may have been read over the years in the Cabinet council, an altogether different, sanitised, overdramatised, and illustrated Gulliver was increasingly viewed in the nursery.[5]

This process probably arose from and then consolidated the increasing focus on certain scenes – such as Gulliver awakening on the shore bound by Lilliputian ties, being shot at with tiny arrows, or towing the Blefuscudian fleet – which lent themselves particularly well to illustration, thereby determining the imagery, themes, and ideas associated with Gulliver. That trend has continued over the centuries, with children's publishers such as Usborne, Penguin, Ladybird, and others producing simplified, colourful picture books which reduce Swift's *Travels* to what Samuel Johnson dubbed a tale of 'big men and little men'.[6] By deleting the extensive dialogues between Gulliver and his hosts, these illustrated editions forego the dialectic structure which elicits comparison and critical contrast between the imaginary societies and real ones, thus reducing the satiric charge, sometimes to nought. The 1975 book version of Disney's 1934 cartoon, *Mickey Gulliver*, one of the most radically simplified illustrated adaptations, shows the extremes to which this process was sometimes taken. However, Martin Jenkins's 2004 retelling of the *Travels*, richly illustrated by Chris Riddell, offers younger readers all four voyages and a range of original, at times potentially alarming, images emphasising the text's ironic quality.[7] Riddell also visually updates Swift's satire: the Lagadan projects for political reform include pulling the ears of ministers who forget their promises, illustrated by a picture bearing a remarkable likeness to Tony Blair.

While children became familiar with *Gulliver's Travels* via such illustrated editions, adults were also increasingly provided with editions containing plates that extended well beyond the 1726 maps and plans,

---

[4] Lilliput and Brobdingnag feature alongside Mother Hubbard and Jack the Giant Killer in *Gulliver's Travels, Old Mother Hubbard, etc. A Picture Book for the Nursery* (Edinburgh: Thomas Nelson, 1883).
[5] 'From the highest to the lowest it is universally read, from the Cabinet-council to the Nursery' (*Correspondence*, III, 47).
[6] James Boswell, *The Life of Johnson* (1791; Oxford: Oxford University Press, 1969), 595.
[7] Martin Jenkins and Chris Riddell, *Jonathan Swift's Gulliver's Travels* (London: Walker, 2004).

although the fluctuating frontispiece portrait often simply vanished. In France, the 1838 Furne edition of *Voyages de Gulliver* included numerous drawings by renowned illustrator and caricaturist Jean-Jacques Grandville (Figure 16.2). The two illustrated French translations of the *Travels* – by

Figure 16.2 Illustration by J. J. Grandville, from *Voyages de Gulliver dans des contrées lointaines, par Swift. Édition illustrée par Grandville. Traduction nouvelle* (1838), vol. 2, p. 11, Bibliothèque nationale de France (BnF), département Réserve de livres rares (RES P-Y2-2320 (2))

the Abbé Desfontaines and an anonymous translator – which appeared early in 1727 had already contributed to the propagation of Swift's text in Europe, serving as the basis for the first editions in Italian, Spanish, Portuguese, German, Polish, and Russian,[8] some of which also reproduced the first French illustrations. Analogously, Grandville's drawings were reused in editions published in Italy and Britain, his imagery shaping perceptions of Gulliver for a significant number of European readers. Other French editions of the *Travels* contained illustrations by well-known artists such as Paul Gavarni, Albert Robida, and Bouchet, suggesting that, alongside simplified children's editions, publishers presumed there to be an adult readership for quality illustrated versions of Swift's text.

In the second half of the nineteenth century, the standard illustrated edition in English contained Thomas Morten's drawings, engraved by W. J. Linton; the 1909 edition published by J. M. Dent, during what was dubbed the Golden Age of Illustration, included plates by Arthur Rackham, one of the most successful illustrators of the Edwardian period. These editions successively established emblematic images of *Gulliver's Travels* for generations of readers, whose experience of Swift's text therefore differed significantly from that of his original audience, who had to rely on their own creativity in imagining scenes and characters.

Graphic Novels and Comics

As the book industry evolved, so did the *Travels*, which were gradually adapted to cater to new tastes and trends. One instance of this is the rise in comic or graphic novel editions, which have grown in number and popularity since the early twentieth century. They inevitably maximise the visual while minimising the verbal, often continuing the process of de-satirising Swift's work. One striking example of how far such publications can diverge from the 1726 text is *Betty Boop in Miss Gulliver's Travels* (1935). Presented as a story 'by Wallace West, with a bow to the ghost of Jonathan Swift', it recounts how Betty, presented as Lemuel's great-great-granddaughter, sets off with her dog Bimbo to locate Lilliput, thwarts a Blefuscudian air raid, and then returns home. The title page claims it is 'based on the Max Fleischer Talkatoon', although no episode bearing this name appears to have existed. Whatever its origins, this comic is indicative

---

[8] *The Reception of Jonathan Swift in Europe*, ed. Hermann J. Real (London: Thoemmes Continuum, 2005).

of Fleischer's interest in the *Travels* prior to his 1939 film – which was itself quickly adapted for publication in the Jumbo Book series, reflecting the increasingly tangled network of text and image within which Gulliver and his adventures have travelled far beyond their initial context.

Comic and graphic book versions of the *Travels* have been produced worldwide and continue to be included in series, such as Barron's Graphic Classics in the US or Campfire Classics in India, which aim to introduce younger readers to literary classics. Many, although not all, such editions limit the textual content to focus on the imagery and, following the trend set by the Newbery edition, omit the last two voyages, as well as cutting and often bowdlerising the first two. A graphic novel published in 2008 by Raintree provides an interesting example of how children's editors may continue to excise Laputa and Houyhnhnm-land while nonetheless portraying scenes such as that of Gulliver urinating on the Lilliputian palace.[9]

For an older readership, Martin Rowson's 2012 graphic *Gulliver's Travels*[10] transposes the narrative to Blair's Britain, fitting consciously into the satiric tradition to which Swift's work belongs and using powerful imagery to convey social critique. The crosshatching in the first voyage links the drawings with those of Hogarth, while the Brobdingnagians tramp across ink-splattered pages that reflect an emphasis, common to Rowson and Swift, on the more unpalatable aspects of human nature. Balnibarbi is depicted in imagery reminiscent of war comics and Laputa – a 'World Heritage Site and now permanent host to the Global Diplomatic Perpetual Plenary Summit' – resembles Bruegel's Tower of Babel (Figure 16.3). The Houyhnhnms, after quelling a Yahoo mutiny, have finally managed 'to restore Order, Efficiency and Reason', as evinced by the increasing density of the geometric squares filling each page, while the horses' dialogues in German and blackletter font reflect their status as a self-styled master race who 'economically resource' the Yahoos for slave labour and fuel.

Graphic editions of the *Travels* also bear witness to varying aesthetic and cultural norms as regards literary genres and their imbrication with the visual. Singaporean publisher Youngjin includes *Gulliver's Travels* in its Manga Classics series, for instance, and another manga version by Kiyokazu Chiba, first published in Japan in 2013, became available in translation four years later in France, where the genre is popular with all age groups. Manga *Travels* inevitably tend to reduce text to the bare minimum and highlight the adventurous nature of Gulliver's experiences,

[9] Donald B. Lemke and Cynthia Martin, *Jonathan Swift's Gulliver's Travels* (London: Raintree, 2009).
[10] Martin Rowson, *Gulliver's Travels, Adapted and Updated* (London: Atlantic Books, 2012).

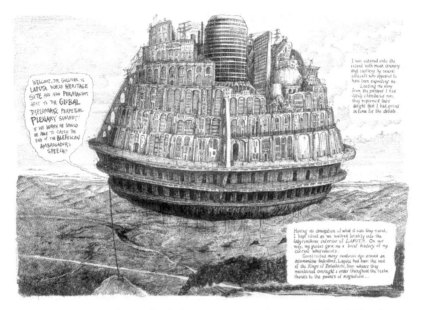

Figure 16.3 The Flying Island of Laputa in Martin Rowson, *Gulliver's Travels, Adapted and Updated* (London: Atlantic Books, 2012), reproduced with the kind permission of the author

presenting them in characteristically stylised format and epitomising a significant shift away from the written word that is so central to Swift's art.

Paintings and Portraiture

From an early date, the imagery surrounding the *Travels* continued the distortion of boundaries that was already so apparent in the various states of the prefatory portraiture. One example of this is found in the 1735 portrait of Swift known as the Brereton Bindon, one of a series of paintings by Irish artist Francis Bindon. Swift is shown pointing at a scroll entitled *Travels by Lemuel Gulliver. A Voyage to the Country of the Houyhnhnums* [sic], while three horses – a foal and what appear to be a sorrel and a grey mare – are visible in the background. Foregrounding the troubling relationship between Swift, Gulliver and the Houyhnhnms that continues to exercise critics to this day, Bindon's portrait not only recalls the complex issues of authorial intent and textual authority that are already central to the *Travels* and their paratext. By setting Swift in the same frame as his Houyhnhnms (who, although obviously a fictional addition to the painting, remain less easily definable as regards their purportedly rational or ideal nature), it also reinforces the Swiftian trope of the uncertainty and unreliability inherent to representations – textual or otherwise – of reality. Stepping out of the text onto the canvas, the horses highlight the disconcerting interplay between Swift's world and his writing.

The Houyhnhnms also unsurprisingly provided inspiration for Sawrey Gilpin, who specialised in painting animals. He produced three works illustrating episodes from the fourth voyage: *Gulliver addressing the Houyhnhnms* (1768) (Figure 16.4), *Gulliver taking his final leave of the land of the Houyhnhnms* (1769), and *Gulliver reprimanded and silenced by his Master* (1771), also sometimes known as *Gulliver describing Fortification to the Horses*. Gilpin's paintings are more standard illustrations of scenes from the text than Bindon's comingling of the real and the fictional, and they offer an interesting contrast between the picturesque of the Romantic

Figure 16.4 Sawrey Gilpin, *Gulliver Addressing the Houyhnhnms* (1769), reproduced
with the kind permission of the Yale Center for British Art

Figure 16.5 Jehan-Georges Vibert, *Gulliver and the Lilliputians*, c. 1870

movement and the mordant satire of Swift's writing. As paintings such as Charles Robert Leslie's *Gulliver being presented to the Queen of Brobdingnag* (1835),[11] and Richard Redgrave's *Gulliver exhibited to the Brobdingnagian farmer* (1836)[12] show, artists continued to draw inspiration from Swift's narrative, creating a web of connections between the written and the visual that is also characterised by the recurrent use of such artworks in modern imprints of *Gulliver's Travels*. A section of Gilpin's *Gulliver taking his final leave of the land of the Houyhnhnms* features on the cover of the 1998 Oxford World's Classics edition, for instance, while the 2003 Penguin Classics and Barnes & Noble editions both use Redgrave's painting.

Like Gilpin's, French painter Jehan-Georges Vibert's portrayal of scenes from the *Travels* reflected artistic trends of the time. His *Gulliver fortement attaché au sol et cerné par l'armée* (Figure 16.5), exhibited at the 1870 Salon de Paris, owes much to the contemporary vogue for Orientalism. The Lilliputians appear to hail from various continents, their robes and foot-wear are decidedly Eastern in appearance, their headgear eclectically includes turbans, conical Asian hats, and exotic-looking military helmets, and in the background stands an Indian elephant. Vibert also takes liberties with Swift's narrative, conflating two scenes from the Voyage to Lilliput to show Gulliver tied down while the inhabitants inspect his pockets.

---

[11] www.nationaltrustcollections.org.uk/object/485039, accessed 3 June 2022.
[12] http://collections.vam.ac.uk/item/O133971/gulliver-exhibited-to-the-brobdingnag-oil-painting-redgrave-richard-cb/, accessed 3 June 2022.

Although most of these paintings related to *Gulliver's Travels* depict scenes, albeit sometimes altered or merged, from Swift's narrative, Olga Hoffman's 2017 acrylic, *Gulliver Trump in the divided land of Lillipublicans and Blefucrats*, operates on a more metaphorical level. An outsized Donald Trump in eighteenth-century garb is set against a backdrop of Blefucrats on the left and Lillipublicans on the right; a large toad sits in the 'Fake News Swamp' and, in the foreground, a blue egg on a chariot drawn by a donkey bears the inscription 'Values' and faces a red egg, towed by an elephant, labelled 'Issues'. Rather than illustrating a scene from the *Travels*, Hoffman uses symbolism deriving from the text to portray contemporary US society, perpetuating in a visual medium the satiric tradition embodied by Swift.

Caricatures and Cartoons

Shortly after *Gulliver's Travels* was published, Hogarth depicted Gulliver being administered an enema with a fire engine, as punishment for urinating on the palace of Lilliput. Although the caption states that it was intended as a frontispiece to the first volume of the *Travels*, no evidence corroborates this; nor does Hogarth's image represent a scene from Swift's text. However, it both alludes to the second voyage and echoes some of the Lagadan experiments – notably a physician's efforts to cure colic with bellows – as well as reflecting and extending Swift's political satire, evoking the excesses of the body politic and suggesting purgative remedies. The presence of Walpole highlights the image's political dimensions, further emphasised when it was reissued in 1757 as *The Political Clyster*.

That first cartoon has been followed by many others reprising the *Travels*. These include Gillray's two versions of *The King of Brobdingnag and Gulliver* (1803, 1804)[13] depicting Napoleon as a diminutive Gulliver, Isaac Cruikshank's 1795 engraving *The Royal Extinguisher or Gulliver putting out the Patriots of Lilliput*,[14] in which Pitt crushes a group of Whigs, and the same artist's *Gulliver towing the Fleet into Lilliput* (1807),[15] drawn together with his son, George. In 1821, the latter produced an engraving whose title echoes his father's work: *The Royal Extinguisher or the King of Brobdingnag and the Lilliputians*[16] shows George IV wielding a paper cone over his estranged wife and various radicals.

[13] www.britishmuseum.org/collection/object/P_1861-1012-46; www.britishmuseum.org/collection/object/P_1851-0901-1149, accessed 3 June 2022.
[14] www.britishmuseum.org/collection/object/P_1868-0808-6487, accessed 3 June 2022.
[15] www.britishmuseum.org/collection/object/P_1868-0808-7593, accessed 3 June 2022.
[16] www.britishmuseum.org/collection/object/P_1862-1217-303, accessed 3 June 2022.

More recognisably linked to Swift's text, a cartoon from 1845 shows a diminutive Disraeli bowing before a Brobdingnagian Peel, epitomising their fraught relations,[17] while in Honoré Daumier's *Lilliputiens essayant de profiter du sommeil d'un nouveau Gulliver*[18] (1850), tiny hordes bind universal suffrage, a commentary on legislation erasing 30 per cent of voters from France's electoral rolls. Evidently appreciating the image's malleability and feeling optimistic before Louis-Napoléon Bonaparte's coup d'état, which overturned those measures, Daumier published another cartoon in 1851, showing the Lilliputians panicking as Gulliver awakens.[19]

Daumier was not alone in finding this image a convenient vehicle for political opinion – many cartoonists whose work includes pictures of Gulliver after the 1850s reference that same scene from the *Travels*, reflecting various, even opposing, viewpoints or situations. Joseph Swain's *Little Gulliver*[20] (1873) showed French President Adolphe Thiers managing political affairs despite being restrained by various factions. Augusto Grosso's *Il Nuovo Gulliver Italiano*[21] similarly portrayed Garibaldi, whose ambitious plans – notably to control flooding by diverting the Tiber – divided opinion, as evidenced by the Members of Parliament tying him down. In a *Historical Caricature of the Cherokee Nation*[22] (1886), a bound Cherokee has his hair shorn by the courts, his skull drilled by missionaries, his feet sawn off by the railroads and his arms, symbolising Indian lands in Alabama and Arkansas, amputated; meanwhile, atop his nose, Uncle Sam represents a coroner, a possible allusion to issues of tribal sovereignty. S. Pughe's *The Boer Lilliputians and the British Gulliver*[23] (1900) uses the trope to show how low the mighty can fall: John Bull is secured with ties bearing the names of battles which the British had lost or failed to win decisively.

Geopolitical tensions around the globe in the twentieth century provided ample material for cartoonists to rework this image. E. H. Shephard's *Dealing*

[17] 'Young Gulliver and the Brobdingnagian Minister', *Punch* (5 April 1845) (www.alamy.com/stock-photo-disraeli-pictured-as-gulliver-among-the-giants-of-the-peel-administration-90843575.html, accessed 3 June 2022).
[18] *Le Charivari* (20–21 May 1850) (www.hermitagemuseum.org/wps/portal/hermitage/digital-collection/04.+Engraving/275441, accessed 3 June 2022).
[19] 'Une panique des Lilliputiens qui ont essayé de garrotter le Suffrage universel pendant son sommeil', *Le Charivari* (28 June 1851) (www.parismuseescollections.paris.fr/fr/musee-carnavalet/oeuvres/actualites-ndeg158-une-panique-de-lilliputiens-qui-ont-essaye-de-garotter, accessed 3 June 2022).
[20] *Punch* (1 February 1873) (www.gettyimages.co.uk/detail/news-photo/little-gulliver-1873-gulliver-exclaims-make-your-game-my-news-photo/463929863?language=en-GB, accessed 3 June 2022).
[21] *Il Pappagallo* (14 February 1875) (www.alamy.com/stock-photo-giuseppe-garibaldi-new-italian-gulliver-by-augusto-grossi-146891858.html, accessed 3 June 2022).
[22] www.loc.gov/pictures/item/2008661841, accessed 3 June 2022.
[23] *Puck* (21 February 1900) (www.loc.gov/item/2010646243/, accessed 3 June 2022).

with Gulliver[24] expresses concern that Mars, god of war, will be unleashed following Hitler's appointment as Chancellor. A 1935 cartoon by William Gropper in *Vanity Fair* shows Uncle Sam immobilised by the agencies of the New Deal,[25] and in *The New Lilliput*[26] (1938), by Hungarian Jewish refugees Derso and Kelen, an outsized Hitler, unrestrained by any ties, lords it over Europe and its diplomats, while Halifax reassures Chamberlain: 'Don't be afraid. I know him personally [...] he's a vegetarian'. In 1941, E. H. Shephard's *The Giant Awakes*[27] portrayed Gulliver as an American casting off Lilliputian Nazi ropes, reflecting renewed hopes that the US would enter the war, and in February 1944, John Collins reappropriated him to represent Allied gains in the Pacific.[28] As the focus of tensions shifted after 1945, this scene allowed Leonard Raven Hill to comment upon the nascent co-operative movement[29] and was repeatedly reworked by Leslie Illingworth: to represent those whose power others wished to limit, like Charles de Gaulle in 1948[30] and trade unions in 1950,[31] or those whose freedom was curtailed, as in a 1953 cartoon presenting Africa breaking free from colonial bonds[32] and another, from 1968, when a black English cricketer was deemed unwelcome by South Africa's Prime Minister.[33]

Too many twenty-first-century cartoonists have created similar images to be mentioned here. Gulliver has been tied down by Lilliputians in order both to predict that Obama would struggle to implement reforms[34] and to comment on Hillary Clinton's presidential ambitions and Republicans' determination to thwart them.[35] French cartoonist Siné imbued the image

---

[24] *Punch* (14 June 1933) (https://punch.photoshelter.com/image/I0000U6sEYzd9xlQ, accessed 3 June 2022).

[25] https://punch.photoshelter.com/image/I0000U6sEYzd9xlQ, accessed 3 June 2022.

[26] www.raremaps.com/gallery/detail/65512jc/the-new-lilliput-kelen-derso, accessed 3 June 2022.

[27] *Punch* (24 September 1941) (https://punch.photoshelter.com/image/I0000SfIMjdRQcUY, accessed 3 June 2022).

[28] 'Gulliver se libère', *Gazette* (Montreal) (21 February 1944) (http://collections.musee-mccord.qc.ca /fr/collection/artefacts/M965.199.2311, accessed 3 June 2022).

[29] *Punch* (date unspecified) (https://punch.photoshelter.com/image/I0000cItoHqwj44U, accessed 3 June 2022).

[30] 'The Man Mountain', *Punch* (29 September 1948) (https://punch.photoshelter.com/image/I0000 tQ_aiIAQh_g, accessed 3 June 2022).

[31] 'Time to get up', *Punch* (27 September 1950) (https://punch.photoshelter.com/image/I00003dII1 H33274, accessed 3 June 2022).

[32] 'Gulliver Africanus', *Punch* (13 May 1953) (https://punch.photoshelter.com/image/I0000lcYmuf G5txs, accessed 3 June 2022).

[33] *Punch* (25 September 1968) (https://punch.photoshelter.com/image/I0000ZGM4FmiL9jk, accessed 3 June 2022).

[34] Rainer Hachfeld, 'Obama in Lilliput', *Neues Deutschland* (10 January 2009).

[35] Héctor Curriel, 'Hillary Clinton, the New Gulliver?', *El Observador News* (May 2014); Taylor Jones, *El Nuevo Dia* (20 March 2015).

with optimism following Syriza's election victory in Greece;[36] then-Speaker Paul Ryan was portrayed bound by pro-Trump Republicans by Chad Crowe.[37] A humbled Jacob Zuma was likened to Gulliver after he agreed partly to reimburse state funds spent upgrading his home,[38] and when in 2018 *Gilets Jaunes* protestors weakened Emmanuel Macron, who had compared his Presidency to the rule of Jupiter, Plantu drew him as a powerless, perspiring Gulliver (Figure 16.6).[39] Paresh Nath portrayed globalisation as a Gulliver inhibited by encumbering forces[40] and, in January 2021, Bart van Leeuwen compared Jack Ma, founder of e-commerce giant Alibaba, to Gulliver constrained by Xi Jinping.[41]

While it is unsurprising that a satire such as the *Travels* should inspire cartoonists, it is striking that they return consistently to the same image: its plasticity is such that it can evoke power curtailed by the underdog, despots

Figure 16.6 © Plantu, drawing published in the issue of *Le Monde* dated 30 November 2018. Reproduced with the kind permission of the artist

---

[36] www.sinemensuel.com/numero-sine/n39-fevrier-2015/, accessed 3 June 2022.
[37] Chad Crowe, *Wall Street Journal* (28 October 2015).
[38] Zapiro, *The Times* (South Africa) (4 February 2016).
[39] Plantu, *Le Monde* (30 November 2018).   [40] Paresh Nath, *Khaleej Times* (17 February 2019).
[41] https://oedipoes.com/, accessed 3 June 2022.

abusing their authority, the oppressed breaking their chains, politicians hampered by opposition, the corrupt brought to justice or the proud cut down to size. Illustrators who imbue Gulliver with such visual symbolism have not necessarily read Swift's text: several of those mentioned above have indicated that they are familiar with Gulliver and the Lilliputians from children's editions, television, or film. In contrast, Henry Morris, who, under the pseudonym Michael Govern Ready, produced an illustrated Twitter journal titled *Goveller's Travels* between August and November 2020, ruthlessly satirising Boris Johnson and his inner circle, was very familiar with Swift's narrative.

Advertising and Merchandising

The same scene from *Gulliver's Travels* has also been used to market an extraordinary range of products. A trade card, probably from the 1870s, shows Gulliver firmly trussed up with Coats' 'Best Six Cord Spool Cotton' (Figure 16.7); on the back is a lengthy quotation from the *Travels*. Despite some quirky anachronisms, such as a photographer snapping Gulliver, the costumes are eighteenth-century. Like Vibert's painting, the image

Figure 16.7 © Photo: R. Menzies & Y. Chiado, 'Gulliver and the Lilliputians'. Advertising card for J. & P. Coats Best Six Cord Spool Cotton, 1870s

conflates two separate episodes from Swift's text to portray Gulliver tied down while an inventory is made of his possessions. A modified version of the card, promoting 'Paisley Spool Cotton', has also survived, as has a separate item, showing 'Gulliver and the Fleet' and advertising 'J. & P. Coats Sewing Cotton'.

Products as diverse as Brazilian insecticide, Micromax mobile phones, and South African audiobooks have all been promoted by reappropriating this image. The first two adverts each include a line of text emphasising the link between Swift's narrative and the product marketed, suggesting that a squirt of chemicals would have altered the course of Gulliver's adventures or that he would have been better off with a mobile phone. In the third advert, the intermedial allusion relies upon an implicit thematic connection between Gulliver, reading, and books: literariness matters more than the text referenced.

Striking a different note, a 2013 advert for Durex lubricant finds suggestive potential in the image of Gulliver bound by Lilliputian ropes,[42] while a Russian example from 2013 depicts the traveller wearing a shirt laundered with Myth washing powder, whose 'Legendary Frosty Freshness' is such that Lilliputians are skiing down the garment.[43] It is significant that this advert for Myth connects Swift's character with the adjective 'Legendary'. Those two terms reflect the process whereby Lemuel Gulliver has acquired a status shared with a handful of other literary characters, such as Romeo and Juliet or Robinson Crusoe, who have achieved their own, autonomous existence in the collective imagination, as myths and legends also do. Gulliver bound by Lilliputians' ropes is clearly considered part of a shared visual lexicon, capable of evoking an array of concepts unrelated to Swift's text.

The image's notoriety and adaptability are such that it can be altered almost infinitely to fulfil advertisers' needs: a poster for a book fair in Vilnius portrays Gulliver as a corpse and unabashedly declares, 'Stories are good. Crime stories are better'.[44] Gulliver is considered so familiar as to be identifiable in amputated or altered form: in an Indonesian advert for Scott's Emulsion, only his hands are visible, while the tagline ('Now even smarter') suggests that the multivitamins would have enabled him to outsmart the Lilliputians. Gulliver's feet, accompanied by the line 'If there really were a Lilliput, AT&T would have you covered', have also

[42] www.1jour1pub.com/wp-content/uploads/2013/09/Pub-Durex-Gulliver.jpg, accessed 3 June 2022.
[43] www.adsoftheworld.com/media/print/myth_gulliver, accessed 3 June 2022.
[44] www.adsoftheworld.com/media/print/vilnius_book_fair_gulliver, accessed 3 June 2022.

been used to advertise a mobile phone network. The literary allusion is presumed clear even when Gulliver is replaced by an eroticised woman to advertise Occhiali Giantess sunglasses, by an egg to promote a financial services company encouraging clients to look after their 'nest egg', or by a Lego brick in a series of minimalist puzzles released to mark the product's fifty-fifth anniversary. Cars are, anachronistically, substituted for Gulliver in several advertising campaigns: in one, from 2006, he is replaced by Ford's F250 pickup, the iconography and slogan ('Built Tough') apparently intended to convey the futility of attempting to immobilise the vehicle. A comparable advert for the Volkswagen Touareg associates Gulliver with exoticism: 'Get far, far away', exhorts the tagline, as though purchasing a German SUV might make one a little more like an eighteenth-century naval surgeon braving distant dangers.

These images raise the question of what is, in fact, being referenced: is it Swift's text, adaptations thereof, or a universal popular culture in which an archetypal Gulliver is considered widely recognisable? One hint might lie in the inclusion of Gulliver in advertising series that use other images from comparably familiar narratives: the Brazilian insecticide mentioned above was also marketed using *David and Goliath* and *Jack and the Beanstalk*; Micromax borrowed images from *Robinson Crusoe* and *Alice in Wonderland*; the 'stories' portrayed by the promoters of the Vilnius Book Fair include *Don Quixote*, *Alice in Wonderland*, and Kafka's *Metamorphosis*. The 'nest egg' series for A. G. Edwards financial services includes *War and Peace*, while Lego's puzzles show the *Three Little Pigs*, Aesop's *Tortoise and Hare*, *Goldilocks and the Three Bears*, *Little Red Riding Hood*, and *Alice in Wonderland*, who again features in Volkswagen's Touareg advertisement. These series suggest that *Gulliver's Travels* is deemed part of a universally recognisable canon. It is notable, however, that a flurry of Gulliver-related advertisements appeared in the years following the release of the 2010 Jack Black film, posters for which included a similar image and perhaps refreshed the collective visual memory.

In some cases, it is evident that those producing such images have a glancing acquaintance with *Gulliver's Travels* at best; for Moncler, Annie Leibovitz photographed a stylised Gulliver against a Nordic backdrop – presumably to clarify why he and the Lilliputians are all sporting Moncler down jackets. The company's promotional literature explains the connection thus: 'Gulliver is a mix of creativity and clairvoyance, capable of overcoming the trends of times, qualities which are perfectly aligned with the spirit of Moncler' – a description which, it is probably safe to say, is not based on close reading of the 1726 text. The company also indicates: 'Nature is once again the true star and *deus ex machina* of the narrative, underscoring the story's value far beyond the traditional methods adopted by the world of advertising'.[45] Valiant attempts to justify his presence notwithstanding, it seems clear that adapting an illustration showing Gulliver bound by Lilliputian ties is so commonplace as to have become one of the 'traditional methods adopted by the world of advertising'.

Conclusion

Gulliver's name and image have also been associated with many other items, including greeting cards, crockery, candy bars, theme parks, IKEA baby furniture, travel agencies, toyshops, puppet theatres, children's clothing stores, shopping malls, and supermarkets. While not all of these are visual in nature, they confirm that there exists a multitude of Lemuel Gullivers, encompassing not only Swift's fictional voyager-narrator and satiric puppet but also a multifarious, shadowy entity embodying a vast range of themes and concepts. In a process begun shortly after publication of the *Travels* and which has intensified exponentially in what Umberto Eco has termed 'a civilization now accustomed to thinking in images',[46] Lemuel Gulliver has come to occupy a place in a gallery of stories, images and archetypes that are incontrovertibly part of the collective visual imagination.

---

[45] www.monclergroup.com/wp-content/uploads/2016/07/MONCLER-SPRING-SUMMER-2016-ADVERTISING-CAMPAIGN_ENG.pdf, accessed 3 June 2022.

[46] Umberto Eco, *Travels in Hyperreality* (New York: Harcourt, 1986), 128.

CHAPTER 17

Screen Media

Emrys Jones

The Appeal and Challenge of Adapting Gulliver

In the almost nine-minute running time of 1934's *Gulliver Mickey*, Mickey Mouse twice gets distracted from Jonathan Swift's satire. First, in the short animation's opening seconds, we see him set aside Swift's book, from which he has avidly read a couple of pages, so that he can instead go and entertain a gang of orphan mice. Then later in the film, having cast himself as Gulliver among the Lilliputians for the story he tells the children, he allows a stray toy spider to infiltrate his imaginative re-creation of the text. Lilliput is mostly forgotten, as the appeal of a fistfight with an overgrown tarantula supersedes Mickey's initial inspiration. When we emerge from his fantasy, we see that story-time has degenerated into an impromptu boxing match between Mickey and a pillow, much to the excitement of his young audience.

Mickey's propensity to distraction and his inability to sustain a retelling of Swift's text are of course indicative of his character and of the kind of production this is, but the film's very interest in the value of distraction might also have useful things to tell us about how film-makers and film audiences approach *Gulliver's Travels* and what they look for in it. In keeping with recent work in the field of adaptation theory, we should be able to acknowledge Mickey's disrespect for his source material without condemning him or the film for it. Rather than fixating on the film's omissions and insertions, we should instead ask why Swift's story is ripe for such unapologetic sabotage, why Mickey feels happy to inhabit the role of Gulliver without having finished reading the book itself. Behind the film's frivolity and silliness, it is after all concerned with the impossibility of faithful adaptation and with the way that certain ideas and images outgrow or overtake their literary origin points. Though he would be unlikely to justify himself in so many words, Mickey would probably agree with Linda Hutcheon that the pleasure of adaptation comes from a combination of 'repetition' and 'variation', even though said variation leads, for Mickey, to the destabilisation and eventual collapse of his narrative.[1] If, like Francesco Casetti, we see an adaptation not simply as 'a work repeating another work', but as 'the *reappearance, in another discursive field, of an element* [...] *that has previously appeared elsewhere*', then the issue of how closely a film adheres to its literary source is no longer pertinent.[2] Instead, we should attend to the types of element that recur, the distortions they undergo, and how such distortions reflect both the preoccupations of the adapter and the challenges inherent in the literary text itself.[3]

What does Mickey take from Swift's book? Most strikingly, if somewhat predictably, there is the image of Gulliver tied down by the Lilliputians. It is visible on the cover of the edition he reads at the outset, an instantly recognisable visual shorthand for all the wonder that *Gulliver's Travels* is understood to encompass. Like the vast majority of screen Gullivers, Mickey will come to recreate that image in the story that ensues; in this, he simply honours the long cultural and artistic tradition that has granted a disproportionate prominence to the events of Swift's very first chapter. But in the meme-like proliferation of the supine and captive Gulliver – the image's simultaneous distillation and simplification of Swift's work – we can also identify the text's more fundamental interest for the modern entertainment industry. Gulliver's experiences, or at least those of the first two parts of the text, which are overwhelmingly the focus of screen adaptations, furnish rich opportunities for technological experimentation on the one hand and for cinematic self-reflection on the other. With their playful approach to perspective and scale, they have held a clear and enduring appeal for some of the medium's greatest innovators: Georges Méliès and Segundo de Chomón[4] in cinema's earliest days; Disney's

[1] Linda Hutcheon with Siobhan O'Flynn, *A Theory of Adaptation*, 2nd ed. (London: Routledge, 2013), 4.
[2] Francesco Casetti, 'Adaptations and Mis-adaptations: Film, Literature, and Social Discourses', in *A Companion to Literature and Film*, ed. Robert Stam and Alessandra Raengo (Oxford: Blackwell, 2004), 81–91 (82).
[3] Karen Bloom Gevirtz adopts the same approach in her publications on 2010's *Gulliver's Travels* (dir. Rob Letterman). See Gevirtz, 'Film Review: *Gulliver's Travels*', ECS, 44 (2011), 559–64; Gevirtz, *Representing the Eighteenth Century in Film and Television, 2000–2015* (London: Palgrave Macmillan, 2017), 17–38. On moving beyond '[q]uestions of accuracy, fidelity, and historical truth' to appreciate 'the constructedness of historical narratives', see also Srividhya Swaminathan and Steven W. Thomas, 'Introduction: Representing and Repositioning the Eighteenth Century on Screen', in *The Cinematic Eighteenth Century: History, Culture, and Adaptation*, ed. Srividhya Swaminathan and Steven W. Thomas (New York: Routledge, 2018), 1–11 (3–4).
[4] Sadly, there is no known surviving copy of Chomón's *Gulliver en el país de los Gigantes* (1903), cinema's second adaptation of Swift's text following Méliès's production in the previous year. For a description of Chomón's technique and how his interest in Brobdingnag initiated a distinctive

would-be rival, Dave Fleischer, in the 1930s; and acclaimed visual effects maestro, Ray Harryhausen, in 1960's *The 3 Worlds of Gulliver*. Fleischer's 1939 *Gulliver's Travels* is so fascinated by the potential of the reclining Gulliver and by his juxtaposition with Lilliputian life that it leaves him unconscious until halfway through its 76-minute running time. Fleischer spends much of the time up until then on the Lilliputian engineering skills required to bind the beached traveller, these sequences seemingly less interested in furthering the plot than in paying homage to the craftsman-ship and teamwork involved in animating the film itself. Indeed, besides the spectacular, mechanical allure of little people and outsized figures, Gulliver's adventures in Lilliput and to a lesser extent Brobdingnag have also been recurring fixtures in cinematic history because of their resonance for the way cinema is created and experienced.

It should come as no surprise that recent theorists of the screen and of its disorientating capacity have turned for inspiration to the figure of Gulliver. Erkki Huhtamo has coined the term 'Gulliverization' to describe a media landscape in which a multitude of screens thwarts 'the idea of a common anthropomorphic scale'.[5] Elaborating on this concept, Martine Beugnet points to the 'estranging, alienating, and marvelous nature' of a modern screen technology that encompasses both the very small (mobile phones) and the gargantuan ('city centers and shopping malls hung with gigantic screens').[6] But one can argue that such dizzying marvels were already inherent in cinematic form from its inception. A film can make Lilliputians or Brobdingnagians of all of us, and can transform us from one to the other at a moment's notice. A close-up shot makes the human performer huge, while threatening to confound the audience member's sense of self and stature. Films also hold us captive, like the shipwrecked Gulliver, in ways that most other art forms cannot. They do so not solely through the conventions of cinema-going, many of which are shared with theatre and opera, but through film's control of what we see and when. This is not to subscribe to a view of the audience as entirely passive, but to acknowledge what Casetti describes as the tension between cinema as a form of thought and cinema as a discipline: 'by giving the audience

tradition of Gulliverian adaptation in Spain, see Ana María Hornero Corisco, '*Gulliver's Travels* on the Screen: Spanish Film Versions', *SStud*, 20 (2005), 111–23 (112–16).

[5] Erkki Huhtamo, 'Walls, Attractions, and Media', in *Ambient Screens and Transnational Public Spaces*, ed. Nikos Papastergiadis (Hong Kong: Hong Kong University Press, 2016), 31–48 (38).

[6] Martine Beugnet and Annie van den Oever, 'Gulliver Goes to the Movies', in *Screens*, ed. Dominique Chateau and José Moure (Amsterdam: Amsterdam University Press, 2016), 247–57 (247–8).

some ready-made formulae, [twentieth-century cinema] guided our eyes. Nevertheless, these formulae were always imposed through entertainment and play'.[7] Film brings our sustenance to us, much as the Lilliputians bring food and drink to the strange giant in their midst. We are the screen's hostages and also the guests towards whom the entire force of its hospitality is directed.[8] Such ironies and contradictions help to explain why cinema has so frequently found itself back on that same beach, watching the impossibly powerful and privileged prisoner, waiting for him to awake.

Of course, there are other reasons for Gulliver's long-standing popularity as a cinematic subject, some of them rather more prosaic. The text's widespread familiarity, even among people who have never read it, makes it an attractive commercial proposition, while its foregrounding of travel, in both its title and narrative, has long invited international appropriation and reinterpretation. The book's misleading reputation as a classic of children's literature heightens its perceived box-office potential. Moreover, Gulliver straddles high and low culture, the dignified and the vulgar, and arguably has done since Swift's book was first published. As proposed by Alan D. Chalmers, we can think about Swift's work as a 'corrupt original', a text held hostage and denied 'textual authority' by its more censorious adapters.[9] By urinating on the Lilliputian palace, Gulliver not only earns the Empress's 'greatest Abhorrence' but confounds expectations from generations of readers about how prestigious literary works ought to behave (I, v, 81). In this sense, he is a perfect and perfectly ambiguous totem for an art form that has wrestled with questions of its own cultural legitimacy from the moment of its inception. When Méliès starred as Gulliver in his *Le voyage de Gulliver à Lilliput et chez les géants*, it was as much the accessibility of the text as its literary credentials that made it a fitting source. When Mickey Mouse gets shot in the backside by a Lilliputian arrow, or when Jack Black's 2010 Gulliver is energetically burped and put in a nappy by his Brobdingnagian captor, neither is descending from quite so high or quite so sacrosanct a cultural peak as audiences may assume.

---

[7] Francesco Casetti, *Eye of the Century: Film, Experience, Modernity*, trans. Erin Larkin with Jennifer Pranolo (New York: Columbia University Press, 2008), 5.

[8] Compare with Gwendolyn Audrey Foster's description of 'captivity as a palimpsest that draws itself as a power/knowledge grid around the history of filmmaking, film study, and film spectatorship, distribution and the like' (*Captive Bodies: Postcolonial Subjectivity in Cinema* (Albany: State University of New York Press, 1999), 1).

[9] Alan D. Chalmers, 'Film, Censorship, and the "Corrupt Original" of *Gulliver's Travels*', in *Eighteenth-Century Fiction on Screen*, ed. Robert Mayer (Cambridge: Cambridge University Press, 2002), 70–87 (76).

Yet, for all the practical and cultural considerations that make *Gulliver's Travels* an irresistible resource for screen adaptation, it also poses significant challenges, predominantly due to the fraught question of its narrative cohesion. Film-makers' almost unanimous focus on Lilliput and Brobdingnag, to the exclusion of Gulliver's other adventures, is not just due to the eye-catching technical opportunities of the text's early locations. It stems as much from an uncertainty about whether we can consider Gulliver's story a single thing, or indeed, whether he himself can be portrayed as a coherent individual. This uncertainty posed few problems for the likes of Méliès in the early twentieth century. The extant four minutes of his silent film betray no anxiety about the need for consistent narrative or characterisation. It is likely that the film at one point began with a shipwreck scene, but the short vignettes that survive – Gulliver stomping around Lilliput, Gulliver tied down, Gulliver being fed, then Gulliver being received by the Brobdingnagians – only carry a loose sense of continuity, greater or lesser depending on one's knowledge of the original text. If he had so wanted, and if technology had allowed, Méliès could probably have carried Gulliver onward to Laputa or to the land of the Houyhnhnms to similarly diverting ends. By contrast, it is hard to imagine most later adapters extending their hero's journey without their conceptions of film narrative being fundamentally altered. For the most part, the history of Gulliver's screen adaptations is a history of attempts to complete his narrative, to make it more obviously fulfilling either for him or for his audience.

Changeable Stories and Changeable Gullivers

The pressures of narrative, the deeply felt need to supply an emotionally or morally complete story on the screen, have had considerable influence on the kinds of Gulliver conjured up by cinema. Fleischer's 1939 animation, despite celebrating 'Jonathan Swift's immortal Tale' in its opening credits, is plainly not content with the narrative threads offered by the eighteenth-century text. In its search for a more familiarly structured plot, it instinctively prioritises Gulliver's Lilliputian hosts over Gulliver himself. The age-old conflict between Lilliput and Blefuscu as described by Swift is replaced with a disagreement over which song should be performed at the royal wedding that is set to unite these two kingdoms. The entirety of the argument is instigated, escalated and resolved during the time of Gulliver's visit, and the star-crossed prince and princess, though shallow in their characterisation, nonetheless account for most of the film's emotional investment. By contrast, as already noted, our title character is out of action until the film's halfway point, and even after this he is deprived of inner life or motivation. Fleischer's Gulliver seems in no particular hurry to get home or to do anything besides laughing, somewhat condescendingly, at the Lilliputians who surround him. His most frequent response to them – a leisurely 'My, my!' – suggests mild, fleeting amusement rather than any profound existential doubt. His main musical number, 'I Hear a Dream', is performed as he gazes out at the night sea. By rights it should convey a sense of his homesickness, but in practice it operates more as a lullaby for the sleeping Lilliputians, and its call for a 'sailor man' to 'come home again' might well leave us confused as to whether Gulliver is the sailor in question or whether Lilliput itself might constitute a viable home for wandering souls.

Such points of indeterminacy in Fleischer's Gulliver make it difficult to pinpoint the audience's anticipated relationship to him. In purely visual terms, the film's use of rotoscoping – an animation technique invented by Fleischer's brother, Max – makes Gulliver the most recognisably human figure in the production. Rotoscoping as practised by the Fleischers was a painstaking process, involving the tracing over of live-action footage so as to insert a performer's features into the animation. Applied to the figure of Gulliver but not to the Lilliputians, this results in a title character who seems to exist in a different representational dimension from the much more cartoonish figures he encounters. But if Fleischer's intention was thus to establish Gulliver as an audience surrogate, our entry point to Lilliput's strangeness, then many of the film's other decisions work against this. The actor who voiced Gulliver and provided his likeness, Sam Parker, is not named in the film's credits; only the singers for the roles of Princess Glory and Prince David are deemed worthy of that honour. More generally, Gulliver's aforementioned lack of motivation and the prevailing uncanniness of his rotoscoped appearance discourage audience members from putting themselves in his shoes or pondering what they would do in his situation. He might come from a world just as strange and different from our own as Lilliput is.

And, in spite of his long sleep, this Gulliver's difference is not simply a matter of passivity. In the later stages of Fleischer's film, he does involve himself more directly in Lilliputian life, for instance by putting out a fire that has been accidentally started by some Blefuscudian spies. Needless to say, his firefighting skills are of a more family-friendly variety than those described by Swift. Fleischer's Gulliver also, ultimately, brings peace to Lilliput and Blefuscu by intervening in a naval battle and by lecturing the nations' respective leaders on the importance of peace and compromise.

With a bit of showmanship surrounding the apparent death and subsequent resuscitation of the Blefuscudian prince, he encourages the opposing
sides to combine their two wedding songs, and everything is fixed in time
for his own nonchalant departure. However, Gulliver is perhaps even
further from us in these moments of decisive action than he is while
submitting indifferently to the Lilliputians' attentions. He is certainly far
removed from the fickle and fallible Gulliver of Swift's text. There is never
any insecurity, either moral or physical, in his condition. Whereas Swift's
Gulliver is filled with 'Doubts and Perplexities of Mind', fleeing Lilliput
with a helplessness conspicuously at odds with his physical power, this
incarnation is practically godlike, and accordingly unfathomable, in his
certainty of purpose (I, vii, 103). 'Poor, poor, foolish little people', he says
of the Lilliputians and Blefuscudians. The anti-war sentiment and disgust
at pointless violence might have some commonality with Swift's book, but
the tone of superiority is particular to this version of the story. Even if it
chimed with a certain vision of American neutrality on the eve of the
Second World War, it does little to convince that straightforward aloofness
could be a workable, ethical antidote to real-world conflict.

As Karen Bloom Gevirtz has noted in response to the most recent
Hollywood *Gulliver's Travels*, Fleischer's introduction of a love plot has
had a lasting influence on screen adaptations of Swift's book.[10] Yet, for the
most part, writers and directors have used this to make Gulliver a more
rounded character, to integrate his personal development more closely
with the rest of their narratives, and to reflect on him as an embodiment
of the audience's own desires and curiosity. Directed by Jack Sher and
starring Kerwin Mathews, *The 3 Worlds of Gulliver* (1960) doubles down on
romantic trappings. Narrative excitement is generated through the plight
of a star-crossed Lilliputian couple closely modelled on Fleischer's prince
and princess, but Gulliver is also given a love interest, Elizabeth, who is
a major impetus for his travels and who stows away on his ship, eventually
reuniting with him in Brobdingnag. Elizabeth's involvement transforms
Swift's narrative into something more resembling a morality tale, albeit
a ham-fisted one. Gulliver sets out on his journey in the first place because
he is unsatisfied with the life he can provide for his beloved on a doctor's
income; they argue over the importance of money, and his clumsily
signposted stubbornness – 'Nothing's going to make me change my
mind, absolutely nothing!' – practically invites the shipwreck and charac-
ter-building experiences that follow. At the film's conclusion, once it has

---

[10] Gevirtz, *Representing the Eighteenth Century*, 26.

become clear that the third 'World' referred to in its title is to be Wapping rather than Laputa, we are treated to a conspicuously desperate attempt to impose didactic order on Swift's wild satire:

GULLIVER: They're always with us: the giants and the Lilliputians. They're inside us, their terrible world waiting to take our lives, waiting for us to make a mistake, to be selfish again.
ELIZABETH: How can we live with such fear?
GULLIVER: With love [...]

As moral exposition, this is barely coherent. It becomes no more lucid a moment later when Gulliver reflects that the goodness of their erstwhile Brobdingnagian protectress, Glumdalclitch, is still 'waiting to be born'. However, the knots into which the film twists itself while trying to mine Gulliver's story for meaning are themselves informative. They return us to the same, barely tenable balancing act between self-fulfilment and self-loathing that has sustained interest in Swift's text and its main character across the centuries. The indictment of both Lilliputians and Brobdingnagians, the latter painted in a rather worse light than in the original book, comes intriguingly close to a renunciation of travel itself, and of the audience's own thirst for vicarious adventure.

A less tarnished, less self-conscious joy in discovery would be the key to Gulliver's character for several adaptations and re-imaginings from the mid-1960s onwards, which tended to target a younger audience. But even these films could find occasional opportunities to contextualise or critique that spirit of adventure, to show it as a source of vulnerability for Gulliver, or at least to mark it out as a negotiable human characteristic rather than, as per Fleischer, a self-explanatory prerogative. The Japanese animation, *Gulliver's Travels Beyond the Moon* (1965), catches up with Swift's hero at a much later point in his life, as he travels on a rocket to the 'Star of Hope', accompanied by a young boy, a talking dog, and a toy soldier. This production's American dub, featuring songs by Anne and Milton Delugg, would turn the whole affair into something chipper and aspirational. Refrains of 'I wanna be like Gulliver!' and 'You gotta think tall!' distract from, but cannot completely offset, the original film's curiously downbeat moments: the boy's violent removal from a cinema screening Gulliver's story, for example; or Gulliver's profound disappointment upon realising that the 'Star of Hope' is actually a 'Devil Star'. By comparison, the 1977 *Gulliver's Travels* directed by Peter Hunt and starring Richard Harris is more consistently jubilant and assured of the dignity of exploration as personified in its hero. Still, it finds moments for reflection upon the broader eighteenth-century social context from which he has emerged. Its earliest scenes show Gulliver giving money to a beggar woman before returning home to explain to his baffled family why he will not pursue a medical career in London. The credits sequence that follows zooms in and out of various Hogarthian street scenes, lingering on the widespread poverty of the world Gulliver seeks to escape, and perhaps implying something other than mere frivolity in his restlessness.

Yet probably the most sophisticated and nuanced engagement with both sides of Gulliver's character – with both his glamour and his unreliability – is to be found in the 1996 Hallmark miniseries directed by Charles Sturridge and starring Ted Danson as Gulliver. It is partly thanks to the production's longer running time that it is able to explore various facets of Gulliver's character and of Swift's text more fully than the films previously discussed. It is after all the only major adaptation to date that has managed to depict all four of Gulliver's journeys, devoting equal time to each. But its greatest interest comes not from faithfulness to the events of the eighteenth-century source; on the contrary, this adaptation is noteworthy precisely for what it must change in Swift so as to build something narratively compelling. The Emmy-winning screenplay by Simon Moore navigates the uncertainty of Gulliver's selfhood by constructing a meta-narrative that is more indebted to Homer's *Odyssey* than to *Gulliver's Travels* itself. The gaps between Gulliver's four voyages are done away with. His account of his travels becomes a disorientating mixture of storytelling, memory, and hallucination, all relayed to disbelieving British society upon his return after nine years away. Especially Odyssean are his attempts to win back his wife, Mary (Mary Steenburgen), from the attentions of his former colleague, Dr Bates (James Fox). Far from the benevolent Master Bates who dies three paragraphs into Swift's work, this villainous figure burns Gulliver's journals and has him incarcerated in Bedlam. Thankfully, just as Odysseus can rely on the loyalty of his son, Telemachus, Lemuel is here saved by young Tom Gulliver, who arrives at the climactic hearing with crucial evidence of his father's sanity: a bleating Lilliputian sheep.

There is much that is impressively elegant in this narrative solution, but it is also worth considering the compromises that even this approach necessitates. A lot of the audience's enjoyment of the production, similar to a reader's enjoyment of *Gulliver's Travels*, stems from our uncertainty of what to make of the hero and his far-fetched stories. Even if this Gulliver is telling the truth, it is still pretty clear that he is mentally unwell through-out, as his past and present bleed into each other and he seems to be living through both at once. The happy conclusion to the miniseries, the Lilliputian sheep's apparently definitive confirmation that everything we have seen was real, risks tipping the scales towards a vision of Gulliver as healthy and whole, at the expense of the productive doubts fostered up to that point. This is Chalmers's central objection to the Sturridge production: that it is 'doomed' by its commercial context to a betrayal both of Swift's satiric project and of his obstinately unheroic narrative structure.[11] But the legal showdown also works oddly alongside the logical progression of Gulliver's flashbacks. The meta-narrative's moment of greatest triumph must necessarily coincide with the travelling Gulliver's time of greatest misery and disgust, his recognition of himself as a Yahoo and his expulsion from the country of the Houyhnhnms. And if we are to understand Gulliver's acts of memory and storytelling as a way of working through traumatic experience, a reliving by the end of which he will be free from his past, then the bleating sheep might offer not vindication so much as a continuation of the traumatic cycle. To point out these ironies and narrative inconsistencies is not by any means to dismiss the production's achievements but to highlight, once again, the inherent difficulty of portraying a truly complex Gulliver while also delivering a gratifying denouement.

Varieties of Otherness

A substantial part of this chapter has been devoted to the figure of Gulliver, how he has been interpreted through film narrative, and what he means to audiences. It is important in this final section to attend to an opposite, but related, question: the ways that various adaptations have conceived of the otherness of the lands visited by Gulliver, Lilliput foremost among them. With the promise of adventure being a central facet of the text's appeal to adapters, it is hardly surprising that this otherness has sometimes been framed through ideas of the exotic. As if it were not outlandish enough to happen upon a country of tiny people, both the 1960 and 1977 films dress their Lilliputians in generically oriental robes and surround them with architecture reminiscent of the Ottoman Empire. Such manoeuvres, while not incompatible with Swift's descriptions, do ignore his repeated emphasis on Lilliput's in-betweenness as well as his interest in establishing it as a thinly veiled representation of eighteenth-century Britain. Gulliver tells us that the fashion of the Emperor's clothes was 'between the *Asiatick*

---

[11] Chalmers, 'Film, Censorship, and the "Corrupt Original"', 84–5.

and the *European*', and that the Lilliputian style of writing was 'neither from the Left to the Right, like the *Europeans*; nor from the Right to the Left like the *Arabians* [. . .] but aslant [. . .] like Ladies in *England*' (I, ii, 46; I, vi, 83). Judging from the details of Gulliver's journey and from the map included in the 1726 publication, Lilliput was actually meant to be situated northwest of Tasmania in the Indian Ocean. The Arabian stylings of both films speak chiefly for the cultural assumptions of their creators and for their eagerness to make Gulliver even more of an outsider than his height already renders him.

Perhaps more interesting, because less predictable, are the other kinds of otherness we encounter in Gulliverian adaptations. There is often a technological distinctiveness to Lilliput – epitomised by the engineering know-how of those who bind, feed, and in some instances shave the captured Gulliver – which exceeds what we are told about Lilliputian ingenuity in the literary source. Such technological otherness might partake of some of the idea, if not the actuality, of Swift's Laputa, despite that location rarely being directly depicted itself. Indeed, one of the few films to put Part III's flying island on the screen, renowned animator Hayao Miyazaki's *Castle in the Sky* (1986), dispenses with all but the name and the technological allure of Laputa, invoking it as a long-abandoned site, guarded by robots and containing forbidden knowledge. Robots feature in *Gulliver's Travels Beyond the Moon* as well, and in the final battle of 2010's *Gulliver's Travels*, which sees Jack Black defeat a Lilliputian antagonist who has constructed a weaponised suit. The recurrence of robotic tropes and imagery might seem coincidental, particularly considering the free-wheeling approach to adaptation adopted by all of these productions, but as Gevirtz's recent work has shown, the drive to confront Gulliver with modern or futuristic technology might actually be the flip side of another variety of otherness manifested in these narratives: a temporal otherness.

The Gulliver played by Jack Black in the 2010 film is in effect a time traveller as well as a discoverer of strange lands. The Lilliput he visits embodies certain ideas of the eighteenth-century past within which Swift lived and wrote, and so it also enables the film to reflect on its own relationship to historical memory and tradition. As James Ward argues, the eighteenth century is 'an important historical source for forms and processes which have become fundamental to the operation of modern memory'.[12] Never mind that the film's ideas of the past are simplistic;

[12] James Ward, *Memory and Enlightenment: Cultural Afterlives of the Long Eighteenth Century* (Basingstoke: Palgrave Macmillan, 2018), 7.

revolving around clichés of excessive formality and social fixity, they clearly have little to do with either the lived experience of Swift or the qualities of his satire. The truth of the past, if it were even salvageable, would not matter, since, in Gevirtz's words, 'suspicion of history and the recognition of its narrativity and flexibility underpin the film'.[13] History is shown to be valuable insofar as it teaches this Gulliver to value himself, and it is rejected wherever its perceived conceptual affiliations – to stale ritual, to corporate identity – become incompatible with twenty-first-century individualism. In this sense, the film is more indebted to Gullivers that have gone before than its character's proud anachronism might suggest. Jack Black follows in the footsteps of Bollywood actor Jaaved Jaaferi, who astounded his own Lilliputian hosts by playing music on his Walkman in 2003's *Jajantaram Mamantaram* (dir. Soumitra Ranade). Indeed, the process of adapting Gulliver for the screen has always been about confronting or celebrating one's own modernity, from Mickey Mouse's unapologetic exploitation of his literary source to Ted Danson's American-accented interactions with an especially regal and execution-happy incarnation of the Lilliputian Emperor (Peter O'Toole).

The temporal aspect of Lilliput's otherness is also apparent, though it assumes a somewhat different form, in one last cinematic Gulliver that should be mentioned here. Nearly contemporaneous with *Gulliver Mickey*, Aleksandr Ptushko's *Novyy Gulliver* (*New Gulliver*) of 1935 could hardly be more different from Disney's vision in either its ideological foundations or its overt reverence for Swift's text, but it is nonetheless similarly invested in the story's potential for constant renewal and novelty, as signposted most obviously by its title. Having received a copy of Swift's book as a prize from his Soviet youth group, Petya (Vladimir Konstantinov) falls asleep as the story is read out, dreaming that he is Petya Gulliver. For Ptushko, the past as represented by Lilliput is not eighteenth-century Britain but an industrial, capitalist society whose abuses his hero is well placed to transcend and denounce. Though one recent analysis of the film has described Petya as a mostly passive witness to the ensuing Lilliputian revolution, he seems, when set against many of the other Gullivers discussed in this chapter, to be a far more assertive figure, at least partially responsible for instigating change in the stop-motion world at his feet.[14] In any case, his significance for a broader understanding of Gulliver's screen afterlife goes beyond his

[13] Gevirtz, *Representing the Eighteenth Century*, 32.
[14] Anne Eakin Moss, 'Cinema's "Miracles": Film Tricks and the Production of Soviet Wonder', *Film History: An International Journal*, 32 (2020), 33–59.

capacity for action. It is felt in his claim to newness, an exhilarating newness brought into focus by the social failings and mechanical inadequacies of Lilliputians who are, for all their cinematic charm, still clumsy imitations of human life.

'Such petty souls', Petya declares of his hosts' corrupt leaders. Here, as in so many cinematic adaptations, the otherness of Lilliput is ultimately in the service of defining Gulliver's character: he is manifestly superior, as Fleischer's hero would be a few years later, but he is also human and humane. The film assures its Soviet audience that they too are different, protected from the callousness of the past. This message takes on retrospective poignancy in light of the Soviet Union's own oppressions and the approaching war which would take the life of the film's young star, along with so many others. Seen through this lens, the film strikes an inadvertently elegiac note, a reminder of the promises that every screen Gulliver makes and struggles to keep. Each new Gulliver prides himself on his singularity while offering audiences something paradoxically familiar and comforting. And each Gulliver tries in some way to assert his newness, his freedom from history, despite being indebted to it, and sometimes haunted by it.

Further Reading

Adams, Percy G., *Travelers and Travel Liars, 1660–1800* (Berkeley: University of California Press, 1962)

Alff, David, 'Swift's Solar Gourds and the Rhetoric of Projection', *ECS*, 47 (2014), 245–60

Alkemeyer, Bryan, 'The Natural History of the Houyhnhnms: Noble Horses in *Gulliver's Travels*', *The Eighteenth Century*, 57 (2016), 23–37

Allison, Alexander W., 'Concerning Houyhnhnm Reason', *Sewanee Review*, 76 (1968), 480–92

Anderson, William S., 'Paradise Gained by Horace, Lost by Gulliver', *Yearbook of English Studies*, 14 (1984), 151–66

Armintor, Deborah Needleman, 'The Sexual Politics of Microscopy in Brobdingnag', *SEL*, 47 (2007), 619–40

Barchas, Janine, 'Prefiguring Genre: Frontispiece Portraits from *Gulliver's Travels* to *Millenium Hall*', *Studies in the Novel*, 30 (1998), 260–87

Barnett, Louise, *Jonathan Swift in the Company of Women* (Oxford: Oxford University Press, 2007)

Barroll III, J. Leeds, 'Gulliver and the Struldbruggs', *PMLA*, 73 (1958), 45–50

Barry, Kevin, 'Exclusion and Inclusion in Swift's *Gulliver's Travels*', *The Irish Review*, 30 (2003), 36–47

Basney, Lionel, 'Gulliver and the Children', in *The Voice of the Narrator in Children's Literature*, ed. Charlotte F. Otten and Gary D. Schmidt (Westport: Greenwood Press, 1989), 148–58

Benedict, Barbara M., 'Material Ideas: Things and Collections in *Gulliver's Travels*', in *Münster 6*, 461–81

Bentman, Richard, 'Satiric Structure and Tone in the Conclusion of *Gulliver's Travels*', *SEL*, 11 (1971), 535–48

Bischof, Janika, Kirsten Juhas, and Hermann J. Real (eds.), *Reading Swift: Papers from the Seventh Münster Symposium on Jonathan Swift* (Munich: Wilhelm Fink, 2019)

Booth, Wayne C., *A Rhetoric of Irony* (Chicago: University of Chicago Press, 1974)

Boucé, Paul-Gabriel, 'Gulliver Phallophorus and the Maids of Honour in Brobdingnag', *Bulletin de la société d'études anglo-américaines des XVIIe et XVIIIe siècles*, 53 (2001), 81–98

'Gulliver's Frenchified Travels to Blefuscu: The First Two Translations', in *Münster* 4, 379–86

'The Rape of Gulliver Reconsidered', *SStud*, 11 (1996), 98–114

Bracher, Frederick, 'The Maps in *Gulliver's Travels*', *Huntington Library Quarterly*, 8 (1944), 59–74

Brady, Frank (ed.), *Twentieth-Century Interpretations of 'Gulliver's Travels': A Collection of Critical Essays* (Englewood Cliffs: Prentice-Hall, 1968)

'Vexations and Diversions: Three Problems in *Gulliver's Travels*', *MP*, 75 (1978), 346–67

Brewer, David A., *The Afterlife of Character, 1726–1825* (Philadelphia: University of Pennsylvania Press, 2005)

Brown, Laura, 'Reading Race and Gender: Jonathan Swift', *ECS*, 23 (1990), 425–43

Bruce, Susan, 'The Flying Island and Female Anatomy: Gynaecology and Female Power in *Gulliver's Travels*', *Genders*, 1 (1988), 60–76

Bullard, Paddy, 'Gulliver, Medium, Technique', *ELH*, 83 (2016), 517–41

Bullard, Paddy and James McLaverty (eds.), *Jonathan Swift and the Eighteenth-Century Book* (Cambridge: Cambridge University Press, 2013)

Bywaters, David, '*Gulliver's Travels* and the Mode of Political Parallel During Walpole's Administration', *ELH*, 54 (1987), 717–40

Carnochan, W. B., 'The Complexity of Swift: Gulliver's Fourth Voyage', *SP*, 60 (1963), 23–44

Lemuel Gulliver's Mirror for Man (Berkeley: University of California Press, 1968)

'Some Roles of Lemuel Gulliver', *TSLL*, 5 (1964), 520–9

Case, Arthur E., *Four Essays on 'Gulliver's Travels'* (Princeton: Princeton University Press, 1945)

Castle, Terry J., 'Why the Houyhnhnms Don't Write: Swift, Satire and the Fear of the Text', *Essays in Literature*, 7 (1980), 31–44

Chalmers, Alan D., 'Film, Censorship, and the "Corrupt Original" of *Gulliver's Travels*', in *Eighteenth-Century Fiction on Screen*, ed. Robert Mayer (Cambridge: Cambridge University Press, 2002), 70–87

Champion, Larry S., '*Gulliver's Travels*: The Framing Events as Guide to Interpretation', *TSLL*, 10 (1969), 529–36

Chow, Jeremy, 'Prime Mates: The Simian, Maternity and Abjection in Brobdingnag', *JECS*, 43 (2020), 315–25

Christie, John, 'Laputa Revisited', in *Nature Transfigured: Science and Literature, 1700–1900*, ed. John Christie and Sally Shuttleworth (Manchester: Manchester University Press, 1984), 45–60

Chudgar, Neil, 'Swift's Gentleness', *ELH*, 78 (2011), 137–61

Clegg, Jeanne, 'Swift on False Witness', *SEL*, 44 (2004), 461–85

Clifford, James L., 'Gulliver's Fourth Voyage: "Hard" and "Soft" Schools of Interpretation', in *Quick Springs of Sense: Studies in the Eighteenth Century*, ed. Larry S. Champion (Athens: University of Georgia Press, 1974), 33–49

Cohan, Steven, 'Gulliver's Fiction', *Studies in the Novel*, 6 (1974), 7–16

Col, Norbert, 'True-to-Life History? What the Dead Say in *Gulliver's Travels*, or: Sensational Disclosures (Gulliver Tells All)', in *Münster* 7, 251–67

Cook, Terry, '"Dividing the Swift Mind": A Reading of *Gulliver's Travels*', *Critical Quarterly*, 22 (1980), 35–47

Coykendall, Abby, 'Cruising Dystopia in *Gulliver's Travels*', *JECS*, 43 (2020), 327–39

Crane, R. S., 'The Houyhnhnms, the Yahoos, and the History of Ideas', in *Reason and the Imagination: Studies in the History of Ideas, 1600–1800*, ed. J. A. Mazzeo (New York: Columbia University Press, 1962), 231–53

Damrosch, Leo, *Jonathan Swift: His Life and World* (New Haven: Yale University Press, 2013)

DePorte, Michael, 'Swift's Horses of Instruction', in *Münster* 2, 199–211

Dircks, Richard J., 'Gulliver's Tragic Rationalism', *Criticism*, 2 (1960), 134–49

Donoghue, Denis, 'The Brainwashing of Lemuel Gulliver', *Southern Review*, 32 (1996), 128–46

Doody, Margaret Anne, 'Swift and Romance', in *Walking Naboth's Vineyard: New Studies of Swift*, ed. Christopher Fox and Brenda Tooley (Notre Dame: University of Notre Dame Press, 1995), 98–126

Downie, J. A., 'Gulliver's Fourth Voyage and Locke's *Essay Concerning Human Understanding*', in *Münster* 5, 453–64

Jonathan Swift: Political Writer (London: Routledge & Kegan Paul, 1984)

'Political Characterisation in *Gulliver's Travels*', *Yearbook of English Studies*, 7 (1977), 108–21

Eddy, William A., *'Gulliver's Travels': A Critical Study* (Princeton: Princeton University Press, 1923)

Ehrenpreis, Irwin, 'The Allegory of *Gulliver's Travels*', *SStud*, 4 (1989), 13–28

'The Meaning of Gulliver's Last Voyage', *A Review of English Literature*, 3 (1962), 18–38

'The Origins of *Gulliver's Travels*', *PMLA*, 72 (1957), 880–99

Swift: The Man, His Works, and the Age, 3 vols. (London: Methuen, 1958–83)

Elliott, Robert C., 'Swift's Satire: Rules of the Game', *ELH*, 41 (1974), 413–28

Erskine-Hill, Howard, *Jonathan Swift: 'Gulliver's Travels'* (Cambridge: Cambridge University Press, 1993)

Firth, Sir Charles, 'The Political Significance of *Gulliver's Travels*', *Proceedings of the British Academy*, 9 (1919–20), 237–59

Fischer, John Irwin, Hermann J. Real, and James Woolley (eds.), *Swift and His Contexts* (New York: AMS Press, 1989)

Fitzgerald, Robert P., 'The Allegory of Luggnagg and the Struldbruggs in *Gulliver's Travels*', *SP*, 65 (1968), 657–76

'The Structure of *Gulliver's Travels*', *SP*, 71 (1974), 247–63

Flynn, Carol Houlihan, *The Body in Swift and Defoe* (Cambridge: Cambridge University Press, 1990)

Foster, Milton P., *A Casebook on Gulliver among the Houyhnhnms* (New York: Thomas Y. Crowell, 1961)

Fox, Christopher (ed.), *The Cambridge Companion to Jonathan Swift* (Cambridge: Cambridge University Press, 2003)

Francus, Marilyn, *The Converting Imagination: Linguistic Theory and Swift's Satiric Prose* (Carbondale: Southern Illinois University Press, 1994)

Franklin, Michael J., 'Lemuel Self-Translated; Or, Being an Ass in Houyhnhnmland', *MLR*, 100 (2005), 1–19

Frye, Roland M., 'Swift's Yahoo and the Christian Symbols for Sin', *Journal of the History of Ideas*, 15 (1954), 201–17

Fung, Julian, 'Early Condensations of *Gulliver's Travels*: Images of Swift as Satirist in the 1720s', *SP*, 114 (2017), 395–425

Fussell, Paul, 'The Frailty of Lemuel Gulliver', in *Essays in Literary History Presented to J. Milton French*, ed. Rudolf Kirk and C. F. Main (New Brunswick: Rutgers University Press, 1960), 113–25

Gevirtz, Karen Bloom, *Representing the Eighteenth Century in Film and Television, 2000–2015* (London: Palgrave Macmillan, 2017)

Gill, James E., 'Beast Over Man: Thereophilic Paradox in Gulliver's "Voyage to the Country of the Houyhnhnms"', *SP*, 67 (1970), 532–49

'Man and Yahoo: Dialectic and Symbolism in Gulliver's "Voyage to the Country of the Houyhnhnms"', in *The Dress of Words: Essays on Restoration and Eighteenth Century Literature in Honor of Richmond P. Bond*, ed. Robert B. White, Jr (Lawrence: University of Kansas Press, 1978), 67–90

Girten, Kristin M., 'Mingling with Matter: Tactile Microscopy and the Philosophic Mind in Brobdingnag and Beyond', *The Eighteenth Century*, 54 (2013), 497–520

Goldberg, Julia, 'Houyhnhnm Subtext: Moral Conclusions and Linguistic Manipulation in *Gulliver's Travels*', *1650–1850*, 4 (1998), 269–84

Goldgar, Bertrand A., *Walpole and the Wits: The Relation of Politics to Literature, 1722–1742* (Lincoln: University of Nebraska Press, 1976)

Gordon, Robert C., 'Jonathan Swift and the Modern Art of War', *Bulletin of Research in the Humanities*, 83 (1980), 187–202

Gottlieb, Sidney, 'The Emblematic Background of Swift's Flying Island', *SStud*, 1 (1986), 24–31

Greene, Donald, 'The Education of Lemuel Gulliver', in *The Varied Pattern: Studies in the 18th Century*, ed. Peter Hughes and David Williams (Toronto: A. M. Hakkert, 1971), 3–20

Griffin, Dustin, *Swift and Pope: Satirists in Dialogue* (Cambridge: Cambridge University Press, 2010)

Halewood, William H., '*Gulliver's Travels* I, iv', *ELH*, 33 (1966), 422–33

Halsband, Robert, 'Eighteenth-Century Illustrations of *Gulliver's Travels*', in *Münster* 1, 83–112

Hammond, Eugene R., 'Nature-Reason-Justice in *Utopia* and *Gulliver's Travels*', *SEL*, 22 (1982), 445–68

Hanlon, Aaron R., 'Re-reading Gulliver as Quixote: Toward a Theory of Quixotic Exceptionalism', *Connotations*, 21 (2011/12), 278–303

Harth, Phillip, 'The Problem of Political Allegory in *Gulliver's Travels*', *MP*, 73 (1975–6), 540–7

Hawes, Clement, 'Gulliver Effects', in *Münster* 6, 523–41

'Scaling Greatness in *Gulliver's Travels*', in *Münster* 5, 407–27

'Three Times Round the Globe: Gulliver and Colonial Discourse', *Cultural Critique*, 18 (1991), 187–214

Higgins, Ian, *Swift's Politics: A Study in Disaffection* (Cambridge: Cambridge University Press, 1994)

Hinnant, Charles H., *Purity and Defilement in 'Gulliver's Travels'* (London: Macmillan, 1987)

Holly, Grant, 'Travel and Translation: Textuality in *Gulliver's Travels*', *Criticism*, 21 (1979), 134–52

Hudson, Nicholas, '*Gulliver's Travels* and Locke's Radical Nominalism', *1650–1850*, 1 (1994), 247–66

Hudson, Nicholas and Aaron Santesso (eds.), *Swift's Travels: Eighteenth-Century British Satire and Its Legacy* (Cambridge: Cambridge University Press, 2008)

Ingram, Allan, 'Doctor at Sea: Gulliver and Medical Perception', in *Münster* 6, 497–505

Janes, Regina, 'Lemuel Gulliver, Map-Maker', *SP*, 118 (2021), 787–826

Jeffares, A. Norman (ed.), *Fair Liberty Was All His Cry: A Tercentenary Tribute to Jonathan Swift, 1667–1745* (London: Macmillan, 1967)

Jones, Myrddin, 'Swift, Harrington, and Corruption in England', *PQ*, 54 (1974), 59–70

Juhas, Kirsten, Hermann J. Real, and Sandra Simon (eds.), *Reading Swift: Papers from the Sixth Münster Symposium on Jonathan Swift* (Munich: Wilhelm Fink, 2013)

Kallich, Martin, *The Other End of the Egg: Religious Satire in 'Gulliver's Travels'* (New York: New York University Press, 1970)

Karian, Stephen, 'The Texts of *Gulliver's Travels*', in *Les voyages de Gulliver: Mondes lointains ou mondes proches*, ed. Daniel Carey and François Boulaire (Caen: Presses Universitaires de Caen, 2002), 35–50

Kelling, H. D., 'Some Significant Names in *Gulliver's Travels*', *SP*, 48 (1951), 761–8

Kelly, Anne Cline, 'After Eden: Gulliver's (Linguistic) Travels', *ELH*, 45 (1978), 33–54

'Gulliver as Pet and Pet Keeper: Talking Animals in Book 4', *ELH*, 74 (2007), 323–49

'Swift's Explorations of Slavery in Houyhnhnmland and Ireland', *PMLA*, 91 (1976), 846–55

'Swift's Versions and Subversions of the Fable Genre: Context for Book Four of *Gulliver's Travels*', in *Münster* 6, 507–19

Kelsall, M. M., 'Iterum Houyhnhnm: Swift's Sextumvirate and the Horses', *Essays in Criticism*, 19 (1969), 35–45

Knowles, Ronald, *'Gulliver's Travels': The Politics of Satire* (Boston: Twayne, 1996)

Korshin, Paul J., 'The Intellectual Context of Swift's Flying Island', *PQ*, 50 (1971), 630–46

Kosok, Heinz, 'Gulliver's Children: A Classic Transformed for Young Readers', in *Münster* I, 135–44

'Stage Versions of *Gulliver's Travels*', *SStud*, 17 (2002), 88–99

Landa, Louis, 'The Dismal Science in Houyhnhnmland', *Novel*, 13 (1979), 38–49

Lenfest, David, 'Checklist of Illustrated Editions of *Gulliver's Travels*, 1727–1914', *The Papers of the Bibliographical Society of America*, 62 (1968), 85–123

Lock, F. P., *The Politics of 'Gulliver's Travels'* (Oxford: Clarendon Press, 1980)

Loveman, Kate, '"Full of Improbable Lies": *Gulliver's Travels* and Jest Books', *BJECS*, 26 (2003), 15–26

Reading Fictions, 1660–1740: Deception in English Literary and Political Culture (Aldershot: Ashgate, 2008)

Lynall, Gregory, *Swift and Science: The Satire, Politics, and Theology of Natural Knowledge, 1690–1730* (Basingstoke: Palgrave Macmillan, 2012)

'Swift's Caricatures of Newton: "Taylor," "Conjurer," and "Workman in the Mint"', *BJECS*, 28 (2005), 19–32

Mackie, Erin, 'Gulliver and the Houyhnhnm Good Life', *The Eighteenth Century*, 55 (2014), 109–15

Markley, Robert, 'Gulliver and the Japanese: The Limits of the Postcolonial Past', *MLQ*, 65 (2004), 457–79

Marshall, Ashley, *The Practice of Satire in England, 1658–1770* (Baltimore: Johns Hopkins University Press, 2013)

Swift and History: Politics and the English Past (Cambridge: Cambridge University Press, 2015)

Mazella, David, 'Husbandry, Pedagogy, and Improvement in Swift's *Gulliver's Travels*', *Studies in Eighteenth-Century Culture*, 45 (2016), 239–66

McKeon, Michael, *The Origins of the English Novel, 1600–1740* (Baltimore: Johns Hopkins University Press, 1987)

McLaverty, James, 'The Revision of the First Edition of *Gulliver's Travels*: Book-Trade Context, Interleaving, Two Cancels, and a Failure to Catch', *The Papers of the Bibliographical Society of America*, 106 (2012), 5–35

McManmon, John J., 'The Problem of a Religious Interpretation of Gulliver's Fourth Voyage', *Journal of the History of Ideas*, 27 (1966), 59–72

McMinn, Joseph, *Jonathan's Travels: Swift and Ireland* (Belfast: Appletree Press, 1994)

Mezciems, Jenny, 'Utopia and "the Thing Which is Not": More, Swift, and Other Lying Idealists', *University of Toronto Quarterly*, 52 (1982), 40–62

Monk, Samuel Holt, 'The Pride of Lemuel Gulliver', *Sewanee Review*, 63 (1955), 48–71

Morrissey, L. J., *Gulliver's Progress* (Hamden: Archon Books, 1978)

Mullan, John, 'Swift, Defoe, and Narrative Forms', in *The Cambridge Companion to English Literature, 1650–1740*, ed. Steven N. Zwicker (Cambridge: Cambridge University Press, 1998), 250–75

Nichols, Mary P., 'Rationality and Community: Swift's Criticism of the Houyhnhnms', *The Journal of Politics*, 43 (1981), 1153–69

Nicolson, Marjorie Hope and Nora M. Mohler, 'The Scientific Background of Swift's *Voyage to Laputa*', *Annals of Science*, 2 (1937), 299–334

'Swift's "Flying Island" in the *Voyage to Laputa*', *Annals of Science*, 2 (1937), 405–30

Nokes, David, *Jonathan Swift, a Hypocrite Reversed: A Critical Biography* (Oxford: Oxford University Press, 1985)

Nussbaum, Felicity, *The Brink of All We Hate: English Satires on Women, 1660–1750* (Lexington: University Press of Kentucky, 1984)

Nuttall, A. D., 'Gulliver among the Horses', *Yearbook of English Studies*, 18 (1988), 51–67

Oakleaf, David, *A Political Biography of Jonathan Swift* (London: Pickering and Chatto, 2008)

'*Trompe l'Oeil*: Gulliver and the Distortions of the Observing Eye', *University of Toronto Quarterly*, 53 (1983/4), 166–80

Orwell, George, 'Politics vs. Literature: An Examination of *Gulliver's Travels*' (1946), in *Jonathan Swift: A Critical Anthology*, ed. Denis Donoghue (London: Penguin, 1971), 342–60

Passmann, Dirk F., *'Full of Improbable Lies': 'Gulliver's Travels' und die Reiseliteratur vor 1726* (Frankfurt am Main: Peter Lang, 1987)

'Gulliver's "Temple of Fame": Glubbdubdrib Revisited', in *Münster* 4, 329–48

'Mud and Slime: Some Implications of the Yahoos' Genealogy and the History of an Idea', *BJECS*, 11 (1988), 1–17

Passmann, Dirk F. and Heinz J. Vienken, *The Library and Reading of Jonathan Swift: A Bio-Bibliographical Handbook. Part I: Swift's Library*, 4 vols. (Frankfurt am Main: Peter Lang, 2003)

Patey, Douglas Lane, 'Swift's Satire on "Science" and the Structure of *Gulliver's Travels*', *ELH*, 58 (1991), 809–39

Peterson, Leland D., 'Gulliver's Secret Commission', in *Swift: The Enigmatic Dean: Festschrift for Hermann Josef Real*, ed. Rudolf Freiburg, Arno Löffler, and Wolfgang Zach (Tübingen: Stauffenburg Verlag, 1998), 201–11

'*Gulliver's Travels*: Antient and Modern History Corrected', *SStud*, 6 (1991), 83–110

Philmus, Robert M., 'Swift, Gulliver, and "the Thing Which Was Not"', *ELH*, 38 (1971), 62–79

Pollak, Ellen, 'Swift among the Feminists: An Approach to Teaching', *College Literature*, 19 (1992), 114–20

Probyn, Clive T. (ed.), *The Art of Jonathan Swift* (New York: Vision Press, 1978)

Quinlan, Maurice, 'Swift's Use of Literalization as a Rhetorical Device', *PMLA*, 82 (1967), 516–21

Quintana, Ricardo, 'Situational Satire: A Commentary on the Method of Swift', *University of Toronto Quarterly*, 17 (1947), 130–6

Rabb, Melinda Alliker, '*Cogito ergo Gulliver*', in *Münster* 6, 483–95

Miniature and the English Imagination: Literature, Cognition, and Small-Scale Culture, 1650–1765 (Cambridge: Cambridge University Press, 2019)

'The Secret Memoirs of Lemuel Gulliver: Satire, Secrecy, and Swift', *ELH*, 73 (2006), 325–54

Radner, John B., 'The Struldbruggs, the Houyhnhnms, and the Good Life', *SEL*, 17 (1977), 427–33

Rawson, Claude J. (ed.), *The Character of Swift's Satire: A Revised Focus* (Newark: University of Delaware Press, 1983)

    God, Gulliver and Genocide: Barbarism and the European Imagination, 1492–1945 (Oxford: Oxford University Press, 2001)

    Gulliver and the Gentle Reader: Studies in Swift and Our Time (London: Routledge & Kegan Paul, 1973)

    (ed.), *Politics and Literature in the Age of Swift: English and Irish Perspectives* (Cambridge: Cambridge University Press, 2010)

Real, Hermann J. (ed.) *Reading Swift: Papers from the Fifth Münster Symposium on Jonathan Swift* (Munich: Wilhelm Fink, 2008)

    (ed.), *The Reception of Jonathan Swift in Europe* (London: Thoemmes Continuum, 2005)

Real, Hermann J. and Heinz J. Vienken (eds.), *Proceedings of the First Münster Symposium on Jonathan Swift* (Munich: Wilhelm Fink Verlag, 1985)

    'The Structure of *Gulliver's Travels*', in *Münster* 1, 199–208

Real, Hermann J. and Helgard Stöver-Leidig (eds.), *Reading Swift: Papers from the Third Münster Symposium on Jonathan Swift* (Munich: Wilhelm Fink, 1998)

    (eds.), *Reading Swift: Papers from the Fourth Münster Symposium on Jonathan Swift* (Munich: Wilhelm Fink, 2003)

Reilly, Patrick, 'Humbling Narcissus: Mirrors in *Gulliver's Travels*', in *Münster* 3, 189–97

Rielly, Edward J. (ed.), *Approaches to Teaching Swift's 'Gulliver's Travels'* (New York: Modern Language Association of America, 1988)

    'Irony in *Gulliver's Travels* and *Utopia*', *Utopian Studies*, 3 (1992), 70–83

Rodino, Richard H., 'Splendide Mendax: Authors, Characters, and Readers in *Gulliver's Travels*', *PMLA*, 106 (1991), 1054–70

Rodino, Richard H. and Hermann J. Real (eds.), *Reading Swift: Papers from the Second Münster Symposium on Jonathan Swift* (Munich: Wilhelm Fink Verlag, 1993)

Rogers, Pat, 'Gulliver and the Engineers', *MLR*, 70 (1975), 260–70

    'Swift and Bolingbroke on Faction', *Journal of British Studies*, 9 (1970), 71–101

Said, Edward, 'Swift's Tory Anarchy', *ECS*, 3 (1969), 48–66

Salvaggio, Ruth, 'Swift and Psychoanalysis, Language and Woman', *Women's Studies*, 15 (1988), 417–34

Seager, Nicholas, '*Gulliver's Travels* Serialized and Continued', in *Münster* 6, 543–62

Seidel, Michael, '*Gulliver's Travels* and the Contracts of Fiction', in *The Cambridge Companion to the Eighteenth-Century Novel*, ed. John Richetti (Cambridge: Cambridge University Press, 1996), 72–89

Shaw, Sheila, 'The Rape of Gulliver: Case Study of a Source', *PMLA*, 90 (1975), 62–8

Skeen, Catherine, 'Projecting Fictions: *Gulliver's Travels, Jack Connor,* and *John Buncle*', *MP*, 100 (2003), 330–59

Smith, Frederik N., 'The Danger of Reading Swift: The Double Bind of Reading *Gulliver's Travels*', in *Reader Entrapment in Eighteenth-Century Literature,* ed. Karl Kropf (New York: AMS Press, 1992), 109–30

(ed.), *The Genres of 'Gulliver's Travels'* (Newark: University of Delaware Press, 1990)

'Vexing Voices: The Telling of Gulliver's Story', *Papers on Language and Literature,* 21 (1985), 383–98

Soupel, Serge, 'Gulliver, Metamorphosis, Gods, Demigods, and Heroes', in *Münster* 5, 429–40

Stepakoff, Shanee, 'Hiding in Plain Sight: Judaeophobia in Swift's Portrayal of the Yahoos in *Gulliver's Travels*', *SStud,* 35 (2020), 106–51

Stubbs, John, *Jonathan Swift: The Reluctant Rebel* (London: Norton, 2017)

Swaim, Kathleen M., *A Reading of 'Gulliver's Travels'* (The Hague: Mouton, 1972)

Swearingen, James E., 'Time and Technique in Gulliver's Third Voyage', *Philosophy and Literature,* 6 (1982), 45–61

Tadié, Alexis, 'Gulliver in the Land of the Hybrids: Language, Science and Fiction in Jonathan Swift's *Gulliver's Travels*', *Etudes anglaises,* 49 (1996), 144–57

Terry, Richard, '*Gulliver's Travels* and the Savage-Critic Topos', *SStud,* 11 (1996), 115–31

Thickstun, Margaret Olofson, 'The Puritan Origins of Gulliver's Conversion in Houyhnhnmland', *SEL,* 37 (1997), 517–34

Todd, Dennis, 'The Hairy Maid at the Harpsichord: Some Speculations on the Meaning of *Gulliver's Travels*', *TSLL,* 34 (1992), 239–83

Torchiana, Donald T., 'Jonathan Swift, the Irish, and the Yahoos: Their Case Reconsidered', *PQ,* 54 (1975), 195–212

Traugott, John, 'Swift's Allegory: The Yahoo and the Man-of-Mode', *University of Toronto Quarterly,* 33 (1963), 1–18

Treadwell, Michael, 'Benjamin Motte, Andrew Tooke and *Gulliver's Travels*', in *Münster* 1, 287–304

'Jonathan Swift: The Satirist as Projector', *TSLL,* 17 (1975), 439–60

'Observations on the Printing of Motte's Octavo Editions of *Gulliver's Travels*', in *Münster* 3, 157–77

'Swift, Richard Coleire, and the Origins of *Gulliver's Travels*', *RES,* 34.135 (1983), 304–11

'The Text of *Gulliver's Travels,* Again', *SStud,* 10 (1995), 62–79

Tyne, James L., 'Gulliver's Maker and Gullibility', *Criticism,* 7 (1965), 151–67

Uphaus, Robert W., '*Gulliver's Travels, A Modest Proposal,* and the Problematical Nature of Meaning', *Papers on Language and Literature,* 10 (1974), 268–78

Welcher, Jeanne K. and George E. Bush, Jr (eds.), *Gulliveriana,* 8 vols. (Gainesville: Scholars' Facsimiles & Reprints, 1970–99)

Wilding, Michael, 'The Politics of *Gulliver's Travels*', *Studies in the Eighteenth Century, II: Papers Presented at the Second David Nichol Smith Memorial*

Seminar, ed R. F. Brissenden (Canberra: Australian National University Press, 1973), 303–22

Williams, Harold, *The Text of 'Gulliver's Travels'* (1952; Cambridge: Cambridge University Press, 2013)

Williams, Kathleen (ed.), *Jonathan Swift: The Critical Heritage* (London: Routledge & Kegan Paul, 1970)

Wilson, Penelope, 'Feminism and the Augustans: Some Readings and Problems', *Critical Quarterly*, 28 (1986), 80–92

Womersley, David, 'Dean Swift Hears a Sermon: Robert Howard's Ash Wednesday Sermon of 1725 and *Gulliver's Travels*', *RES*, 60.247 (2009), 744–62

Worth, Chris, 'Swift's "Flying Island": Buttons and Bomb-Vessels', *RES*, 48.167 (1991), 343–60

Wyrick, Deborah Baker, *Jonathan Swift and the Vested Word* (Chapel Hill: University of North Carolina Press, 1988)

Yang, Xiao, 'On the History of the Chinese Translations of *Gulliver's Travels*', *American Notes and Queries*, 34 (2021), 36–61

Zimmerman, Everett, 'Gulliver the Preacher', *PMLA*, 89 (1974), 1024–32

Zirker, Herbert, 'Horse Sense and Sensibility: Some Issues Concerning Utopian Understanding in *Gulliver's Travels*', *SStud*, 12 (1997), 85–98

Index

Authors

Topics

Arthurian Legend edited by Elizabeth Archibald and Ad Putter
Australian Literature edited by Elizabeth Webby
The Australian Novel edited by Nicholas Birns and Louis Klee
The Beats edited by Stephen Belletto
Boxing edited by Gerald Early
British Black and Asian Literature (1945–2010) edited by Deirdre Osborne
British Fiction: 1980–2018 edited by Peter Boxall
British Fiction since 1945 edited by David James
British Literature of the 1930s edited by James Smith
British Literature of the French Revolution edited by Pamela Clemit
British Romantic Poetry edited by James Chandler and Maureen N. McLane
British Romanticism edited by Stuart Curran (second edition)
British Romanticism and Religion edited by Jeffrey Barbeau
British Theatre, 1730–1830, edited by Jane Moody and Daniel O'Quinn
Canadian Literature edited by Eva-Marie Kröller (second edition)
The Canterbury Tales edited by Frank Grady
Children's Literature edited by M. O. Grenby and Andrea Immel
The City in World Literature by Ato Quayson and Jini Kim Watson
The Classic Russian Novel edited by Malcolm V. Jones and Robin Feuer Miller
Comics edited by Maaheen Ahmed
Contemporary Irish Poetry edited by Matthew Campbell
Creative Writing edited by David Morley and Philip Neilsen
Crime Fiction edited by Martin Priestman
Dante's 'Commedia' edited by Zygmunt G. Barański and Simon Gilson
Dracula edited by Roger Luckhurst
Early American Literature edited by Bryce Traister
Early Modern Women's Writing edited by Laura Lunger Knoppers
The Eighteenth-Century Novel edited by John Richetti
Eighteenth-Century Poetry edited by John Sitter
Eighteenth-Century Thought edited by Frans De Bruyn
Emma edited by Peter Sabor
English Dictionaries edited by Sarah Ogilvie
English Literature, 1500–1600 edited by Arthur F. Kinney
English Literature, 1650–1740 edited by Steven N. Zwicker
English Literature, 1740–1830 edited by Thomas Keymer and Jon Mee
English Literature, 1830–1914 edited by Joanne Shattock
English Melodrama edited by Carolyn Williams
English Novelists edited by Adrian Poole
English Poetry, Donne to Marvell edited by Thomas N. Corns
English Poets edited by Claude Rawson
English Renaissance Drama edited by A. R. Braunmuller and Michael Hattaway, (second edition)
English Renaissance Tragedy edited by Emma Smith and Garrett A. Sullivan Jr.
English Restoration Theatre edited by Deborah C. Payne Fisk
Environmental Humanities edited by Jeffrey Cohen and Stephanie Foote

For EU product safety concerns, contact us at Calle de José Abascal, 56–1°,
28003 Madrid, Spain or eugpsr@cambridge.org.

www.ingramcontent.com/pod-product-compliance
Ingram Content Group UK Ltd.
Pitfield, Milton Keynes, MK11 3LW, UK
UKHW020335140625
459647UK00018B/2149